Pagan
Astrology

"*Pagan Astrology* combines a practical and easy-to-understand overview of the basics of Western Astrology with techniques and ideas to build astrological altars, work rituals, and perform magic using the unique forces and qualities of the astrological signs. Astrologers will particularly appreciate the magical prescriptions to counteract the energies of afflicted planets. This is a book that could grace the shelf of any student of the planetary mysteries."

ELLEN EVERT HOPMAN, AUTHOR OF
A DRUID'S HERBAL OF SACRED TREE MEDICINE,
A DRUID'S HERBAL FOR THE SACRED EARTH YEAR,
AND *BEING A PAGAN* (WITH LAWRENCE BOND)

Pagan Astrology

Spell-Casting, Love Magic, and Shamanic Stargazing

RAVEN KALDERA

Destiny Books
Rochester, Vermont • Toronto, Canada

Destiny Books
One Park Street
Rochester, Vermont 05767
www.DestinyBooks.com

Destiny Books is a division of Inner Traditions International

Library of Congress Cataloging-in-Publication Data

Kaldera, Raven.
  Pagan astrology : spell-casting, love magic, and shamanic stargazing / Raven
Kaldera.
     p. cm.
  Includes bibliographical references (p.   ) and index.
  ISBN 978-1-59477-302-0
  1. Astrology. 2. Neopaganism. I. Title.
  BF1729.R4K36 2009
  133.5'94994—dc22

                                                                 2009027180

Printed and bound in the United States by Lake Book Manufacturing

10   9   8   7   6   5   4   3   2   1

Text design and layout by Virginia Scott Bowman
This book was typeset in Garamond Premiere Pro and Agenda with Diotima,
Baskerville, and Gill Sans as display typefaces

To send correspondence to the author of this book, mail a first-class letter to the
author c/o Inner Traditions • Bear & Company, One Park Street, Rochester, VT
05767, and we will forward the communication.

Contents

PART THREE

Magical Prescriptions

Tools, Holidays, Altars, and Practices

AUTHOR'S NOTE
REGARDING PLANET PLUTO

The International Astronomical Union's 2006 decision to reclassify Pluto from a planet to a dwarf planet presented a challenge for astronomers who clearly consider it a strong planetary force. The International Astronomical Union's planet classification system is far from "watertight" and most certainly does not represent any type of agreement among astronomers. Only 4 percent voted on their planet definition, and most are not planetary scientists. Their decision was immediately opposed by hundreds of other professional astronomers in a formal petition. There are various inconsistencies in their nomenclature; their definition states that dwarf planets are not simply a type of planet, but are not planets at all. This is entirely inconsistent with the use of the term "dwarf" in the rest of astronomy, where dwarf stars are still stars, and dwarf galaxies are still galaxies. Their definitions also define objects solely by where they are while ignoring what they are. If Earth were in Pluto's orbit, according to the IAU definition, it would not be a planet either. A classification scheme that takes the same object and makes it a planet in one location and not a planet in another location is essentially useless.

Many astronomers favor a broader planet definition that includes any non-self-luminous spheroidal body orbiting a star. The spherical part is important because it means an object is large enough for its own gravity to pull it into a round shape—a characteristic of planets and not of shapeless asteroids. Astrologers, in general, have rejected the IAU definition, because for us the important part isn't even the size of the rock, it's the strength of the effect of the cosmic force marked and interpreted by that planet. The force that Pluto marks for us is awesome and powerful, and we find no reason not to refer to it as a planet, regardless of the transient squabbling of astronomers.

Stars and Stones

Astrology is the art and science of calculating cosmic currents by observing heavenly bodies. That's the nutshell description . . . and to most outside observers, that smacks terribly of magic. Most astrologers, though, would disagree. Starting with Evangeline Adams (the first astrologer to try to scientifically prove the validity of astrology in a court of law in 1914), the astrological community has been attempting for a century or more to prove that astrology is completely scientific, with nothing spooky or supernatural about it.

Of all the divinatory methods, from tea leaf reading to Tarot, astrology is the one that attracts the most "left-brained" types. After all, it's got more math than any other method, except maybe the I Ching. If one could grade divinatory methods the way one grades sciences—with physics on the "hard science" end and psychology on the "soft science" end—astrology would unquestionably be the "hardest" (with maybe scrying as the "softest"). It lends itself better than any other method to statistics and lab testing, and the hope of most of its practitioners is to someday allow it to join the ranks of ordinary sciences, like long-lost-twin astronomy.

In order to do this, the practice of Western astrologers has been to pare off and throw away anything that reeked of the Mysteries. This included anything remotely religious—after all, the existence of deities and spirits can't be proved scientifically—and anything associated with magical practice. Of course, this is nearly impossible in the end, because every divination method in existence sooner or later brushes up against the human need to explain the spiritual nature of the Universe . . . and that includes astrology. To the desperately bowdlerizing scientists in the astrological community, I can only point out a truth about that hardest of sciences, physics. The further into esoteric physics that physicists go, the "spookier" their theories become. Everything comes around in the end.

Some astrologers, seeking something a little more spiritual, gravitate toward the Vedic astrology practices of India. In studying traditional Indian astrology, they run smack up against the practice of astrological "remedies," which is an ordinary and expected part of the Indian astrologer's daily repertoire. The practice goes like this: The astrologer looks at your chart, checks it against the current planetary positions in the sky, and figures out if any of those moving planets are contacting yours in a way that messes with them and makes your life miserable (or, conversely, make things more fortunate). For the nonastrologers in the audience, we call these "transits" and speak of a transit of heavenly Planet X "afflicting" your natal Planet Y if it's bad.

So far, so good; this is exactly what a Western astrologer is likely to do. The difference is that the Vedic astrologer then consults a chart of "remedies," which are actions you can take to "propitiate" the injurious transiting planetary energy and lessen its effect on you. These can be as varied as wearing a particular gemstone or giving hay to a sacred cow. Sound like magic to you? It did to me, when I read about it, and I wasn't surprised to find that most Western astrologers dismiss the Vedic remedies as bunk. Frankly, I suspect that they work as well as any spell, and probably better than most, given the long history of their use. The one problem I have with them is that they are culturally specific; we don't have a lot of sacred cows wandering around, nor can we donate a cow to the local temple of Shiva, usually. That's why I've worked out a modern Western version of the astrological remedies that any of us can use without trouble. More on that later.

In the meantime, while India had a large number of lay astrologers giving out religious rather than magical advice, in medieval Europe astrology was used extensively on the magical side of things . . . but only for certain kinds of magic. Throughout the European medieval period, being an astrologer meant that you were a literate, educated individual with access to a great number of unusual books and other reading materials. This almost guaranteed that you were not a member of the lower classes, which were the huge unwashed bulk of European humanity at that time. If you were upper class and educated, and you had access to astrological materials, chances were that you also had access to magical textbooks such as grimoires. Greek and Roman and Arabic writing, Qabala, Christian demonology, and other trappings that became associated with the amalgam we now refer to as "ceremonial magic." Such magicians used astrological charts and symbols to add power and "kick" to many of their spells, be it timing the magic by the planets or invoking their energies to a particular purpose.

In the meantime, some of the common folk were practicing magic, too. They were mostly illiterate, so they couldn't read books on strange Greek and Roman names for stars or constellations, or stories of the Greek and Roman gods and goddesses for whom they were named. They couldn't do much math, so they couldn't read ephemeris charts, and anyway, books were only for the rich. Their magic was based on keen observation of nature—plants, animals, trees, stones, and humanity. They were not unaware of the heavenly bodies above them; they figured out that the Sun meant life and joy, and the Moon meant mystery and the feminine cycles. They might not know Venus's name, but they knew that one could wish for love on the morning and evening star. They might not know when the Moon was void of course, but they knew that aboveground herbs were best harvested on the Full Moon, and root crops on the New Moon.

When the modern witchcraft revival started in the 1960s, most of its first public practitioners had experimented with ceremonial magic— some, like Gerald Gardner, had been long-term members of groups such as the Ordo Templi Orientalis—and they borrowed heavily from those traditions. However, as the various Pagan sects progressed and modern Paganism got more and more embroiled with movements such as environmentalism and feminism, the magical practice started to turn back to the old hedge-witch-inspired spells and traditions. The green magic of old— peasant magic, kitchen magic, the work of granny witches and cunning men—didn't use a lot of astrology because of the previously mentioned class issues. Many of the modern folk who looked into astrology noticed that it seemed to be mostly used by ceremonial magicians and decided that it must not be "natural" enough to be of any use in folk witchery. The fact that astrology does look complicated, with lots of numbers and charts and complex combined symbols, often puts off people who are looking for a simpler, more "instinctive" system of magical practice.

So the lines got drawn . . . and a chasm grew between astrology and the magical practice of both modern witches and Pagans. But there are many commonalities that bridge that chasm, if anyone bothers to notice. The first obvious point is that of the four elements—earth, air, fire, and water. They are not only the basis of the natural world and of folk magic—most folk magic can be sorted by element, if you try—they are also the basis of astrology. Everything in this divinatory practice lives and dies by the four elements. In both astrology and modern witchcraft, the elements also symbolize—and are bound up with—the same qualities. Air is the mind, intellect and words; fire is will and passion and action; water is the emotions of the heart; earth is the physical body and everything used to maintain its life and comfort. This sacred quadrangle is reflected over and over in Western occult practice of any kind, from the suits of the Tarot to the Guardians of the Four Quarters of the Earth.

Modern witches do sometimes grudgingly use astrology in gardening, especially gardening by the Moon. Traditionally, plants are better off when planted on Waxing Moons and harvested during Waning Moons; the astrological sign of the Moon will also affect growth, so certain plants should be sown or transplanted during certain Moon signs. However, even some die-hard green-thumb witches are put off by the complicated dance of sign and phase, and most almanacs, while useful, don't allow for the varied planting dates in a large area with many climatic zones. One of the things that I felt would be most useful to gardeners who are intimidated by astrological gardening is a simple, straightforward chart that could be adjusted to their particular area.

Astrology is most frequently used magically to find out *when* rather than *why*—meaning that it is used to figure out when the best time for a ritual or working might be. While doing a spell at a nonpropitious time doesn't mean that it won't possibly work, the addition of astrologically appropriate energy gives it some extra grease, so to speak. Sometimes that extra bit of juju makes the difference in a spell with a lot of probability stacked against it. Using propitious times can also make a difference for rituals, because the very atmosphere will be saturated with a particular energy that can be tapped for the efficacy of the ceremony.

One classic method of scheduling rituals is the practice of choosing an astrologically auspicious time for a wedding, checking Venus and its aspects and rulerships, as well as comparing the potential happy day with the charts of the bride and bridegroom. I wrote about this practice in my book *Handfasting and Wedding Rituals,* but at the same time I was using astrology to schedule the right day—or the right time of day—for all sorts of regular rituals as well.

Rituals can also be created to celebrate the astrological currents themselves and to give the participants a better idea of what kind of cosmic flux is swirling about them. For example, a fellow astrologer and I created a ritual called "Changing the Dream, Dreaming the Change." We first conceived of it when Neptune, the planet of dreams, went into Aquarius, the sign of change. While transits do color everything with their energy, we as human beings do have free will as to how we respond to those energies, thus tilting the future in a way that we would prefer. We chose to design a ritual that would harness the energies of these two forces in combination, and thus use the power of the cosmic currents to carry our will.

We first did the ritual years ago, when slow-moving Neptune entered Aquarius. Now, as Uranus (the ruler of Aquarius and the planet of radical change) has passed into Pisces (the dreamy, mysterious sign ruled by Neptune), the two are in mutual reception. That's an astrologer's way of saying that two planets are in each other's signs, which usually means that they are working together in some way. This is a doubling of the Uranus-Neptune energies. Recently, we performed a larger and more elaborate version of the ritual during the summer of 2009 at a major Pagan gathering, as the two planets are currently in a semisextile (mildly positive) aspect to each other, as well as in mutual reception. We think that this will give us the best possible energy for creating change in the world through creating new images, visions, archetypes, and dreams.

Here's another important application for astrology: it provides a complex and highly useful symbol system for creating spells that are more complicated than just "love" or "money." If "bring me love" isn't enough (especially if you've tried it before and only managed to get attractive but unsuitable dates), and what you really want is "bring me intense, deep, radically honest love that will see and honor my darkest parts," then perhaps using the symbolism of Venus in Scorpio—including its associated stones, plants, and color—will give more magical specificity to your spell. If what you really want is "bring me casual, friendly love that will be straight with me, and be a good traveling companion," then you might want to look at the attributes of Venus in Sagittarius. Sure, you could just stick in various objects that symbolized those things to you, and it'd work . . . but using the astrological associations lends the strength and power of the actual cosmic clock to your spell.

By learning the language of astrology and applying it to magical work, you give yourself a much wider and variegated vocabulary to work with. You also give yourself the chance to learn about the universal currents of life and what they are doing to you on a daily basis. As astrologers have found, it can give you a jump on life.

Astrologers themselves have a lot to learn from magical practice, because it involves taking direct action in places where most astrologers are only watching passively. A friend of mine with a science background, upon learning astrology, commented that it was really "applied astronomy," so to speak—doing more than just observing the planets, actually working with the patterns that their motion betrays to us. Doing astrological magic takes the application process one step further. These energies are here already; we know what they look like and a good deal about their effects, although there's always more to learn. We might as well use them to the fullest, even if it may seem to cost astrology what pathetic scraps of scientific reputation it already has. After all, I've always believed that it is bad science to disbelieve in magic. No matter what anyone does, we will not be able to sever astrology-as-divination from the spiritual—and magical—arts, because it is and always has been one of them.

> *Above you are the stars,*
> *Below you are the stones.*
> *As you go through life, remember:*
> *Like a star should your love be constant,*
> *Like a stone should your love be strong.*
> —TRADITIONAL NEO-PAGAN WEDDING RITE

PART ONE

Charts

1
Deciphering a Chart
For Beginners

This chapter is for people who don't know much about astrology, so if you already know how to read the basics of a chart and apply transits to it, skip ahead to the next chapter.

Astrological charts can be pretty intimidating. They resemble nothing so much as an overdecorated Spirograph, surrounded with arcane symbols and complex numbers. At first glance, most people are taken aback and worry that they will never be able to make sense of them. And it is true that they contain a great deal of information crunched into a single symbol set, on a single page.

This chapter is not going to tell you how to interpret your chart for your own personality, which is what one normally associates with charts. There are plenty of other books on the market for that. (See Recommended Reading.) Instead, this chapter explains how to use your own chart, or that of a particular day, for magical purposes.

Another thing that I'm not going to teach you here is how to cast a chart yourself, using an ephemeris. That's also material for a different book, and anyway there are plenty of ways to get a chart done. You can use a computer program—several are out there, Solar Fire being the best of all in my judgment—and you can get free charts online from astro .com and a number of other websites, if you can get onto the Internet for a few minutes. If you don't intend to become a serious astrologer, but only want to know enough to use it magically, don't bother to learn the art of chart erection. We'll assume that you are sitting here with "Spirograph" in hand, looking quizzically at the weird lines and glyphs.

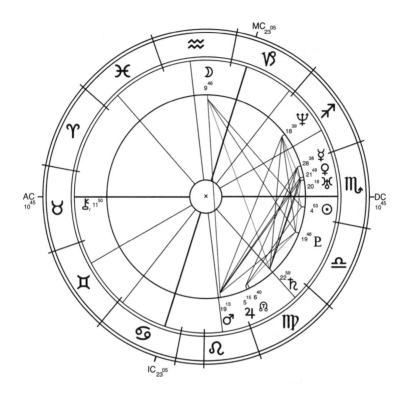

Figure 1. A typical computer-generated astrological chart.

WHAT'S GOING ON HERE?
MAKING SENSE OF ASTROLOGICAL SYMBOLS

The first thing that I've found it useful to do, especially if you are getting a badly printed black-and-white chart from some computer program or website, is to sit down and redraw the whole thing with colored pens, pencils, or markers. Make it large. Draw the circle and divide it into twelve pie slices, making sure to include one horizontal line and one vertical line. It should look like this:

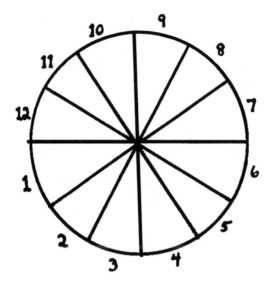

Figure 2. A simple hand-drawn chart.

Around the outside of your computer chart, you'll see a ring of numbers and glyphs. Twelve of these number-and-glyph combinations will coincide with the twelve pie-slice lines. Those lines are the separations between the astrological houses, which are basically twelve arenas of life. These twelve lines rotate like a wheel, changing degrees every few minutes in the sky, and they are superimposed on a pie of twelve zodiac signs, each of which is 30 degrees wide. The number-and-glyph combos tell you where, in the 360-degree circle of the sky, the houses fall onto the signs.

However, put those aside for the moment. The next ring is more important. Here you'll find glyphs of the planets as they appeared at the moment for which the chart was cast. You'll see them in groups that contain a planetary glyph, a sign glyph, and two numbers. One is the degree of the sign that the planet falls into, and the other is the minutes, which are a subdivision of the degrees—60 minutes for each degree. Ignore the numbers for the moment and concentrate on the glyphs.

In each combination, one of the glyphs symbolizes the planet, and the other glyph symbolizes the sign that it happens to be immersed in. For example, in my birth chart, ☉06♐23 indicates that the Sun (that's the first glyph, the planet in question) had gotten 6 degrees into Sagittarius (that's the second glyph, the sign), and then gone 23 minutes toward the 7th degree when I was born. Most computer charts put the information in this order: Planetary glyph, numbered degree, sign glyph, numbered minutes. (For a list of planet and sign glyphs, see chapter 3.)

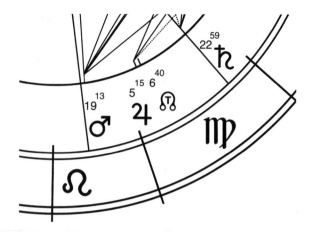

Figure 3. Planetary glyphs, house cusps, and sign cusps.

The sign colors the planet's energy temporarily, for a long or short time depending on the planet. (Inner planets move quickly in relation to the Earth, have short orbits, and don't spend a long time in each sign. Outer planets move slowly and may spend decades in each sign.) When you were born, the positions of the planets crystallized something in your nature. The planets themselves kept going, passing into other signs, going in their endless circles, but inside of you there will always be the reflection of that moment of birth. The Sun that was at 6 degrees of Sagittarius at the moment I first drew breath became part of me. Every time the real Sun passes a point in the sky that forms a special angle with my Sagittarius Sun, it affects me in some way. It's as if the planets are plowing over the points where your natal planets "froze" and temporarily "splashing" them with their energies. They also "splash" them with their energies when they form certain specific and exact angles with them. These are called transits, and they are how predictive astrologers figure out the coming trends of your life.

I'm going to give you a couple of examples of what this looks like, but first I have to explain that we don't have the time and space to go into detailed descriptions of each planet and sign and how they interact. For that, you need an entire book on basic astrology, not just a mere chapter. For poetic and magical imagery of the energies of each of the planets, you can check chapter 15, I'll give examples here of what these interactions look like, but be advised that the natures of the planets and signs are much more complex than the information I have presented here.

First, let's say that the Moon was in Aquarius when you were born. That means that your "lunar" functions (emotions and nurturing, among others) run in a very Aquarius way (intellectual and nonconformist). Meanwhile, one day Mars, the planet of aggression, makes its way along its path and hits a point in a perfect 90-degree angle to your Moon—one of those special "affecting" points that I mentioned. (We call that a square, as in "Mars is squaring your Moon.") This point happens to be in Scorpio. Suddenly, your Aquarius Moon is flooded with both "alien" Mars energy and "alien" Scorpio energy. Circumstances appear in your life that would feel much more familiar to someone who had the Moon in Scorpio, or perhaps Mars squaring the Moon in their ordinary natal charts. You, however, don't. Out of nowhere, "Mars-type" things and "Scorpio-type" things begin to happen to you . . . but only in the areas of your life associated with the Moon.

As another example, let's say that instead of forming a 90-degree angle, Mars instead forms a 120-degree angle, which is called a trine. These angles are much more comfy than squares, because the energy of a trine is made up of two planets in the same element, and they get along much better. Let's say that Mars is trining your Moon in the sign of Libra. This time, your Moon and the sky's Mars are in partnership; they form a temporary team that does something good for your life. Because they are in the same element—this time, air—they speak similar languages. They're still somewhat alien to each other, because Mars and the Moon are quite different planetary energies, but they manage to work together harmoniously.

For a third example, let's say that the sky's Pluto skulks up and sits directly on top of your Moon. That's a conjunction, two planets sharing the same space. It's rather like locking them in an elevator together for a while.

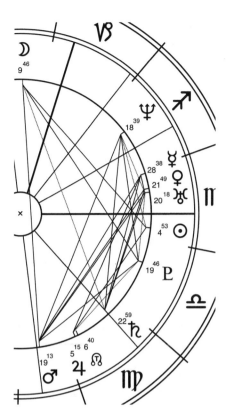

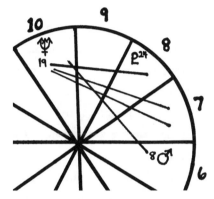

Figure 4. Aspects between planets in same chart, computer version.

Figure 5. Aspects between natal and transiting planets in a hand-drawn chart. Notice how planets are drawn differently between the two charts, and interchart aspect lines are drawn thicker than intrachart lines.

They're in the same sign, so they definitely speak the same language. Do they get along? That depends on the planets in question. Pluto is pretty darn alien to the Moon in a lot of ways, so they may clash, or they may not.

ASPECTS
Relationship and Conversation

Astrologers tend to refer to the difficult angles—squares, which we mentioned above, and oppositions, which place the two planets directly opposing each other—as "challenging" aspects. In the old days, they called them "afflicting" aspects, and I still call them that, because when they're on top of you, it feels pretty much like an affliction. (Yes, I know that we're all supposed to look for silver linings in the storm clouds and learning experiences in disasters, but sometimes being able to call it the wretched problem that it is can help you survive it with your sense of humor intact.) I have long been referring to the easier aspects, such as the already mentioned trine and the sextile (which is 60 degrees away and basically half a trine, a sort of mini-trine), as "enhancing." A conjunction can go either way, depending partly on the planets involved and partly on how well you choose to handle the transit.

I like to think of aspects as relationships and conversations. Are they difficult relationships, where the conversations are mostly arguing (like a square), or are they lovey-dovey with lots of "Let's do this!" "Oh, yes, let's!" (like a trine), or are they rather love-hate, with people who are so alike that their few differences grate on each other even more (like a conjunction)? I'm certain that you've experienced all three types of relationship in your life. Imagine that your planets have many of these various relationships with each other and also with the transiting planets that drop in and camp on their couches for a while. Sometimes they may love the houseguest, sometimes they may spend every moment wishing that they'd leave. All those lines in the middle of a chart just show who's talking to whom, and whether that conversation is happy or argumentative.

Conjunctions—planets on top of each other—are easy to see in a chart, even when you're looking for transits. Transiting planets that are trining, squaring, or otherwise at angles to each other are more difficult and take more perusing to get used to. There are many, many sorts of aspects, but most are minor, and there's not enough space to talk about them here. Here's a basic list of major aspects, skinned down to their most general use:

★ **Conjunction** (on top of each other, same sign and thus the same element): Good or bad, depending on the planets involved and what you choose to do about it. When looking for suggestions in the tables in this book, use either or both the "afflicting" and "enhancing" directions.

★ **Trine** (four signs apart, same element, 120-degree angle): Really friendly, like family. The planets are having a love affair, and it's a great time to propitiate either or both energies. You may also want to connect with the energies of those signs, those planets, or signs that those planets rule, in order to "borrow" energy you'd like but don't have.

★ **Sextile** (two signs apart, harmonious elements, 60-degree angle): Still quite friendly, sort of like a mini-trine—actually, it's half a trine. Use it like a trine, but expect weaker effects.

★ **Opposition** (six signs apart, harmonious elements, inharmonious signs, 180-degree angle): Difficult for a transit, as this energy forces you to confront an opposing viewpoint about familiar things, sort of like a cosmic devil's advocate. Such a transit can be very good for you, or drive you nuts, or both. Magically, propitiate the sign/planet that is transiting you, and ask it to teach you what you need to learn in order to more skillfully ride out the transit.

★ **Square** (three signs apart, inharmonious elements, inharmonious signs, 90-degree angle): The most difficult of the major aspects. Square energy forces you to confront an entirely alien view of how things are. Although such mind-stretching exercises are good for us, they are never comfortable and are often painful, and most of us, being lazy, would rather skip the pain and the improvement as well. That's why squares have their bad reputation. Magically, propitiate the sign/planet that is afflicting you, and ask it to teach you what you need to learn. Sometimes it helps to talk to people who have that sign/planet combination in their charts or who have those planets squaring each other natally. Remember that doing something nice for them counts as propitiation and can be a promise to the Universe that you really value that alien energy and want to do your best to understand it, even if the lesson is hard.

You can actually do magic to bring the alien energy of the contacting planet in a square or opposition into your being, and experience it, but this is only for the brave. It's rather like going to cramming school; it can get you through the transit quicker, but it will be a much more intense and up-close study of something that you may feel uncomfortable enough with already.

When the sky's planets zap yours, it's a one-way effect. They get you, but you don't affect them. (Two human beings can and do zap each other with their own planets, but that's called *synastry,* and we don't get into that until chapter 6.) This means that the planetary energy to look at is always the sky's, not your own. In other words, if you have Mars in Taurus in the seventh house, and it's being squared by Venus in Aquarius, which happens to be sitting in your fourth house, the keywords to look for are Venus, Aquarius, and fourth house, not the signifiers of your own afflicted planet. You already know all about being a seventh house Taurus Mars, because you've lived with that all your life.

With a conjunction, the sign energy will be familiar, but perhaps not the planet, so you concentrate on the "alien" planet. If it's a matter of the same planet coming around again to the point at which you were born, well, that's called a return (as in Mars Return or Uranus Return). A return is a call to Look at Your Own Issues; it's dealing with the problems you've carried around forever, not slapping you with new challenges. Some, like Venus and Jupiter returns, are generally times for rejoicing. Some, like the dreaded Saturn Return—which asks you, "Are you really grown up now?"—rubs your face in things about yourself that you'd rather not look at.

When it comes to computer charts, some programs use different colored lines for the different sorts of aspects. Some use lines that are dotted or somehow spaced differently. (There ought to be a key somewhere in the program that will tell you what's what, if it's a good program.) Some will use straight lines with the glyph of the aspect stuck in the middle, which makes for a more cluttered chart, but one that is the easiest to figure out. When I draw charts myself, I make the lines for squares red, trines blue, sextiles green, and oppositions purple. I save the other colors for minor aspects (such as quincunxes and semisextiles, which we won't go into here) and don't bother with dotted lines and such. For conjunctions, I might draw a curved line that connects them.

The next thing that you'll want to look at is the houses. That's those twelve pie wedges that your chart is laying on top of. The houses carry the energies of twelve basic areas of life, and they are constantly turning in the sky, minute to minute. They really only come into play when you have a "snapshot" of the sky—say a birth chart or a chart of any given moment that you call up on a program. Your natal houses, like your natal planets, are "frozen" in time. The sky's planets drift through them, and as they go into each house, they affect you in that area of your life. For example, when Saturn passes through any given house, since its energy is slowing, retarding, blocking, and disciplining, things may get more difficult for you in that area. Passing through the ninth house, which is the house of travel, Saturn might give you multiple ongoing car repair problems; passing through the seventh house, which is the house of partnerships, it might encourage a breakup, herald a time of celibacy, or make you suddenly want to get serious and marry your sweetheart. Jupiter passing through a certain house might bring good fortune in that specific area of life, while Uranus might spread general chaos and randomness. (Check chapter 3 for more information on the houses.)

BUT NOW WHAT?
COPING WITH YOUR TRANSITS

But what can you do about a transit, magically? You can't stop the planets from moving. You can't stop them from affecting you. What you can do is to connect your own self, and thus your contacted natal planet, with the energy of the transiting planet. If you do this willingly, if you throw yourself into it with the resolve to learn everything you can about this planetary and sign energy—including how to appreciate it—things will go a lot better for you.

This is, in a very real sense, a form of propitiation . . . because some of the ways of making peace with this "alien" energy are the sorts of things that one would do to propitiate the favor of a god or goddess. In fact, it really works best if you try to think of the planets as divine archetypal energies and treat them that way. This could include creating an amulet with the symbol of your natal planet on one side and of the contacting planet on the other, or perhaps the two entwined. It could include making

an altar to the transiting planet, and meditating before it, to better understand its energy and thus better navigate the transit. It could include carrying items that the planet has an affinity with or doing certain actions
that it would approve of.

You can also contact the energy of a planet in a particular sign when
that planet is not actually currently in that sign (although it's always easier when it is) or when it is not contacting anything in your chart. Why
bother to do such a thing? Well, sometimes we run into problems that
stem from our being unskilled at accessing certain energies, and we need
to ask them to come into our lives. For example, if you have Mercury in
Pisces and you are constantly plagued with a vague memory that tends to
lose details, invoking the powers of organized, precise Mercury in Virgo
into your life and inviting it to teach you more about those things (even if
that's a hard lesson) can be useful.

Your first task is to go through your chart and list the planets and
their signs and houses, and check them out in chapter 3, Planetary Gifts.
This will give you a better idea of your own potential magical talents and
how to use them. It will also give you an idea of the gifts that don't come
naturally to you and the energies and symbols you need to use to bring
them into your life.

We humans are often irrational beings, and we are often ambivalent
about talents and affinities that we don't have. We may devalue them, either
because we don't understand their worth or because we want to feel better
about the fact that we're bad at those things. We may long for them, but
find ourselves struggling whenever we attempt to develop them. We may
get reasonably good at them after a long period of work, only to find that it
stifles us and feels alien to our natures to practice them, causing us to resent
them even if—perhaps especially if—they are important to our survival.

It's impossible to be good at everything, and no matter who you are
or how multitalented, there will always be some trait beyond your reach,
and I am not suggesting that magic can make you different from who you
are. If you have a Pisces Moon, you will never not have a Pisces Moon.
When dealing with lunar issues—home and family, for example—you
will always *react* in a watery Piscean way, if only quietly. You will never

react on a deep level as if you had a detached Aquarius Moon . . . but if you are in a situation where being detached is the only way to protect yourself, you can learn to *act as if* you had one, and magic is useful for such things. Astrological energies can be like a tool, or a disguise . . . they aren't you personally, and you wouldn't want to be dependent on them all the time, but they can get you by in emergencies.

So how does one do it? Let's say, for example, that you have your Jupiter in any sign except for Leo. Having a Leo Jupiter means having natural access to that quality that both Hollywood and medieval folk storytellers referred to as *glamour*. Hollywood uses the term to talk about stars, and old storytellers used it to talk about deceptive faeries, but the two uses are kin at bottom. Let's say that you have no glamour, and you wish that just once you could summon up that gift, perhaps for a big date. If Jupiter happens to be in Leo, you're good—just make an altar and an offering. However, given that this configuration only happens every twelve years, if it's not going on at the moment, you may not want to wait so long for that date.

One option is to check for when Jupiter is making a positive aspect to the Sun, such as a trine or sextile. (Why the Sun? Because the Sun "rules" Leo, meaning that it gives it its energy. The rulers of each sign are listed in chapter 3.) To figure this out, check your astrology program; look at the ephemeris and at charts for periods over the next few years. See if you can figure out, visually and by the numbers, when Jupiter and the Sun are a third of the chart away from each other, four signs apart, with the degree numbers less than 3 degrees apart. That's a trine. A sextile is two signs apart, again with the 3-degree allowance, which astrologers call an *orb*.

If that's still too long to wait, try a more local tack. Find someone with Jupiter in Leo in their chart and do something nice for them. This is like making an offering to that planetary energy via one of their walk-ing, talking avatars. Give them a gift that shows how much you appreciate that energy in them. Do it while consciously asking the Universe to gift you with some of that same glitter and glamour. By giving them a gift of some kind, not only do you earn good karma and propitiate that planet through them, you also show the Universe that you really do value that gift, even if it's not naturally yours.

More likely, though, you will not be going out and looking for planetary energy so much as dealing with what the Universe is constantly throwing at you. When it comes to dealing with transits of the sky planets knocking into and zapping your natal planets, the first line of defense is knowing what's going on. This means that you have to get reasonably good at figuring out when a specific transit is happening and remembering to check on them regularly.

There are a few different ways to check on transits to your chart. The first is, simply, to either consult an ephemeris chart or create pie charts for random days in the present and future and compare them with your chart. This method can also be used for specific occasions—if, for example, you want to know the best time to schedule a wedding, or a funeral, or a party, or an initiatory ritual, or the conception of a child, or a particular magical working. If you are trying to do propitious scheduling, you don't compare the day's chart with your own chart, you go through it looking at the planets, signs, houses, and aspects to see if they resonate with the purpose of your event. For example, for a wedding, Venus should be prominent and not too riddled with squares and oppositions. For a cathartic ritual, look at the placement of Pluto. For any magical working that will require you to utilize strong feelings about your need, look at the Moon's sign and house.

Some computer programs will do chart comparisons; some won't. To find out what's going to happen in your own life, you take a future chart and compare it with your own chart. If transiting planets are about to run over your own planets, look them up in chapter 15, and figure out their nature and how to honor them. If they are really giving you a hard time, check chapter 16 for ideas on how to properly propitiate them with actions. Conjunctions are the worst offenders for strongly affecting you, but if you can learn to calculate squares and trines and oppositions as well, you'll do even better.

Other astrology programs will simply calculate all the transits to your chart for a set period of time and give you a list. Go through it and check them out. Remember that inner planets move fast, and their transits are quick. Outer planets move slowly, and their transits can last months, so you might want to concentrate on them. It's unlikely that you'll have the time to magically use, or even honor, every transit anyway. You'd be doing nothing else.

FIGURING OUT
THOSE TRANSIT THINGIES

An easy way to see clearly which transits are affecting your life is to make a chart of tomorrow's date (don't do today, because it may take you all day to put the darn thing together) on a clear plastic page protector and superimpose it onto your own chart. This is especially good for people who are visual in nature and really need to see what's where in relation to their planets. Turn the clear plastic until the signs and degrees line up with your own chart. The first things that will stand out are the transiting planets that are on top of, or about to go over, your natal planets. Check the numbers of the degrees to see how close they are. Remember that although some astrologers allow as much as 10 degrees between aspects in a natal chart, they generally agree that transits get a smaller window. Most concur that you really start to feel a transiting planet when it's about 3 degrees away from the natal planet it's contacting, that its influence is strongest when the aspect is exact, and that it goes on for about 3 degrees farther. That means that if Saturn is at 25 degrees of Pisces, and Mars is directly across from it in Virgo, in order to be really connected and zapping away in an opposition, it would have to be between 22 and 28 degrees. That's 7 degrees where you'll feel it . . . but many astrology programs only give you the date of the middle where they match exactly, and they don't tell you about the lead-up and trail-off. For outer planets, that period of time might be months or even years.

If a transiting planet is coming up on one of your natal planets, and you have access to a program or website that does charts, order a bunch of charts for dates further into the future to find out when the transit will be exactly on your planet and when it will fade away entirely. Ideally, you should be able to look at charts that are cast for many points over a period of time and see how a given planet meanders its way around the sky. Make a list of the dates when a transiting planet is within the 3-degree orb of messing with you, so you'll be warned. Another way to do this is to buy an ephemeris book, which will have charts that show where any planet is likely to be. Using an ephemeris, you can track a planet by the degree numbers and figure out when it pops into any of your houses or when it goes over your planets. Some astrology programs come with good ephemerises; some don't.

So that's the basics. The rest of this book is all about the specific magic that you can do for and with the various combinations of planets in signs and houses. But really, you should start by getting used to charts—looking at them, figuring out what is moving where. It's a lot less complicated than it sounds, once you start doing it. And if you get too confused, you can always consult an actual astrologer to tell you what transits are coming up for you. Ask them to write down the actual planets, signs, houses, and aspects in a list, and then you can check through this book for useful things to do with them. And hopefully, by the time you've done a few, you'll be on your way to becoming an amateur astrologer yourself.

2
Using Your Chart
For Astrologers

I'll assume, if you've skipped to this section, that you already know the basics of chart erection and interpretation, that if I talk about a planet in a particular sign or house or aspect you'll have a basic idea of what I'm talking about, and that you can compare charts and figure out transits with reasonable facility. I'm also going to assume, for the sake of those who fit this description, that you know very little about magic and may, indeed, have your doubts that it can work. Astrology is a science, or so many astrologers would like to pretend (and perhaps prove), and this witchcraft stuff is fuzzy, unclear, and tainted with centuries of murky and bizarre occult trappings and secrecy. Isn't conflating the two just a way to drag astrology down again into that disreputable muck?

I'm not even going to try to convince you, because I can't. What will convince you, or not, is trying the magical techniques in this book and seeing whether they work for you. I will let them and their efficacy stand alone, and you can take that challenge or not, as you will. However, do keep in mind that although the current trend is to make astrology entirely into a left-brain activity, there is still a good deal of right-brain work in it. Interpretation is still terribly right-brained, whether we admit to it or not. "But," you say, "it's right-brain intuition working within a set framework of symbols!" You're correct, and I submit that this is what magic is as well. The symbol set of Western Neo-Pagan magic is far more concrete than you might realize; for example, as I mentioned in the introduction, the four elements are wonderfully concrete and yet amazingly intuitive symbols for four ways of being in the world, whether you are a physical object (solid, liquid, gas, energy) or a soul quality (practical, emotional, intellectual, spirited), or both.

As I discuss in chapter 16, astrologers around the world have combined the study of the stars' synchronicity with that of magic. One of the few forms of Vedic propitiation that has started to catch on is the use of *Jyotish stones* (expensive gems worn to avert negative astrological influences) partly because crystals are all the rage right now and partly because it's easier for some lazy first-world Westerners to buy a piece of pretty jewelry than to do inconvenient community service work. I did include, in chapter 15, a stone for every planet in every sign that can be carried as a talisman to work with that combination, either as propitiation or as a way to bring it into your life. With the exception of the black stones relevant to Saturn, I have not gone into detail about every rock in the list; that would take a whole 'nother book! I have also, after much thought, not listed the traditional Jyotish stone associations. Since this is a book geared toward Western practitioners, I have instead decided to work with the Western meanings for the various stones.

But let's go on to what you can actually do, magically, with a chart. If you study ceremonial magic texts, you'll find that most of what they do is to time magical activities for propitious times. This is the most basic form of astrological magic. As the wise-woman character Aughra says as she contemplates her orrery in the movie *The Dark Crystal,* "This is how to know when, that's what!" Any spell, even if it has no astrological components, can be given a better push by checking the timing. You can do this the same way that you can schedule any other event. For those who are new to this technique, I'd work it this way: Figure out what house this problem would fall under. Figure out what planet's energy would best serve the situation (Venus for love, the Moon for family issues, etc.). Use your ephemeris to find out (in order of desirability):

1. When the target planet will be transiting that house. If this will take seventy years, keep going down the list.

2. When that planet's ruler will be transiting that house and in aspect to the target planet, if only as a quincunx or semisextile. If possible, avoid square angles, although that's better than nothing.

3. When the target planet will be in positive aspect to the ruler of the sign on that house cusp.

4. When the target planet will be trining the first cusp of that house.

5. When the target planet will be trining any planet in that house.

6. When any planet will be transiting that house and in major positive aspect to the target planet.

So far, so good. The next thing, and the more controversial, is using astrological energies to aid your life, even when they aren't touching you at the moment. It's a way of working with those energies instead of simply charting them, ducking, and hoping for the best. Astrological energies are well mapped, complex, and there for the using. It harms no one to do work to draw them to you. The spell technique works like this:

1. Start with the house that best contains the area affected by your spell. For instance, a spell for romance is fifth house, a "get-me-a-McJob-to-pay-my-bills" would be sixth house, a career-promotion spell would be tenth house, and a spell to keep a child safe would be fourth house. (For other suggestions, see chapter 3.) Look at what transits are going on in that house currently for you.

2. If the answer is "not much," then think of what you'd like to be going on. Let's say that you want to get a well-deserved raise and promotion at the company you've worked for these last ten years. Right now nothing worth speaking of is transiting your tenth house of career ambition, which is mostly in the sign of Cancer. What would be the ideal planet to be transiting there? Jupiter? Mars? While the ideal would be to wait until these planets actually made it into your tenth house and then do magic to make the most of that energy, the whole

point of doing magic now is that things aren't going easily and they need a boost. So you'll do things to pull a shadow of that energy into the appropriate house.

Check for other transits to see if there's actually something that can be worked with. Are either Jupiter or Mars going to be trining or sextiling the cusp of your tenth house anytime soon? Is the Moon (Cancer's ruler) going to be making a strong positive aspect to either of them in the near future? If so, schedule a spell or ritual for that date. If none of these things works, then just go it alone.

First, you can go to chapter 8 and do the Jupiter in Cancer spell to bring that energy into your life. If you combine it with symbols of your tenth house, so much the better. This will bring in the energy that would be happening in your life if Jupiter were actually up there in your tenth. It's a temporary thing, not as long or strong as actually having a transit, but it can be just enough to trigger something positive. Second, you can go to chapter 15 and set up an altar with an offering to invoke that energy further into your life. For the above situation, I'd make a combination Jupiter-Mars in Cancer altar to pull the energy of such a profitable conjunction into your empty house. Third, you can carry an amulet with the colors and symbols of that combination. Fourth, you can consult chapter 16 and make an offering of your time, money, or effort, which shows to the Universe how much you value these energies and what they themselves find valuable. (For looking this up in chapter 16, I'd use either Mars transiting Jupiter or Jupiter transiting Mars, in Cancer and in the tenth house, for an enhancing aspect.)

3. If the problem isn't that there's nothing going on in a particular house, but that something is there and it's no fun at all, that too can be dealt with. Let's say that you're trying to get pregnant, but so far it has eluded you. Your body checks out all right; the circumstances just aren't working out. You look at your chart, and lo and behold transiting Saturn is parked in your fifth house of children, in Leo. While you can't get rid of Saturn, and you can't make him go any faster, you can do some things to help.

First, you have to propitiate the planet that is in the way. Make a Saturn in Leo altar, leave an offering, and dwell hard on Saturn's lesson for you here. When you meditate before it, divination may help you to understand this situation better; it may be a karmic issue that simply won't budge no matter how much magic you pour onto it until you've absorbed what has to be learned. (For a divination method that is properly Capricornian/Saturnian, check chapter 11, Neptune Magic, and look under Capricorn.) Consulting a diviner, or doing the augury yourself, can show you whether it's futile and what needs to be learned before Saturn will be satisfied. In the meantime, check chapter 16 for an astrological remedy. Since the Moon is in charge of children, use the remedy for Saturn transiting the Moon in afflicting aspect, in Leo and in the fifth house. If you do it with a respectful attitude, it will show the cosmic Saturn forces that you respect that work and that presence. After you do it, ask yourself what you learned from doing it, even if only a small and trivial lesson. If you learned nothing, do it again. Only when you've done the propitiation can you then do the positive energy importation.

If you were to come up with a combination to soften Saturn's edges there, it would probably be a combination of Jupiter and the Moon (abundance and children). Look to see when either of these are going to be conjuncting or trining transiting Saturn as he sits there grimly. (The Moon moves fast enough that you'll have a shot at it once a month at least.) Schedule your spell or ritual for that day, if possible. Do the Moon in Leo and the Jupiter in Leo spells, as that is the energy that would be flooding your life if they were there. Set up altars and make offerings to these two planets. Make a talisman that combines Saturn, Jupiter, and the Moon in Leo, and carry it. Look in chapter 16 and find the offerings for the Moon and Jupiter transiting Saturn, enhancing aspect, in Leo in the fifth house. Do them happily and willingly. This adds to your conscious good karma and throws out a certain flavor of positive energy to the rest of the Universe. Since what you give out, you get back, it will hopefully return as a flood of Moon-Jupiter energy coming into your fifth house, and there's little better for making babies. Even if the earlier divination says that there's no moving Saturn until he's done, it can be a good thing to do the positive energy-drawing work anyway. All transiting planets keep moving, and it means that as soon as he's gone off to your next house, all that energy will pop up.

4. Other ways to bring those planetary energies into your life include wearing the colors of the planets in question (if you're combining planetary energies, look for a print cloth or garment with all those colors); eating the food associated with them; ingesting the herbs associated with them (or carrying them in a mojo bag if they are not safe for you to eat); planting a tree that is associated with them; or working with an animal spirit associated with them. You can combine any or all of these techniques.

You can see how some of these instructions could seem strange to someone who knew nothing about the energies involved. You can imagine the reaction if I, as a shaman/astrologer, do a client's transits and say to them, "Pluto is about to go over your Sun next year. The likelihood is good that your life will change drastically, whether you want it to or not. You can fight it and lose, or move with it and make it easier on yourself. First, we'll do a reading with a different sort of divination; since this is a Pluto problem, we'll put down slips of paper with poems and sayings written on them and use dowsing, a Scorpio method. In two weeks, Pluto will go over the house cusp into the house of your Sun, and at the same time the Moon will be within orb of a trine to both Pluto and your Sun. At this point, you should set up an altar with a cloth of dark orangey brown—oh, and by the way, try to find and wear that color as much as possible for the next year—and put animal skins and wild animal traps on it. Find something that you ought to have given up a long time ago, but you didn't because it was too painful. Give it up now, and put it or a symbol of it on the altar as an offering. Then you want to sit in front of it and meditate on whatever comes out of the reading we're about to do. If you see a toad, consider it a serious omen of change and transformation. Try talking to a toad spirit and see what advice it has to give you. Find some horsetail in the local health food store, and drink it in a tea. Find some bittersweet growing wild, and carry it in a bag on your person, but don't eat it—it's poisonous. Carry some malachite, or wear it in jewelry. Check nurseries for a staghorn sumac and plant one out somewhere, preferably in a place where wild animals are hunted or near the local deer-checking station during hunting season. Tell the truth more than usual, even if it's harsh. Lies will be discovered sooner and look worse than usual. Oh, and above all else, you need to contact an organization that helps refugees from countries in turmoil, and give them some kind of aid toward getting the refugees proper housing. You should do more than just cut them a check; get involved somehow and really find out what's needed, how these people are uprooted and alone in a strange place. You need to meditate on that in front of your altar, too."

After all this, some modern Westerners would simply decide that I was a nutball, give me the hairy eyeball, and leave, probably to call up whatever friend recommended me and give them an earful. On the other hand, maybe that friend will tell them that when it was their turn, they did the things that I suggested and they really helped, and not just because it was busywork to take their minds off the transit.

As a reader, I tend to be straightforward and not very subtle. It's not an approach that works for everyone (which is one reason I don't do it professionally for my own pay), and I'm sure that the more diplomatic of the astrologers who read this (perhaps the ones with even one planet in Libra or Cancer, which I don't have) will be able to suggest these things in a way that might actually convince the skeptical Yuppie across the table. Then again, if you're talking to someone from a third-world country, they are much more likely to be very receptive to it. This is the sort of thing that they expect to get from a spiritual provider, and they don't expect to be able to understand much of it. All they care about is that it works.

In order to tell them with conviction that it works, you will need to try it yourself and get used to the idea that astrological energies can be used as the excellent and versatile tools that they are. Astrology is a complex tool kit, and if you turn the diagnostic tools around, you'll discover that they have application bits at the other ends. It's a different sort of helping than that of astrologers who are trying to model themselves on the Western therapist model, which comes out of Western medical practices. It's more akin to the granny witch with her folk charms or the shaman who works with the spirits to invoke their aid. The two are very different archetypes and job descriptions, as I well know, having started out as a witch and ended up as a shaman . . . but they have in common the use of both divination and magic to aid those who call upon them.

Three years ago, I wrote *MythAstrology* as part of a practice that I slowly began to see as shamanistic astrology. The first part of the practice had to do with presenting chart interpretation not as a series of random characteristics with which the querent might identify or not, but as a series of stories to tell them about what that energy looks like archetypally. Shamans don't give cookbook-style lists of qualities to their clients, they tell stories. Clients remember a story a lot better; whether or not they identify with it immediately, it gets under their skin, stays with them, makes them say years later, "Oh! So that's what that reader meant by that!" If they do identify with it, they can often get an object lesson out of it: "You mean if I do X, Y will happen? Well, actually, it already has. You mean that if I keep doing it, I can expect more of the same?"

The stories in *MythAstrology*—and the stories in its two sequels, which are currently under construction—are the shamanistic tools for simple interpretation. However, transits needed a whole different approach, one not just of power-stories but of power-actions. This book is for shamanistic astrologers who want to help their clients not just to be ready to duck reality, but to shape it and dance with it. Although the cosmic currents are much bigger than we are, and we have no hope of changing their nature or their clock (and nor should we, as it was designed by forces that know a lot better than we do), it is not true that we cannot affect their effects. To work magic in a way that honors the energies of these cosmic forces is to see them as sacred, as worthy of a kind of deep respect that we would call worship if we didn't know that too many people associate that word with negative things. No, on second thought, I'll say it: they are worthy of worship, in the sense that they are of the ever-unfolding and yet never completely knowable Mysteries, and to come humbly before them is to admit that there are things in the Universe greater than myself, and that this is how it should be. Frankly, if being an astrologer doesn't ever put you in awe of the grand cosmic system, you've missed the point and should go back to playing with Sun sign horoscopes. Use that awe. Harness it. Study it. It is the key to the door that opens on as much understanding as we mere mortals can handle.

PART TWO

Planets in Motion

3
Planetary Gifts
Those Glyphs in Your Chart

This is the part that I promised to the beginners in chapter 1—the section that would tell them what those strange glyphs on the outer ring of their chart mean. Since I'm including explanations of their magical usages so that you can use them for amulets if need be, experienced astrologers might also want to take a look at the list. For beginners, though, read the planets, read the signs, read the houses . . . put them together, like a sentence, or a paragraph. If you still don't have a good understanding of the energy, that's all right . . . go to chapter 15, build an altar to that energy, and meditate on it. Let it speak to you and it will tell you its story.

THE PLANETARY GLYPHS

1. The Sun. Really obvious. It's a dot in a circle. Its metal is gold, and any amulets with this sigil should be of gold or brass. The Sun symbolizes identity, the core of your personality. It also symbolizes warmth and life itself. When your Sun is affected by a transit, it's your core personality and way of seeing the world that is affected by the energy of the contacting planet. An amulet with the Sun glyph and its sign in your natal chart protects and reaffirms your identity and worldview. An amulet with the Sun glyph with a different sign helps you to learn and access other qualities of identity and worldview.

2. The Moon. Again, obvious; a crescent Moon. Its metal is silver. The Moon symbolizes your emotions, your inner child, your inner parent or source of nurturing, and your intuition. When your Moon is affected by a transit, the contacting planet affects your emotional judgment and your ability to feel. An amulet with the Moon glyph and your natal Moon sign glyph protects and reaffirms your inner self, your inner child, and your intuition. An amulet with the Moon glyph with a different sign helps you to learn and explore new ways of dealing with your emotions.

3. Mercury. The symbol here is a little guy with wings on his head, symbolizing the Greek god Hermes (Roman Mercury) with his winged hat. Its true metal is mercury, which is toxic, dangerous, and not recommended for an amulet, although you could theoretically attach a thermometer to a Mercury amulet. These days, aluminum is accepted as a decent substitute for quicksilver. Mercury symbolizes your mind and your speech. During transits, the contacting planet affects your ability to think and speak. An amulet with the Mercury glyph and your natal Mercury sign will reinforce and strengthen your current mental and verbal processes. An amulet with the Mercury glyph and a different sign helps you to learn and practice new ways of thinking and talking.

4. Venus. This symbol is well known in our culture as the sign for "woman," and it supposedly comes from the figure of a hand mirror. Its metal is copper. Venus is associated with your ability to love, your preferred form of romance, and what you consider aesthetically beautiful. A transit to your Venus, not surprisingly, affects your love life. If you are the artistic type, it may also have an effect on your creative work. An amulet with the Venus glyph and your natal Venus sign nourishes and reaffirms your current view and practice of love and romance, and helps you be a better lover. An amulet with the Venus glyph and a different sign helps you to learn different ways of loving and can also be used to attract someone with that style of handling love.

5. Mars. This is the traditional "male" symbol, which supposedly comes from the warrior's spear and shield. Its metal is iron. Mars is the planet of energy, of get-up-and-go, of doing and acting rather than feeling and reacting. When it is contacted by a transiting planet, your style of taking action, and your decision-making ability, are affected. An amulet with the Mars glyph and your natal Mars sign strengthens and reinforces your natural style of moving to act. An amulet with the Mars glyph and a different sign teaches you about different ways of taking action.

6. Jupiter. This glyph is the lightning bolt that strikes from above—not just of terror, but of inspiration. Its metal is tin. Jupiter is associated with knack, with talent, with that thing you do that comes so easy to you, and you can't understand why others have such a hard time with it. Jupiter is the big gift-giver, the freebie, the place where you shine and skate by. When it is contacted by a transiting planet, your luck changes, for better or worse. An amulet with the Jupiter glyph is an all-around luck charm for the area of talent indicated by Jupiter's placement in your chart. An amulet with the Jupiter glyph and a different sign can bring you luck in other areas of life.

7. Saturn. The glyph is the relentless scythe of Father Time. Its metal is lead, but if you find that too dangerous, the soft stuff referred to as "pot metal" will do, as will nickel. (Although amulets made from lead weights are very Saturnian.) Saturn is the planet of discipline, of limitation, of eat-your-vegetables. It is the single most disliked planet of all, but it is painfully necessary to our survival; we cannot all be grasshoppers all the time; sometimes we must be ants. When your natal Saturn undergoes a transit, it tends to shake loose old feelings and opinions and beliefs and wounds that have been buried, frozen, or otherwise put into stasis. Whether this will be a gentle shaking or a rough one will depend on the planet and the angle. An amulet with the Saturn glyph and the sign of your natal Saturn will help you work on your own personal limits and difficulties, and help you develop discipline in those areas . . . or it can reinforce your fears and emotional biases, depending on the spirit in which it is created. An amulet with the Saturn glyph and a different sign will teach you about other people's pain and other paths of discipline.

8. Uranus. The glyph is a stylized H, from William Herschel, the astronomer who discovered it. (Yes, I know, how unromantic.) Its true metal is uranium, which is of course impossible to put into an amulet, but like Mercury it has an affinity for aluminum. Uranus rules the way you see change and innovation, the way you look toward the future, and where you have trickster energy. An amulet with the Uranus glyph and the sign of your natal Uranus will nourish your innate ability to change to meet the future. An amulet with the Uranus glyph and a different sign will allow you to see different futures from perspectives you might not have thought of.

9. Neptune. The glyph is a trident, for the Greek sea god Poseidon (Roman Neptune). Although it supposedly has an affinity for the radioactive and impossible-to-get heavy metal neptunium, I've found that Neptune doesn't much seem to like metals at all. Instead, it has a strong affinity for glass, and I suggest etching glass for a Neptune amulet. Neptune rules your ability to merge—with another person, with higher spirituality, and with illusion (the latter gift also ruling addictions, insanity, and general self-delusion). An amulet with the Neptune glyph and your natal Neptune sign can push you naturally in any of these three directions, depending on the spirit in which it is made. (I suggest concentrating on the higher-spirituality intent while making it.) A Neptune amulet with a different sign will open up the paths of other spiritual perspectives to you and perhaps also help you to understand the illusions of other people, so as to better help them.

10. Pluto. One of the glyphs is a combination of the letters PL, the other a combination of the letters UTO. Either can be used. Its true metal is radioactive plutonium, and in fact any radioactive metal. Most people use steel, tempered iron, as a stand-in for Pluto. This planet rules power, control, and intensity; your inner volcano; and what you would bleed and starve for. An amulet with the Pluto glyph and your natal Pluto sign will help you master and control the intense energies within you. A Pluto amulet with a different sign will introduce you to different forms of intensity and give you lessons in alternate means of self-empowerment and self-control.

11. South Node. The glyph is the tail of a dragon. The Nodes are mathematical points, always opposing each other. There are no particular associated metals, and if you use something colored, make sure to use opposite colors for the two Nodes. The South Node has to do with the qualities that you came into the world instinctively knowing and that you revert to in times of crisis and laziness. This is often blamed on past lives, and many astrologers feel that the sign and house of your South Node describes your recent past life. Carry the glyph, with your natal South Node sign, on an amulet in order to better remember the lessons learned in that lifetime. Carry the glyph with a different sign on an amulet to help you understand the past-life experiences of those close to you (in other words, use their South Node sign) or to find out if you had past lives with those energies.

12. North Node. The glyph is the head of a dragon. The North Node is your karmic lesson for this lifetime. Carry its glyph, with your natal North Node sign, on an amulet to better learn and accomplish this lesson. Carry its glyph with a different sign to learn about a karmic lesson that you think would be useful to you.

13. Part of Fortune. This comes from Vedic astrology, which has many, many "Parts," all of them mathematical points made by adding and subtracting the degrees of various planets. Western astrologers sometimes stick on the Part of Fortune because it's the most "fun" and "pleasant" of the Parts. It describes the place to go for your best luck. Carry its glyph and natal sign as an amulet for getting the most out of that lucky activity. Carry its glyph and a different natal sign as an amulet for getting some luck out of a different activity where you are not normally lucky.

14. Ascendant. Not a glyph—it's just the horizontal line to the left of the center point of the chart. It's the beginning of your first house, the place where the Sun rose on the day of your birth. The Ascendant is your outer shell, your "mask," the way that you interact with the world. If it's in a sign that's harmonious with your Sun and/or Moon, then you're a "what you see is what you get" sort of person. If it's not, then you're the sort who is different underneath your outer persona.

15. Descendant. The horizontal line to the right of the center point of the chart—the beginning of your seventh house. This symbolizes the people that you are drawn to in order to feel "complete" . . . at least until you own those qualities for yourself.

THE SIGN GLYPHS

1. Aries. A fire sign, ruled by Mars. The glyph is the horns of a ram. Aries is both warrior energy and fresh, new infant energy. An Aries amulet would add the energies of the warrior to any venture that required courage and adventurousness, while it would also add the energies of new beginnings, idealism, and enthusiasm to a stagnant situation. It's also good for athletes to wear during competitive games.

2. Taurus. An earth sign, ruled by Venus. The glyph is a bull's head. Taurus is earthy energy, slow and practical and physical. A Taurus amulet would help with physical endurance, with success in material projects such as making money through hard work or starting a business, and with developing patience.

3. Gemini. An air sign, ruled by Mercury. The glyph is a Roman numeral 2, symbolizing the Twins. Gemini is quick, verbal, and lives very much in the head. A Gemini amulet would help with teaching, studying, talking your way out of things, and multitasking. Since it is also the sign of the Twins, it would be useful for allying the dark and light parts of yourself.

4. Cancer. A water sign, ruled by the Moon. The glyph is two crab claws. Cancer is emotional and deals strongly with the feeling side of things. A Cancer amulet would help someone to notice, acknowledge, and express their feelings (perhaps a good thing to wear to the therapist appointment) and would also be useful for learning to nurture and take care of oneself, healing wounds caused by bad parenting, and helping children to feel loved and cared for.

5. Leo. A fire sign, ruled by the Sun. The glyph is a lion's tail. Leo energy is self-expressive, confident, and loves to be the center of attention. A

Leo amulet would be the thing to wear to combat stage fright, gain confidence in public arenas (especially if it's you up there giving the speech), and develop self-esteem. It's the "I'm in charge; look at me!" amulet.

6. Virgo. An earth sign, ruled by Mercury. There's a lot of argument about what the glyph is—some say that it's the Scorpio glyph with a bar through it to suggest the sexual energy blocked, some say that it is a symbol of Pallas Athene, some have other suggestions. At any rate, Virgo energy is quiet, precise, disciplined, and detail oriented. A Virgo amulet would be the thing to carry when you have to organize complicated tasks that are boring, or niggling, or repetitive, or must be done with absolute perfection. It's also good for developing in yourself a discipline of maintaining bodily health.

7. Libra. An air sign, ruled by Venus. The glyph is a set of scales. Libra loves beauty and harmony, yet is moved by injustice and argues for fairness. This would be a good amulet for a lawyer to carry (but only if they are honestly on the side of justice), or for someone who is embroiled in a court case (but only if a fair outcome would actually serve them), or for someone who wants to create beauty and harmony in their life.

8. Scorpio. A water sign, ruled by Pluto. The glyph is a scorpion with a barbed tail. Scorpio energy is intense, emotional, and tends toward extremes. This is the amulet for the person whose life is in the midst of transformation and upheaval, and who needs to learn to welcome the intense changes (and the feelings that they bring up) rather than just struggling futilely against them or trying to pretend that they are not happening. A Scorpio amulet can also lend passion to an otherwise dry and repressed life. It may come out as sexual passion or some other sort.

9. Sagittarius. A fire sign, ruled by Jupiter. The glyph is an arrow, for the archer. Sagittarius is a fiery, adventurous, and straightforward sign. A Sagittarius amulet would aid in discerning truth from lies, help one find one's own individual path, and lead one into and out of adventures.

10. Capricorn. An earth sign, ruled by Saturn. Capricorn is practical, persistent, and goal oriented, and can endure a good deal of hardship and deprivation in pursuit of a goal. Obviously, then, this is the amulet to carry if you're pushing your way through to a difficult long-term goal, and you need the strength and endurance to keep going day to day even when all seems miserable. It can also help you get through times of poverty and scarcity, help you find practical ways to survive, and temporarily hold back overwhelming tides of emotion that threaten to paralyze you.

11. Aquarius. An air sign, ruled by Uranus. Aquarius energy is intellectual, coolheaded, nonconformist, and somewhat preoccupied with its place in the group, either insider or outcast. An Aquarius amulet brings inspiration and mental focus, as well as strength of purpose and principle, for the person who is suddenly finding themselves cast out of a group due to controversial opinions and values.

12. Pisces. A water sign, ruled by Neptune. The glyph is two fishes facing each other. Pisces is a sensitive, self-sacrificing water sign that is adept at merging with others, including the divine, or addictions and delusions. A Pisces amulet would be useful for healing, developing compassion, or achieving altered states.

THE HOUSES

While there are no glyphs for the astrological houses—those twelve pie slices on your chart—and therefore no amulets, they are important to know about for purposes of magic. Each of them rules a different area of life, and planets falling in that area (in your natal chart or in daily charts) will help with magical and ritual workings. I am listing the house meanings, not as they would be listed in a book on chart interpretation, but for their magical uses.

All of your planets fall into a house, and that means that you have a knack in accessing a specific kind of magic. The Sun or Jupiter in a particular house suggests a strong natural talent in general in that area.

The Moon means that you will need to access that talent in a particularly intuitive rather than logical or methodical manner. Mercury here means that you should concentrate on the power of the spoken or written word to access this knack. Venus suggests that the talent is best utilized through the arts, or the "art" of relationships. Mars here is a powerhouse of energy, but one that needs to be carefully aimed or it will go off in the wrong way. Pluto in a house speaks of a gift that can be reached only through underworld methods, such as intense experiences, sex magic, or deep psychology work. Neptune is the sign of the gift that is accessed only in conjunction with some spiritual path. Uranus suggests an erratic gift, one that can best be accessed by unusual means. Saturn here means that you have a powerful gift in this area, but it is deliberately blocked as part of your karmic lessons. In order to access it, you will have to put in years of training and discipline, and you will need to learn to use difficult techniques as crutches.

1. House of the Body. Glamour magic, making yourself appear different, magic to change bodily habits or physical traits.

2. House of Finance. Money magic, spells to get expensive items cheap, magic to change people's materialistic values.

3. House of Communication. Message spells, magic for better communication, wind magic, short-journey safety spells.

4. House of Home. Peaceful-home magic, home-finding and home-protection magic, spells to acquire land, rituals to deal with leftover childhood issues, protection for parents.

5. House of Creativity. Fertility spells to conceive children, safe pregnancy spells, enhancing-creativity magic, gambling magic, sex magic for pleasure or practical purposes, general happiness magic to lighten hearts.

6. House of Service and Health. Physical healing spells of all kinds. Spells to get survival jobs; spells to get good hired help; magic to find ways to give honorable service; magic to help you get through rotten daily jobs like cleaning your house, taking out the garbage, changing the cat-box, getting your car inspected.

7. House of Partnerships. Magic for attracting and maintaining a romantic or business partnership, spells for better understanding between partners, marriage magic.

8. House of Death. Sex magic for connecting with deeper powers; spells for getting through spiritual crises; spells for contacting the dead, laying ghosts, communicating with Underworld deities, dealing with karma; magic to ensure inheritances.

9. House of Long Journeys over Water. Travel charms for long trips, study magic for higher education, rituals to propitiate deities, spells to find hidden written knowledge, divination with traditional tools of symbol sets (Tarot, runes, etc.).

10. House of Career. Success in business spells. Fame and fortune spells. Creating, destroying, and repairing one's reputation magic. Magic for determining the best real-world path for you.

11. House of Friends and Groups. Spells to make friends and find new peer and interest groups, magic to promote "tribal bonding" within a group of unrelated people, magic to achieve long-term goals for groups and organizations.

12. House of Dreams. Dream magic and dream interpretation; intuitive-type divination such as scrying, spellwork, and energy work for exploring the unconscious and bringing up hidden thoughts and memories; magic work for knowing yourself more deeply.

Go through your chart and see where each planet lies and what that means about your own psychic knacks. Then, armed with charts of future times for you, see what planets are transiting your various houses. During the time that a transiting planet goes through a particular house, it's easier for you to do certain magic or spells that you don't have a natal "knack" for. It's as if the transiting planet lends you a bit of a knack. For example, if you really wanted to find a spouse and not just another short-term fling, then doing a spell when Venus is transiting your seventh house, the house of partnerships—or even when Saturn, the planet of commitment, is transiting it—is more likely to get results.

Pay special attention to outer planets, since they stay in one particular house for a very long time, sometimes several years. This will give you a chance to mine their energy for magical uses. It's also a good way to have a better attitude about a planet mucking about in some area of your life. See it as an opportunity for magical work rather than merely an annoying interference to be endured.

4
Moon Magic
Lunar Cycles

Most witches and Pagans have at least some kind of surface-level reverence for the Moon, which they usually associate with the Goddess and feminine energy, although there have been many Moon gods in ancient cultures as well. They wear Moon symbols on their heads, around their necks, and tattooed on their bodies . . . but most really have no idea what the lunar cycle is really about. If you asked the average Pagan to name the phases of the Moon, most couldn't get past New, Crescent, and Full; perhaps they'd know Waxing and Waning, but that's likely all. If you asked them how many days were in a lunar month, many would parrot the old fallacy of twenty-eight days, "just like a woman's menstrual cycle ought to be." I've even found that error written into many books on Pagan and Earth-centered and (especially) women-centered spirituality.

The actual lunar cycle is twenty-nine and a half days long. There are twelve to thirteen moons in the period of a solar year, and they do not line up with that solar year (or rather, they take 18.6 solar years to do so). There's really no such thing as a "lunar year," because the 365-day concept of "year" is a solar pattern. The Moon may reflect the Sun's light, but it doesn't work on the Sun's schedule. It keeps spinning along, doing its thing, and annoying the solar-centered calendar-makers who would like for it to line up properly (28 times 13 is 364, much closer to the solar year, which accounts for why so many people cling irrationally to the 28-day error). Yet to attempt to make it fit the solar year is to deny the Moon's own nature, just as so many of us try to force our own erratic, annoying, feeling natures into a logical left-brained ego-control pattern.

Many ancient civilizations calculated the solar and lunar calendars at the same time—the ancient Greeks, for one, and the Celts for another. They used different means to account for the difference. The Greeks counted only twelve lunar months and then started over, which meant that after a couple of years, the seasonal harvests were beginning to slip noticeably, so they would stick in an extra month every three years. The Celtic lunar tree calendar started with Beth, the birch month, and ended with Ruis, the elder month; their solar year began with the Winter Solstice. Generally, the modern Celtic practice is to start Beth at the next New Moon after the solstice, so Ruis gets truncated, sometimes to only a few days. (If you have Internet access, a useful lunar calendar with both the Greek and the Celtic holidays—and explanatory commentary on lunar calendars—can be found on the Pagan Book of Hours site, at www .cauldronfarm.com/bookofhours/index.html.)

The lunar cycle itself has eight phases—New, Crescent, Waxing Quarter, Gibbous, Full, Disseminating, Waning Quarter, and Balsamic. Does this remind you of anything? It sparked a memory in my mind, when I saw it . . . that of the Pagan solar year, which we also divide into eight sections, marked by the solstices, equinoxes, and cross-quarter days. It seems that although the Moon refuses to work on the Sun's calendar, they do have an eightfold wheel in common, if one chooses to divide it that way. That might also imply that the eight quarters of the lunar month have a resonance with the eight quarters of the solar year. (For astrological information on these, check the Astrology of Pagan Holidays, chapter 14.) This concept merits further investigation.

Each of the eight lunar phases also moves through each of the twelve signs, creating a total of ninety-six possible combinations. (Ninety-six, now there's an interesting number. Not only is it a multiple of three, the "magic number," but it is written with the numerals that contain both circles and crescents.) As the Moon goes through each sign in approximately 2½ days, that means that the phases will cover, in some cases, a sign and a half—45 degrees.

One easy thing to remember is that when the Moon is New, it is in the same sign as the Sun. (See, it's not exactly true that they don't work together on a calendar. It's just that they do a dance together, touching and then whirling apart, and then coming together again on a set schedule. Just like the lunar and solar parts of your soul ought to do.) When it's Full, it's in the sign opposing the Sun. In other words, if it's August and the Sun is in Leo, the New Moon during that time will be in Leo, but the Full Moon during that time will be in Aquarius. If you know that Taurus and Scorpio are the signs that square those two, you'll also know that the Waxing Quarter will be in Scorpio (at a right angle to Leo) and that the Waning Quarter will be in Taurus (at a right angle to Aquarius). For the actual times when the signs change, don't be ashamed to have to check an ephemeris or a calendar; even experienced astrologers do that.

To do a spell utilizing Moon magic, the ideal way would be to line up the appropriate sign and the appropriate phase, and to do this, you need a Moon sign calendar. You also need to go outside on every clear night, if only for a moment, and take a look at the Moon. This way you'll get a feel for her cycle, and it won't just be a theoretical thing to you. In fact, you may eventually become adept at estimating the sign from the Moon's face.

The list that follows explores the archetypal energy of each sign and phase of the Moon. As the Moon passes through its various phases, you'll feel the pull of each kind of energy and perhaps see it happening in your life. Each series of same-sign Moon phases tells a story, a cycle of growth and maturing in a specific way. Of course, they aren't in order in any given lunar month, but then that's part of the Moon's magic. Feeling experiences are rarely orderly. They often come upon you seemingly out of nowhere, with no context. Checking up on what part of the great story the Moon is playing out may help you to better connect with what's going on in your life from day to day.

I. NEW MOON

During this phase, the Moon is in the same sign as the Sun, having circled back around to meet its solar partner once more. Its energy continues a little ways after the sign has changed. The New Moon, the time when the Moon is not yet visible, is the time of beginnings. It is the point when the seedling breaks out of its shell, but has not yet broken out of the dark earth. Everything is just an unformed idea with no manifestation apparent. All spells done on the New Moon pertain to beginnings. The archetypes here are of children and adolescents, not yet formed in their own identity, but already bearing qualities that will become the basis for what is yet to be.

In Aries: Infant's Moon. The Aries energy is the first breath of spring at the equinox, and it is the youngest of all the signs, so its New Moon manifestation is the Infant—tiny and helpless, crying and waving its powerless fists, but full of all possibilities. *Do magic for the beginnings of any project.*

In Taurus: Dryad's Moon. The Taurus lunar energy starts out as the Dryad, a tree spirit, an earth faery, the child of nature and the woods. *Do magic for planting trees, reforestation, or reclamation of polluted land.*

In Gemini: Little Brother's Moon. The Gemini energy starts out as the archetypal Little Brother—mischievous, rambunctious, always into everything, but eager to learn. *Do magic to assist the start of any educational beginning, such as a new school, a new class, or a new area of learning.*

In Cancer: Mother's Daughter Moon. The Cancer energy begins as the Mother's Daughter—shy, clinging, oversensitive, innately kind and trusting. *Do magic to bless any emergence from the home into the outer world or to bless the birth of any girl child.*

In Leo: Sun Child's Moon. Leo energy begins as the Sun Child, blessed with divine charisma from birth, open and trusting and joyful. *Do magic for confidence in being in the public eye for the first time.*

In Virgo: Maiden's Moon. Virgo energy starts out as the solitary Maiden, reserved and private, keeping her thoughts to herself. *Do magic to assist the beginning of any endeavor that must be done entirely by oneself and that will gain no approval from the outside world.*

In Libra: White Knight's Moon. The Libra energy begins with the adolescent White Knight, full of ideals and high principles, sure of his ability to take on any opponents and win. *Do magic to help begin to defend what you feel is right.*

In Scorpio: Raging Moon. The Scorpio energy begins with a child who is born in shadow and born angry. Wounded and misused, the Raging One starts life with a fearful and vigilant attitude, but also with a hidden will that has been tempered by early sorrow. *Do magic to defend abused children and to open negotiations with one's own shadow side.*

In Sagittarius: Gypsy's Moon. The Sagittarius energy starts out with the careless, freedom-loving Gypsy, who has no goals other than experiencing whatever comes up on one's wandering travels. *Do magic to assist any long journey undertaken for fun or experience, or to broaden one's horizons.*

In Capricorn: Forgotten One's Moon. Capricorn energy starts out with the Forgotten One, the child noticed by few, dismissed by many, and undervalued by all, but who bears the potential to achieve greater things than more showy peers. *Do magic to aid those who are underestimated by those who judge by surfaces.*

In Aquarius: Father's Son Moon. Aquarius energy starts out with the Father's Son, the Bright Boy upon which hopes and ambitions are heaped, but who is destined to rebel and reject the values of his early caregivers. *Do magic to aid any project whose acceptance is uncertain or to bless the birth of any boy child.*

In Pisces: Dreamer's Moon. Pisces energy begins as the Dreamer, the child who is full of fantasies, who can barely tell them from reality at times. *Do magic for any project that has been longingly dreamed of for years.*

II. CRESCENT MOON

The Crescent phase starts about halfway into the sign following the one that matches the Sun and continues through the end of the third sign. The narrow Crescent Moon shows in the sky, and we go from a place of not-moving to one of motion. This is the time of the first step, and generally we go in the direction that we were pointed at the New Moon, for good or ill. The time for changing direction is not yet here; we have taken our first steps and are now hastening along the path in front of us, happy in our ability to be moving at last. The archetypes of Crescent Moons grow out of the New Moons; they are the logical continuation of those energies, learning to do and create as well as be.

In Aries: Torch-Bearer's Moon. Aries has grown from the Infant to the Spirit of Fire, the enthusiastic runner who carries the torch of his dreams and ideals. *Do magic to aid projects that require a good deal of ongoing enthusiasm from the participants.*

In Taurus: Gardener's Moon. Taurus has gone from the wild, innocent Dryad to the Gardener, who realizes that it is possible to plant your own seeds and make an impact on the world around you. The Gardener, busy learning the lessons of patience and care in order to make things grow, loses sight of the fact that in making a garden, you lose the wilderness. *Do magic to make gardens flourish.*

In Gemini: Little Sister's Moon. Gemini now becomes the Little Sister—smart, inquisitive, sharp, able to figure out the right thing to say to the grownups to get out of trouble. *Do magic to impress a superior who has something you need.*

In Cancer: Mother's Son Moon. The next phase of Cancer is that of the Mother's Son—quiet, clinging, cuddly, sensitive, but silently perceiving all the feelings of those around him. *Do magic for family bonding or for blessing the first spoken words of any boy child.*

In Leo: Clown's Moon. The Sun Child becomes the Clown, trying hard to impress people and be seen, and learns the lesson of the joy found in bringing laughter to the hearts of others. *Do magic to make someone happier and to lift depression.*

In Virgo: Apprentice's Moon. The Maiden becomes the Apprentice, learning the skills of a new trade. The Apprentice is taken with the details of the new craft and throws herself into it, making it her whole life. *Do magic to assist with learning new skills and studying.*

In Libra: Dancer's Moon. Libra now becomes the Dancer, learning to balance and be graceful, and to understand beauty in movement. This balancing will eventually lead Libra to learn the lesson of moving back and forth between opposing sides. *Do magic for grace, for poise, and for balancing many things without dropping them.*

In Scorpio: Blood Moon. The Scorpio youth begins to learn the lessons of blood—sexual maturity, passion, death and the food chain, and the rites of passage that come as ordeals. *Do ritual rites of passage at this time, especially ones that are ordeals or commemorate hard times.*

In Sagittarius: Traveler's Moon. The Sagittarian Gypsy decides that the next step is to actually have a goal, and so becomes the Traveler, moving purposefully from place to place, perhaps as a messenger or for business. *Do magic for moving one's home and for seeking aid on any journey that is undertaken for a serious purpose.*

In Capricorn: Mountain Climber's Moon. The Forgotten Child grows older and notices the mountain, and he decides to climb to its top like so many other youths in faery tales. What magic will he find at the peak? *Do magic to aid any far-reaching goal that others scornfully say is impossible for you.*

In Aquarius: Father's Daughter Moon. Aquarius becomes the Father's Daughter—serious, intelligent, and willing to support and explain the values of the family, tribe, or culture from which she came, as Athene supports her father Zeus. *Do magic to protect the welfare of one's own family, tribe, or culture.*

In Pisces: Mermaid's Moon. The Dreamer becomes the Mermaid, sitting on an island in the ocean of dreams and feelings, attempting somewhat incoherently to put all those dreams into words and song. Sometimes the songs draw in others, sometimes they just sail by, looking askance at the mythical creature. *Do magic to help communicate poetic and mystical truths to others.*

III. WAXING QUARTER MOON

This phase begins with the fourth sign and continues until somewhere halfway through the fifth sign. At the Waxing Quarter Moon, things reach a period of crisis. Sometimes it's because we realize that our former path has gone as far as it could go, and perhaps it went somewhere that we didn't expect or want. Oftentimes we find ourselves in a situation where we have betrayed and compromised the ideals of our New

Moon period or where we must betray them to keep from falling into stagnation. The Waxing Quarter Moon is the difficult place, the point of tears and treachery and mutiny. In each of the archetypes of this Moon, the joyful pathwalkers of the Crescent period find themselves in painful and intolerable situations for the first time; they learn about suffering and about taking responsibility for one's bad decisions. It's the time where we scream, "Why do I deserve this? How did I get here?" and we scramble, panicked, for a way out, even if it means justifying some action that will later come back to haunt us.

In Aries: Brigand's Moon. In this phase, Aries has become the Brigand, a rogue, a strong but selfish desperado, a highwayman who is as likely to romance and leave ladies as he is to attack and rob people on the road. The ideals of the Torch-Bearer have become tarnished through cynicism, and the Brigand cares only for his own gain and his own adrenaline rush. The warrior spirit of the Brigand is strong, but he has yet to learn a code of honor. *Do magic to protect against attackers and to develop raw courage.*

In Taurus: Woodcutter's Moon. The Gardener decides that she needs more room in which to plant, and so begins to cut down the trees of the forest, thus betraying her origins as the Dryad and killing the very trees from which she sprang, in the name of commerce and expansion. *Do magic to expand a business or moneymaking project.*

In Gemini: Liar's Moon. Also called the Moon of the Evil Twins, the Little Brother and Little Sister have learned that they can manipulate others through fast talking and lies that start out small and soon grow into whoppers. At the same time, they fight over the lies that they tell each other and themselves. *Do magic to uncover the truth beneath fluff and glitter or to add an especially bright edge to your own blarney.*

In Cancer: Weeping Moon. In this phase, the Cancerian is forced away from the home that has been their entire world up until now and wanders forlorn and homesick on the road. Unlike Sagittarius, for the Mother's Children to be denied their hearth is a terrible thing, and Cancer becomes the Weeping One, the homeless orphan who will never be happy until home is achieved once more. *Do magic to aid homeless people, orphans, and foster children.*

In Leo: Actor's Moon. The Clown has become a polished performer with many masks, but Leo has forgotten how to take them off. In his desperation to be loved, he hides his true self behind dramatic displays and then is desolate when no one truly sees him. Leaping from one costume to another, he begins to lose who he really is and becomes his shallow personas; in his panic he becomes more histrionic and overdramatic. *Do magic to conceal yourself for some good purpose or to see behind the masks of others.*

In Virgo: Counting Moon. The Apprentice has learned her job down to the last detail, and now she is obsessed with perfection in doing it. She becomes an accountant, the Counting One, who tallies up only flaws and criticizes every imperfection, in herself and others. Trapped in the coldness of perfectionism, she loses contact with humanity and her own human frailty. *Do magic to become more organized and to get details in order.*

In Libra: Black Knight Moon. In this crisis phase, Libra learns that there is another perspective to every ideal and swings hard in the opposite direction to balance out the White Knight's one-sidedness. Here, Libra becomes the Black Knight, the Adversary, the one who stands in the path and presents a challenge to the naive and the complacent . . . but often coldly slays them when they fail to give sufficient respect to his new perspective. *Do magic to assist in any challenge to another whose views oppose yours and who sees you as wrong and dangerous.*

In Scorpio: Executioner's Moon. Also called Lichtor's Moon. Learning about death leads the Bloody Youth to take a job as the Executioner, beheading those he sees as evil and an enemy. He reacts from his own pain and fear, seeing enemies everywhere, and drawing on ruthless imagined laws that no one can live up to. Sooner or later, he will realize that he cannot kill the real enemy, who lies within. *Do magic to work with inner violence in oneself and others, and to honor the internal predator.*

In Sagittarius: Seeker's Moon. Here the journeys of the Sagittarian energy take on a desperate flavor. He has been the carefree Gypsy and the purposeful Traveler, but the more he moves, the more he realizes that something is missing. The Seeker despairingly rushes from one place to another, driven by an urgency that hunts for inner truth, but his external journeys avail him nothing. *Do magic to help someone find their true path.*

In Capricorn: Miner's Moon: The Climber of Mountains has reached the top and sees a precious jewel half-buried in the stone. Delving into the mountain, he finds a wealth of jewels and precious metals, but soon loses himself in dark, close tunnels, piling up more and more gold and gems that no one else can see, and perhaps finds himself trapped in his own unhealthy burrows. *Do magic to uncover possible wealth from unexpected places.*

In Aquarius: Rebel Moon. The Father's Children see the flaws in what has been taught to them, and Aquarius becomes the Rebel, smashing any idol that looks too familiar. Armed with a keen nose for hypocrisy, a vague dream of how things could be, and no real plan on how to get there, the Rebel raises an insurrection and is cast out from the tribe. *Do spells to help people survive a rebellious time in their lives.*

In Pisces: Martyr's Moon. Pisces longs to give of herself to others, and here she gets her chance: she is thoroughly martyred and forced to selflessly aid others until there is practically nothing left of herself. The magical Mermaid is captured and bled of her magic until almost nothing is left of the Dreamer's hopes. Dull and washed out, the Martyr continues to offer herself up to others, believing that this is all she is good for. *Do magic to help someone who has let others overcome their boundaries.*

IV. GIBBOUS MOON

The Gibbous Moon starts halfway through the fifth sign and continues until the end of the sixth. At the Waxing Quarter, all the hopes of the New and Crescent Moons fell apart, and we found ourselves in a terrible mess. At the Gibbous Moon, we figure out what we have to do to get out of that mess. It is never anything easy. The Gibbous Moon is the period where we struggle, but at least we are struggling toward a goal and not just thrashing around. More often than not, the direction that we end up taking to save our souls is nothing like what we intended back at the beginning, but it is what turns out to be necessary. The Gibbous Moon is a time of applied, conscientious effort in the face of obstacles. The archetypes of this Moon phase all work hard, internally and externally, to perfect something and to have something to offer up to the world.

In Aries: Adventurer's Moon. The Brigand has found an outlet for his aggressive energy, instead of frittering it away in meaningless and destructive fights. As the Adventurer, he explores new lands, pioneers new territories, and pits himself against hardship and the elements instead of against other people. *Do magic to help someone who is "going where no one has gone before."*

In Taurus: Farmer's Moon. The Gardener has expanded into being the Farmer, who owns and cultivates a large area of land . . . and discovers, to his dismay, that his farm is an ecosystem unto itself, which must be carefully kept in balance. He learns that to control the land is to take the place of all the natural controls that exist in the wild. *Do magic to help a flourishing business or a family farm.*

In Gemini: Mercenary's Moon. Gemini is now the Mercenary, an expert swordsman and duelist who will fight for anyone, at any time, as long as the pay is good. While the Mercenary's ethics are still flexible, during this time there will be lessons in who it is more honorable to defend, and Gemini will learn the art of discernment and mental self-control. *Do magic to enhance any project where careful verbal or written communication is necessary or to win a debate.*

In Cancer: Life-Giver's Moon. Here Cancer is the Life-Giver, the pregnant woman and her mate who create the next generation. By making her own family, the Life-Giver heals the wounds of the Weeping One, creating a hearth of her own that salves loneliness and takes in other lonely souls. *Do magic for conceiving children and for healthy pregnancies.*

In Leo: Singer's Moon. The Leo Actor has learned to do more than simply act out a persona. In this phase, Leo learns the art of genuine self-expression and becomes the Singer who puts heart and soul into the performance. People are moved, rather than merely dazzled, and the Singer wins acclaim as a real, unique person and not a collection of masks. *Do magic to be better able to express oneself through art.*

In Virgo: Housewife's Moon. Here the self-enclosed Virgin is forced to become a Housewife, perhaps as a step-parent caring for orphaned children. Although she keeps house beautifully, she is not used to taking human needs into account, and she learns painfully that people are, in the end, more important than numbers or a perfectly clean floor. *Do magic to motivate people to clean up their messes.*

In Libra: Lover's Moon. In this phase, the Black Knight finds love, and it turns him entirely around. Instead of being on one side or another, he learns the give-and-take of real relationships and becomes the Lover. This has a softening effect on both his ideals and his reactions. *Do love spells, of all kinds.*

In Scorpio: Cloaked One's Moon. After the bloodthirsty crisis of the Executioner, Scorpio realizes that the demons lie inside and decides to go after them there. The Cloaked One is the one who passes into the dark places, the hidden and unseen cracks in a soul, and quietly digs out all that has lain rotting and gangrenous. *Do magic to assist in introspection.*

In Sagittarius: Scholar's Moon. Having exhausted all that his travels can offer, the Seeker turns to the writings of others concerning their own travels . . . and becomes the Scholar, studying and collecting the many particles of truth contained in the libraries of the world. His journeying continues, but it is a journey of the mind rather than of the body. *Do magic to aid any educational endeavor and to help students concentrate.*

In Capricorn: Smith's Moon. The Miner realizes that all his hoarded precious metal is of no use in raw form, so he becomes the Smith, whose creative powers of manifestation turn the gold, silver, and gems into tools, coins, and jewelry to be used and worn and traded to others for yet more riches. *Do magic to bless the hands of those who do craft work.*

In Aquarius: Trickster's Moon. The Rebel realizes that he cannot change people's minds, either by force or by direct persuasion, so he turns to the teaching methods of the Trickster. In this phase, Aquarius learns to use humor and the absurd to make people laugh, and then to make them think, and to get away with it in a way that the Rebel cannot. *Do magic to* *hide a lesson that you are subtly trying to teach someone or to bless a direct action that uses humor as a teaching tool.*

In Pisces: Poet's Moon. In this phase, Pisces finally learns to articulate those long-lost dreams and fantasies, and in doing so manages to communicate them to the world. The Poet may live in a poor garret, but she has learned to keep enough of her Source to fuel and feed her own creativity, and she serves others indirectly, by bringing them into contact with that Source through her writing. *During this phase, write spiritual poetry and liturgy.*

V. FULL MOON

The Full Moon—the sign that is in opposition to the Sun's sign, and a little way past that—is the time of culmination, when things reach their peak, or at least as far as they can go on their own thrust. It's the crest of the hill, the halfway point, the place where you know it's all going to be downhill from here . . . for good or ill. The archetypes of the Full Moon are the signs at their best, come to full fruition. They have matured past their crisis and their educational struggle, and they are now "adult," fully come into their powers.

In Aries: Warrior's Moon. Aries has now become the Warrior, skilled and fearsome and competent . . . but he has learned how to follow a code of honor and is a true defender of the helpless rather than merely an opportunist. Instead of being a loner, he leads a small band of equally honorable warriors who respect him deeply. *Do magic to bring the energy of the honorable warrior into your life.*

In Taurus: Earth Mother's Moon. The Farmer—controller of domestic growth—and the Dryad—embodiment of wild growth—have come together in the form of the Earth Mother, who embodies and honors all growth. She blesses both the cornfields and the forests, and she spreads fertility wherever she goes. Flowers spring up in her footsteps. *Do magic to bring fertility to lands, animals, or people.*

In Gemini: Storyteller's Moon. Here Gemini has learned to tell stories that are more than just interesting lies. The self-control learned as the Mercenary has brought the Gemini mind to a point of intellectual blossoming, where everything spills forth brilliantly and is instinctively put into a form that is most understandable to others. People follow the Storyteller around asking for more stories, which in turn inspires Gemini's imagination, and the former Liar becomes a fountain of powerful and subtle truths. *Tell sacred tales during this phase.*

In Cancer: Sea Mother's Moon. The Sea Mother is the incarnation of the nurturing, receptive maternal instincts. She has a multitude of children and enough room in her heart to love every one of them. Her life is built around her loved ones, giving to them of her ever-flowing waters and receiving in turn their love and adoration. *Do magic to promote bonding between parents and children.*

In Leo: Queen's Moon. Here Leo goes from one who performs to one who rules, either as the Queen Consort chosen off the stage for her charm like the Empress Theodosia or as a ruler in her own right. As Queen, she is a mother to an entire country, caring for the needs of many and inspiring them with her stable, confident presence. *Do magic for any woman in a leadership position.*

In Virgo: Spinner's Moon. Also called the Spinster's Moon. Here Virgo goes back to her solitude, but she is not utterly detached from human contact. As the Spinner of Threads, she partakes in the nature of the youngest of the Fates, who creates all life impartially with her spindle. On a practical level, the Spinner supports her family with her own hands, neither relying on another nor forgetting the ultimate purpose of her work. *Make and/or consecrate magically crafted items during this phase.*

In Libra: Artist's Moon. Inspired by the experiences of the Lover, Libra becomes the Artist and blossoms into the fullness of aesthetic inspiration. The Artist is a master of vision, creating works that move everyone who sees them and help them to understand the nature of both Love and Justice. *Create magical artwork during this phase.*

In Scorpio: Priestess's Moon. After years of introspection, the Cloaked One stumbles across the Mysteries, finds deeper spirituality, and emerges as the Priestess. Like the figure on the Tarot card, she understands both internal mystery and external esoteric lore, and finds the connections between the two. She devotes herself to her Gods and Goddesses, and in doing so finds purpose in the world. *Do ritual to honor the Gods and Goddesses during this period.*

In Sagittarius: Priest's Moon. While Scorpio finds spirituality through inner introspection, Sagittarius finds religion through the collected words of the ancients and dedicates himself to being a Priest. Where once he spurned the routine, he now finds comfort in the tethers of tradition. The empty place inside him is filled by divine communion. *Do ritual to honor the Gods during this period.*

In Capricorn: Matriarch's Moon. Also called Grandmother's Moon, although Capricorn is as much mother as grandmother. Here the former loner Capricorn is the center not just of a family, but of a tribe. As the Matriarch, she imparts values and wisdom to the next generation and prepares them to deal with the outside world. *Do magic to assist any woman with family problems.*

In Aquarius: Friendship Moon. Outcast Aquarius finds the unthinkable: people of like mind who want to be friends. This is the height of the Aquarian lesson, as the former Rebel and Trickster becomes the center of an affinity group and declares that all of humanity ought to be friends as well. *Do magic to help friends heal their differences.*

In Pisces: Healer's Moon. In this phase, Pisces discovers a gift as a Healer and realizes also that in order to do this job she need neither give herself away nor hide herself away. She learns to give of her Source up closely and personally, yet she also manages to maintain boundaries and not allow herself to be too overused. *Do magic for healing.*

VI. DISSEMINATING MOON

The Disseminating Moon starts somewhere in the eighth sign and continues to the end of the ninth. After the revelation of the Full Moon, the time comes to carry the message out to the rest of the world. Up until now, the entirety of the struggle has been internal, as we bring ourselves to the pinnacle of our abilities, but now our gifts need to belong to more than just us. The Disseminating Moon is the time when one asks the questions "So what good is all this? How does it serve the world? Are you going to let it die with you?" In this phase, the archetypes go out into the community of humanity to serve the greater good.

In Aries: Soldier's Moon. The Warrior joins up with larger forces to fight for a Cause and goes off to battle in a team. Finding a place to fight for something larger than himself and his own ideas seasons him, and the Soldier is a defender of cities, the Warrior in service to the greater good. *Do magic to assist bonding and camaraderie among people fighting for the same cause.*

In Taurus: Builder's Moon. Bringing the security and stability of the Farmer and Earth Mother to the outside world requires Taurus to become the Builder, first creating homes out of wood and clay, and then great edifices out of stone that will last for centuries. *Do magic to aid the expansion of a business or the construction of a building.*

In Gemini: Scribe's Moon. Gemini's way of bringing the Storyteller's words to the outer world is to write them down, and the Scribe spends his time translating those words of power for a wider audience. Aware that he will not know the worldviews of his readers, he hones his craft for the least possible chance of misunderstanding. *Do magic to help people write.*

In Cancer: Shield-Father's Moon. The Water-Mother is vulnerable while she has young children, and so the Shield-Father must protect her. Here Cancer dons his crab's shell, picks up his weapons, and stands guard outside the home, making sure that his loved ones are safe. The love he has learned from the secure hearth inside gives him a strong passion to defend its sanctuary from the outer world. *Do magic to defend one's home and one's personal boundaries.*

In Leo: King's Moon. The Leo archetype matures to that of the King, who rules and is a father to his people. He protects them and wages war when necessary; he trades with other countries, but not to feed the people, as the Queen does, but to enrich the country as a whole. His eyes are on his future and that of his dynasty. *Do magic to aid any man in a leadership position.*

In Virgo: Weaver's Moon. The Spinner moves on to the mature aspect of the Fates, which is that of the Weaver who weaves the thread of people's lives. Where the Spinner brings forth raw material, the Weaver brings forth a finished product, a craft to make people gasp with pleasure and one that will protect their bodies and keep them warm—practical considerations that mean a lot to Virgo. *Do magic to bless crafters and their work, especially those who make clothing of some kind.*

In Libra: Ambassador's Moon. The Artist takes the message of peace and harmony on the road and becomes the Ambassador or Diplomat, who artfully arranges relationships instead of mere paint or clay. *Do magic to increase harmony among others.*

In Scorpio: Witch's Moon. The Priestess feels the need to aid the suffering peasants, and she does this by becoming the Witch, whose knowledge of the Mysteries is useful in creating charms for healing, love, vengeance, and many other things. *Do magic to heighten one's own powers or the powers of others.*

In Sagittarius: Philosopher's Moon. Here the Priest mellows and becomes the Philosopher, writing and speaking his truths to an audience of interested disciples, much like a college professor. Unlike his younger incarnations, the Philosopher no longer travels, but is attached to an academic or ecclesiastical institution; the world travels to him for his wisdom and learning. *Do magic to aid with higher education or with teaching something new and complex.*

In Capricorn: Patriarch's Moon. Also called Grandfather's Moon, although Capricorn is as much father as grandfather. Matriarch becomes Patriarch, who goes out into the world and supports his family, providing for them as best he can and passing on his values and work ethic. *Do magic to assist any man with family troubles.*

In Aquarius: Apostle's Moon. Aquarius goes out among the people, speaking of the doctrine of universal friendship to all and sundry. The Apostle can be the bearer of any creed, even an antispiritual one, but it is always deeply believed and sincere. *Do magic to change people's ideas about something controversial.*

In Pisces: Moon of the Angel of Mercy. Having learned to heal, Pisces goes out among the people, determined to save as many lives and souls as possible. The Angel of Mercy leads many back from death and pain, but she must always guard against the hubris of attempting to be a messiah. *Do magic to help anyone in need.*

VII. WANING QUARTER MOON

The Waning Quarter Moon starts with the tenth sign and continues through to the middle of the eleventh. The Quarter Moons are both times of crisis. In the Waxing Quarter, the crisis was personal and internal; now, after the Disseminating Moon has forced us out into the greater arena, the crisis revolves around our interaction with the outer community and society. Instead of Man against Himself, it is Man against Man. The archetypes of this phase are in conflict once again, but they are older and wiser and have learned to better handle strife and turmoil.

In Aries: Survivor's Moon. The Soldier comes home shell-shocked from battle, with wounds that will be with him the rest of his life. He will be a long time healing, but he has survived, and he has no more fear of what the world might throw at him . . . and no more need to prove himself or act aggressively without dire need. However, those he tells about his battles don't really understand, and they dismiss his difficulties with tales of how they would have done better in his shoes. *Do magic to help someone who has survived a difficult battle of some kind.*

In Taurus: Merchant's Moon. The Builder has grown wealthy, and his needs for material security are all well met, but he has slowly become a slave to the materialism that surrounds him. The Merchant runs the risk of forgetting about the future in the effort to keep piling up wealth and comforts in the present. *Do magic to make money.*

In Gemini: Magician's Moon. The Scribe has found ancient written magical secrets, and in a flutter of intellectual hubris, he becomes a Magician. However, he has no sense of the deeper mysteries under the magic, and no connection with the Gods or Goddesses, and he must learn the lesson that the Universe is not his to push around. *Do magic to strengthen psychic powers.*

In Cancer: Widow's Moon. Here Cancer comes to a place of bereavement and mourning again, with the death of a spouse, and children who leave home and do not come back. After so many years of seeing herself as the center of a family, the Widow must now decide who she is now that she is alone. *Do magic to aid someone who is mourning the loss of a loved one.*

In Leo: Usurper's Moon. Leo plays out the myth of the fall from hubris, overreaching his territory and usurping the power of others, and having his throne usurped in turn. Falling from power, he must abandon all that he has achieved and find value in what he once was. *Do magic to prevent someone from becoming overextended or to pick up the pieces after a fall from pride.*

In Virgo: Fate's Moon. Here Virgo transitions to the third face of the Fates—that of the older woman with the scissors. As such, she becomes the one to say the sacred No, to draw the line and cut the cord and mark the boundary. Unlike her earlier archetype who merely criticized imperfections, the Waning Quarter's Virgo face understands people well enough to make allowances for their flaws . . . but the job makes her cold, and frays her nerves, and makes her want to retreat into solitude. *Do magic to understand one's destiny.*

In Libra: Judge's Moon. The Ambassador has been made a Judge, with the power to cast wrongdoers into prison or order their deaths. In this phase, Libra runs the risk of reverting to the ruthless justice of the Black Knight, only with all the power of law and society behind each decision . . . unless there has been sufficient maturity to create a Judge whose justice is tempered with mercy. *Do magic for winning court cases.*

In Scorpio: Madwoman's Moon. Oppressed by external enemies and still tormented by the inner demons of childhood pain, the Witch loses her grip on reality and goes insane. As the Madwoman, Scorpio runs amok through the wilderness, hysterical, seeing enemies everywhere . . . but unlike the Executioner, there is no law to hide behind, and she is too far gone even to protect herself. The good she has done as Witch and Priestess, however, gives her friends and allies who care for her until she recovers, forcing her to learn a humble lesson about dependency on the love of other flawed human beings. *Do magic to aid the mentally ill.*

In Sagittarius: Hunter's Moon. Seeker has matured to Scholar, then to Priest, and then to Philosopher, but something is still missing, and

Sagittarius sets off once again to find it. This is the time of the Hunter, who is old and hard and skilled and knows where to track. The Hunter also, at the end of the Hunt, intends to bring something down. In matters of the soul, the Hunter has no mercy for those who deny what he pursues as truth, and fanaticism may ensue. *Do magic to hunt down things that have gone astray or things that are needed.*

In Capricorn: Miser's Moon. Beaten down by the pressing need to provide for his family and tribe, even at the cost of his own happiness, the Patriarch clutches his resources desperately to his breast and becomes the Miser. He sinks into a depressed solitude, alienating himself once again from the loved ones he has tentatively embraced. *Do magic to prevent spendthrift behavior.*

In Aquarius: Heretic's Moon. Here Aquarius finds himself once more an outcast, but this time it is not for simple political rebellion against the family or tribe, but spiritual rebellion against the entire worldview of his society. The Heretic questions not just the actions of others, but the social and spiritual underpinnings that motivate them, and as such he is even more dangerous and even more of an outlaw. Still, this time he is wise enough to gather a group of like-minded people who look up to him and who will carry on his work. *Do magic to change society, in any way you think necessary.*

In Pisces: Moon of Lost Souls. Once again Pisces has extended herself too far, and she finds herself lost, as lost as the souls of those she tried to save as the Angel of Mercy. True compassion comes out of a knowledge that your soul is like that of others, including their flaws; if Pisces gets too caught up in saving people, she forgets this fact and loses herself. *Do magic to help those who are lost and missing and to find missing things.*

VIII. BALSAMIC MOON

This Moon phase finishes the cycle, from midway through the eleventh sign to the end of the twelfth, when the Moon returns to the Sun's position. At the Balsamic Moon, everything has run its course for good or ill. This is the final phase of the lunar cycle, and it is usually marked by peace. This may be the peace of mindfulness and contentment, or it may be the silence of things rotting down into the earth, decaying to become something else. The archetypes of this phase are the Wise Elders, the figures who have been through the fire and returned better for the tempering.

In Aries: Veteran's Moon. Aries has become the old Veteran whose job is to train the youngsters in the ways of fighting and survival. This is the archetype of the gunnery sergeant, the sword teacher, the sensei, who must send their charges out into the cruel world and pray that they have learned enough. *Do magic to aid oneself in martial arts or to find a teacher to help with confidence and strict training.*

In Taurus: Ancestor Moon. Taurus becomes the wise old one who has created a legacy for those who come afterward, a heritage for many descendants to honor and value. Also called the Inheritance Moon. *Do magic to honor ancestors and to gain an inheritance.*

In Gemini: Teacher's Moon. In old age, wordsmith Gemini finds the role of Teacher. Of what? Of anything; it doesn't matter. It's the passing on of words of wisdom that matters. The Balsamic Moon in Gemini is the long-lived witness, speaking to the younger generation in timeless words. *Do magic to help any teacher.*

In Cancer: Moon of the Keeper of Memories. The Widow spends the end of her life collecting the memories of all her feelings, and her memoirs eventually become part of history. People come to her hearthside again, looking for her elder wisdom, for she lives more and more in the past, yet can speak to the present from that place. *Do magic to deal with suppressed or painful memories.*

In Leo: Bard's Moon. Leo goes back to his prerulership origins and ends his days in the role of respected Bard, speaking out against tyrannical kings. In Celtic myth, no one could be a king and a bard at the same time, for only a bard could judge a king and vice versa. As the Bard, Leo uses his experiences of kingship to judge other leaders, but he does it from a place of finally allying himself with the commoners instead of setting himself apart. *Do magic for eloquence in public speaking for a cause.*

In Virgo: Monk's Moon. At the elder stage of her life, Virgo retires to a convent, monastery, or ashram, a place of quiet contemplation and gentle service to the Gods or Goddesses. The Monk has learned to find the spiritual worth in repetitive labor, meditatively raking sand or hoeing potatoes in the monastery garden. *Do ritual to bring inner peace while doing simple labor.*

In Libra: Whore's Moon. Here Libra has found a way to integrate sexuality with spirituality and not lose herself in the partnership: she becomes the Sacred Prostitute, the Holy Whore and temple dancer. She is able to give of her charm and warmth and skill at relationship in order to serve and heal the sexually wounded, yet she manages to keep a healthy distance with impersonal love and is not drawn in to intrigues and drama. *Do magic to aid sex workers, to improve your own experience of sexuality, and to facilitate sexual healing.*

In Scorpio: Phoenix Moon. The Phoenix is the symbol of rebirth, and in this phase Scorpio comes back from the edge of darkness with enough self-knowledge to start over again as a new and whole person. This is the sign and phase of real transformation, the point at which Death claims the old life and the new life is ready to start anew. *Do magic to drastically change your life or to get ready for a serious life change.*

In Sagittarius: Shaman's Moon. The kills of the Hunter become the skins worn by the Shaman, and the eyes that can see in the dark have learned to see the spirits as well. This is the phase where Sagittarius discovers that true wisdom is found not only in experience or books or dogma, but in the world of the instinct and the spirits. The Shaman does not merely connect with the Gods or Goddesses, he takes them into himself and brings their presence straight to the tribe, removing any need for missionary work. *This is the phase for working shamanic magic and honoring the spirits.*

In Capricorn: Dragon's Moon. After spending a lonely time as the Miser, Capricorn learns wisdom and integrates as the Dragon. While the Dragon still keeps a hoard of jewels, he carries also a fund of esoteric knowledge that draws people as intently as his riches. The Dragon may still be cautious as to how he gives either away, and he is able to guard his resources fiercely, but he does dispense both wealth and wisdom to the worthy. *Do magic to find a teacher who you can respect and who will respect your boundaries.*

In Aquarius: Prophet's Moon. In this final phase, Aquarius becomes the Prophet, whose words will be someday remembered as truth. This phase requires coming to terms with the fact that the world will never change as fast as Aquarius would like it to, and that some changes can only be prepared for, that they will happen long after one has left this life, and that this is the long view of changing culture. *Use this phase for divination.*

In Pisces: Mystic's Moon. In this final phase, the Lost Soul finds herself by opening up and merging—not with another, but with the cosmos itself—and becomes the Mystic. This is the ultimate experience of Pisces, and it does not resolve itself quickly, but must be learned over time and through the cycle. *Do ritual to open oneself to the All That Is.*

5

Mercury Magic

Words of Power

Throughout the ages, bards and skalds and other workers of words have spun poetry with such skill that it dug grooves into our minds when we heard it. This chapter collects many different words and short phrases that hold the power of the twelve signs within them. Each of these words rings with its own magic and can be used for creating one's own invocations. Speak them aloud, and you will understand the currents of each sign.

ARIES—*I AM*

Dawn Flame Spring Equinox Quicken Unfold Uncurl Blossom Uprising Heroic Lance Spear Steel Brushfire Blaze Spark Clamor Charge Fierce Reflex Innocence Open Headstrong Daring Dauntless Epic Legendary Valiant Ardent Dynamic Cavalier Front Line Flag Face First of All

TAURUS—*I HAVE*

Stone Oak Garden Moss The Unhewn Dolmen Roots Bedrock Endure Solid Mighty Cliff Hearty Thick Sturdy Mass Gather Pile Brick Continent Covet Value Immovable Fertile Verdant Lush Flourish Thrive Colossal Impervious Mammoth Rough Muscle Patience Century Millennium

GEMINI—*I THINK*

Wind Wings Flutter Hurricane Mind Knife Cutting Edge Black and White Duality Double-Time Pair Two-for-One Razor Tongue Slash Mercurial Games Player Multiply Multitudes Marvelous Glitter Gleam Hover Dart Skate Smooth Nimble Fingers Mischief Skill Dazzling Bright Eyes

CANCER—*I FEEL*

Moon Tides Sand Mother-of-Pearl Hearth Cooking Pot Soup Sipapu Mother's Milk Crescent Nourishment Quilt Thistledown Shell Infant's Cheek Petal Bud Wail Loneliness Desolation Enfold Fruit Orchard Mercy Devotion Sensitive Cling Security Blanket Silver Unspoken Serenity

LEO—*I WILL*

Noonday Heat Bonfire Castle Heart Assurance Radiance Charisma Sunflower Sceptre Throne Golden Gilded Ornate Magnificent Nobility Noblesse Oblige Expand Luxury Example Model Attention Generosity Savage Pride Lash Explosion Exalted Performance Costume Solar Flare

VIRGO—*I ANALYZE*

Wheatfield Sheaf Sickle Scythe Maiden Earth Leafy Delicate Cleanse Clear Cold Springs Pure Undefiled Unsullied Immaculate Hourglass Sands Time Timekeeper Beekeeper Servant Scour Broom Fences Walls Ditches Narrow Accounting Precision Numbered Broken Fix Mending

LIBRA—*I BALANCE*

Scent Breeze Sword Rose Thorn Knight Honor Faery Tale Crane-Dance Grace Poised Charm Bubble Cloud Glossy Feather Sway Decision Coax Seduction Court Jury Negotiation Law Parchment Scroll Cool Smile Eloquence Fluent Evenhanded Compromise Happy Ending

SCORPIO—*I DESIRE*

Twilight Cave Deeps Ice Steam Smoke Trickle Blood Flesh Chrysalis Transformation Mourning Web Spider Bind Bound Trapped Hunger Rot

Decay Desert Iceberg Frozen Torrential Crack Descend Shudder Strive Yearn Thirst Cloak Conceal Shadow Implosion Rebirth Regeneration

SAGITTARIUS—*I SEE*

Arrow Hoofbeats Thunder Lightning Flight Stampede Winding Road Sandals Dust Horse Wild Lantern Staff Horizon Tome Learning Fugitive Wanderer Wayward Vagrant Neighbor Scatter Tumble Stride Caravan Sail Sunset Unbounded Unchained Freedom Luck Faith Providence

CAPRICORN—*I USE*

Mountain Cliff Canyon Sheer Steep Dragon Hoard Cold Scaly Coiled Clinking Forge Hammer Tongs Chisel Chain Ambition Excellence Creaking Bones Weathered Crush Buried Riches Dedication Resolution Conviction Frost Winter Opaque Indomitable Matured Ripened Season

AQUARIUS—*I KNOW*

Electric Solitary Tribal Community Global Holistic Inspiration Rise Soar Faraway Tower Star Balloon Billow Reverse Turnabout Change Upside-Down Insurrection Skyrocket Meteor Galaxy Nebula Ludicrous Lunatic Absurd Outrageous Transgress Whimsical Zany Esoteric Serendipity

PISCES—*I BELIEVE*

Ocean Wave Mists Pearl Gray Minnow Shark Foam Formless Limitless Obscure Quiver Vast Flux Flow Current Sweep Cycle Spiral Mystery Curtain Veil Fade Dissolve Undulate Yielding Merge Selflessness Charity Barefoot Openhanded Coral Reef Sunken Treasure Ship of Souls

6
Venus Magic
Synastry and Love Spells

Of all the spells that people ask for when they visit the local hedge-witch, the most frequent ones are love spells. They want that perfect someone to appear out of the blue and love them. They want the unrequited love to fall madly head over heels for them. They want the current flame to be romantically trapped and never leave them. They want the stalker-lover to give up on them. They want the abusive or unfaithful lover to shape up and become someone different, someone who is better to them. They want to rekindle love that has gone sour or cold. They want the straying lover's eye off the new flame. They want the fleeing lover back. They want the ex-lover punished, that he or she may never find love again. They want to be free of the dead lover so that they can love again. And so on. There's nothing quite so tortuous as love when it comes to people attempting to wrestle the Universe down and force its laws to bend for their convenience.

Venus understands all this and has sympathy with every one of them. She's the force of Love itself. She's also the force of beauty, aesthetic considerations, and art—all things that you can fall in love with. She deals in feelings and images, not rules and ethics. In every culture, the Love Goddesses have similar characters: They value feelings and aesthetics over all else, including right and wrong. Aphrodite is just fine with you cheating on your spouse to get your needs met. Ishtar sees nothing wrong with cruelly discarding your lovers when you're tired of them. Inanna sends her lover to Death when he isn't glad enough to see her come back from the Underworld. Freya sells her charms for the world's most beautiful necklace. Eros shoots his arrows randomly, taking delight in mismatched couples. Oshun has been known to strike with venereal disease those who insult her flamboyantly dressed horses. Ezili Freda is the archetype of the mulatto mistress who wants to move up in social class by marrying her already-married white lover. The cow-eyed Hathor turns into lioness-goddess Sekhmet when she is enraged and devours entire cities. The love deities are all unapologetically irrational, as is Love itself.

As a diviner, you will have to deal with people who have Love Problems, and you will have to make peace with the fact that Love is not reasonable, and sometimes there will be no reasoning with them. From the starry-eyed second-daters who thinks that their lover walks on water, to people desperately trying to make an unsuitable relationship work out, they will often be unable to see their lover and their situation clearly. Sometimes, if you are that sort of practitioner, they will ask you to do magic—or to teach them to do magic—to salvage something that is clearly unsalvageable or to manipulate someone into doing what they want. It can be difficult not to fall to the extremes of either empathizing with them and agreeing to something that is in no one's eventual best interests or being horrified or disgusted and lecturing them with words they will probably not be able to hear through the clamor of Love. It can be difficult to maintain a detached compassion, to say, "Yes, I know that you feel helpless, but part of the mystery of Love is that it makes us helpless, if only for a time. But the more we thrash around, the harder it is to hear the real message. Love tells us to live in the moment, but let's try to look ahead of the moment and see if that makes things clearer."

The first thing that you're going to look at when someone comes in with Love Issues is, of course, the Venus placement in that person's chart. If you're not a professional, but just someone who is having Love Issues of your own—and it's rare to find someone who has made it to adulthood and not had any—the first thing that you want to do is to look at your own Venus. What sign is she in? Is that the energy you want in a lover, or would you rather embody that Venus and have your lover be someone different? Look down the list of invocations below and see which one jumps out at you. If more than one stands out, that's all right.

You might also look at the sign on your descendant, the line opposite your ascendant. This often indicates people who we are attracted to. Find the invocation for that sign and see if this appeals to you. If the one that you like best isn't a sign that's found much in your chart, that's not too unusual; it might be an energy that you are missing in your life or one that is in harmonious aspect to some of your important planets.

Love spells aren't just for single people who are looking to find the right person. An existing relationship can lack important qualities, or have lost them, and calling a particular kind of Venus energy into your lives can help with that. Using spells for Venus is a reasonably ethical way to go about a love spell; you aren't trying to directly mess with a specific person's free will. If it's not meant that you are to have someone of the type you request, it simply won't happen. If that energy cannot come into your relationship for some reason—for example, your partner is not ready to accept it—then it won't work, but you'll be ethically clean. If it does come in, it may be in subtle ways, or it may take a while. If you've got Pluto or Saturn currently aspecting your Venus, it may be hard for soft Libra or Cancer energy to get through immediately.

Using more than one of the Venus energies at once is perfectly acceptable. After all, we are all a blend of various astrological energies, as is every lover you will ever have. If what you really want is an Aries-Scorpio-third house mix, well, people like that are out there, and at least one of them might be right for you. Just read them carefully and understand what you're asking for.

VENUS INVOCATIONS

VENUS IN ARIES INVOCATION

Light a candle or torch and speak into the flame

Hail the Power of Love!
I call into my life Fire Love,

First morning's love, adventurous love,
Love that is fearless in the face of adversity,
Ardent love that blows the ashes
Once again into a dancing blaze!
With your vital spirit bless me,
With your courage take my hand,
With all your boundless energy love me now.

VENUS IN TAURUS INVOCATION

To be said while turning over the earth in a garden or at least potting a plant

Hail the Power of Love!
I call into my life Earth Love,
Solid as bedrock, bound in rings of metal,
Commitment loyal as the turning seasons,
Love you can depend on.
With your patience stand beside me,
With your body worship me,
With all your worldly goods may I be endowed.

VENUS IN GEMINI INVOCATION

To be called while releasing flower petals into a stiff wind

Hail the Power of Love!
I call into my life Eloquent Love,
The meeting of the minds, the synergy of words,
The lover who will always talk to me,
The feather-light bliss of total communication.
With your words stroke me,
With your mind excite me,
With all your fondest thoughts may I be included.

VENUS IN CANCER INVOCATION

To be spoken while standing in the ocean or while immersed in water

Hail the Power of Love!
I call into my life Nurturing Love,

The feeling of ultimate safety, the connection of the heart,
The one who will take care of me
And allow me to care for them in turn.
With your tides roll into my life,
With your waves envelop me,
With the love of all the ages hold me tight.

VENUS IN LEO INVOCATION

To be spoken into a bonfire

Hail the Power of Love!
I call into my life Sun-Drenched Love,
The brightest star, the grandest gesture,
The romantic who takes my breath away,
Sweeping me off my feet with ease.
With your glance heat me,
With your brilliance awe me,
With your heart of golden flame fill me with light.

VENUS IN VIRGO INVOCATION

To be spoken while fixing or mending something

Hail the Power of Love!
I call into my life Mending Love,
The one who will fix my cracks, stitch my tears,
Polish the scratches off my heart until it shines,
Who will set themselves gladly to the work between us.
With your sharp eyes seek out my inner self,
With your gentle hands darn up my holes,
With the purest of intentions cleanse my life.

VENUS IN LIBRA INVOCATION

To be spoken while gazing into a mirror

Hail the Power of Love!
I call into my life Mutual Love,
Eye to eye, the bond of a couple,

Giving and taking in perfect consideration,
The vows spoken and unspoken that tie us
In a dance of fairness and equality.
With your light touch balance our needs,
With your beauty paint my world,
With your hand held firm in mine walk with me now.

VENUS IN SCORPIO INVOCATION

To be spoken into a glass of wine

Hail the Power of Love!
I call into my life Passionate Love,
Hunger for my flesh, longing for my spirit,
Intensity that rips me from my placid life,
The hot struggle for power that ends in joyous lust.
With your ardor take me,
With your craving remake me,
With the heat of your desire burn my soul.

VENUS IN SAGITTARIUS INVOCATION

To be spoken to the horizon

Hail the Power of Love!
I call into my life Trusting Love,
The open hands, the heart that does not hide,
The one who will speak only truth to me,
Seeing the divine within my mortal flesh.
With your quest find me,
With your vision see into me,
With your trust free the bonds of my spirit.

VENUS IN CAPRICORN INVOCATION

To be spoken while climbing to a higher place

Hail the Power of Love!
I call into my life Ascending Love,
The goals we share, the life we build,

Believing in us and our power to achieve,
Looking forward to aging together.
With your determination help me climb,
With your endurance pull me through,
With your quiet strength warm my old bones someday.

VENUS IN AQUARIUS INVOCATION
To be spoken while letting a brightly colored cloth or ribbons fly in the wind

Hail the Power of Love!
I call into my life High Winds Love,
The challenge to my assumptions, the allure of a new
  road,
Opening me up to a myriad of possibilities,
The one who will never bore me with sameness.
With your genius enlighten me,
With your lightning strike me,
On the winds of inspiration lift me high.

VENUS IN PISCES INVOCATION
To be spoken standing in the ocean or bathing one's face and hands with salt water

Hail the Power of Love!
I call into my life Ocean Love,
Merging into my arms, heedless of my flaws,
Rescuing each other from the horrors of the world,
With love enough between us to encompass the Universe.
With your fathomless depths enchant me,
With your healing touch redeem me,
With the waves of your compassion bathe my soul.

VENUS IN THE FIRST HOUSE INVOCATION
To be spoken while watching the sunrise

Hail the Power of Love!
I call into my life Pride Love,
Defending my honor, proud to be with me,

Taking my hand where others can see,
Standing at my side against the forces of malice.
With your sword speak out for me,
With your shield protect me,
With the force of all your confidence let us shine.

VENUS IN THE SECOND HOUSE INVOCATION
To be spoken while holding something made of gold

Hail the Power of Love!
I call into my life Worthy Love,
Treating me as precious, willing to earn my heart,
Knowing our love for your greatest treasure,
Never once taking me for granted.
With your actions woo me,
With your principles win me,
With the gifts of all you offer shower me.

VENUS IN THE THIRD HOUSE INVOCATION
To be written in your best handwriting and spoken while throwing the paper into the wind

Hail the Power of Love!
I call into my life Mind-Sharing Love,
The tumble of ideas, the fascination,
The rush of intellectual challenge,
The long conversations far into the night.
With your knowledge intrigue me,
With your wit delight me,
With your keen perception show me myself.

VENUS IN THE FOURTH HOUSE INVOCATION
To be spoken in the center of your home or in the home you grew up in

Hail the Power of Love!
I call into my life Love of Family,
The safety of the hearth, the laughing little ones,
I long to be a keeper of generations

And to pass on my own blood through the act of love.
With your children bless me,
With your strong arms gather me,
Within the circle of our loving may we live.

VENUS IN THE FIFTH HOUSE INVOCATION
To be spoken while dancing

Hail the Power of Love!
I call into my life Butterfly Love,
The Maypole's dance, ephemeral as a mayfly,
Landing like a moment to brighten the heart,
Then flying on to become a fond remembrance.
With your bright wings bless me,
With your light feet dance with me,
With my open hands I set you free again.

VENUS IN THE SIXTH HOUSE INVOCATION
To be spoken while doing work you wish you were not doing alone

Hail the Power of Love!
I call into my life Working Love,
The fingers that toil with mine, the back that bends with
*   mine,*
The caring touch that keeps us both from falling,
The working partnership where neither shirks the labor.
With your willing hands serve me,
With your willing heart support me,
With your persistence in the face of toil bear me up.

VENUS IN THE SEVENTH HOUSE INVOCATION
To be spoken to a ring

Hail the Power of Love!
I call into my life the Love of the Marriage Bed,
The promises exchanged, the knotted cord about two
*   hands,*

The thrust and parry of the phrases
Between two who meet each other with love and respect.
With your words bind me,
With your lips kiss me,
With the very breath we share may we be one.

VENUS IN THE EIGHTH HOUSE INVOCATION
To be spoken in total darkness

Hail the Power of Love!
I call into my life Shadow Love,
Sharing hidden wealth, tasting the blood of secrets,
Welcoming of each others' dark places,
Joyfully coupling in the shadow of the grave.
With your flesh torment me,
With your mysteries feed me,
With your naked soul welcome me to my fate.

VENUS IN THE NINTH HOUSE INVOCATION
To be spoken while driving or riding down a road

Hail the Power of Love!
I call into my life Journeying Love,
The traveling companion, the stranger's touch,
Our wonder in the shared amazement of the new,
Friends even if eventually our paths drift apart.
With your enthusiasm greet me,
With your awareness guide me,
With your feet upon the road let me follow you.

VENUS IN THE TENTH HOUSE INVOCATION
To be spoken softly in a public place

Hail the Power of Love!
I call into my life Enthroned Love,
The one who stands at my side
Before the masses, before the public eye,

The mate to decorate my arm and spirit.
With your discretion earn my trust,
With your dignity earn my respect,
With your knowing wisdom see behind my mask.

VENUS IN THE ELEVENTH HOUSE INVOCATION
To be spoken while ringing bells

Hail the Power of Love!
I call into my life Loving Friendship,
Where no matter what the passion
Or tears, at the end of the day
You will still be my best friend in fellowship.
With your steadfast heart stand by me,
With your playful words salute me,
With your caring remind me of all my hopes.

VENUS IN THE TWELFTH HOUSE INVOCATION
To be whispered into the night

Hail the Power of Love!
I call into my life Mystical Love,
Soul to soul, the sacred above and below,
Bringing out the blissful depths I never knew I had,
Bringing me to a holy place I never knew could be.
With your singing silence heal me,
With your vast serenity open me,
With the touch of the Divine aid my rebirth.

SYNASTRY
Two Charts in One

The second likely thing that you'll be looking at with issues of Love is chart comparison. For this, which is an art unto itself, I strongly recommend Steven and Jodie Forrest's wonderful book *Skymates,* which has everything you ever wanted to know about the basics of comparing two people's astrology. For the beginners in the audience, I'll go on to say that there are two main ways to do this: comparisons and composites. Both are useful in different ways, and anyone who wants to give astrological relationship advice—including advising yourself—ought to be able to do both.

The first consists of placing one person's chart over the other. Remember how we discussed doing this with transits, using clear plastic if necessary? You can do the same thing with two people's charts. Line up the houses with each other and look at how the planets fall. You should be able to see conjunctions between the charts instantly—they're where the planets pile up on top of each other. Draw lines between the two sets of planets to see aspects; it helps to have the two charts in different colors, so you're always drawing from red to blue or some such.

Looking at the comparison between the charts, you'll read them just like you would a transit chart. In fact, you can think of it that way: two people, when they come together, are "transiting" each other, for as long as they are in each other's presence. If they form a strong full-time relationship, those transits overshadow each others' lives. The difference is that two people are theoretically equals, or at least when compared with a human being and a giant cosmic force. While the planetary forces don't take much notice of us mere mortals, two people will always be affecting each other at the same time. While your critical Saturn is squaring his cranky Mars, that Mars is giving it right back to you.

Also unlike a planetary force, you're not going to be propitiating each other, exactly. What you will be doing instead is the equivalent of diplomatic work between each others' planets. For enhancing aspects, it will be more of a celebration. Plan activities with each other that directly appeal to that Moon-Pluto trine or that Mercury-Mars sextile. For afflicting aspects, you could try making separate altars to each aspect and then combining them. It's especially effective if each makes the altar for the other person's planet and sign, as a way of both getting to know that energy in their lover and openly honoring it. Then the combining of the two is an activity to do together.

The second method, that of composite charts, consists of making a chart of the midpoints between each two pairs of planets—halfway between the two Suns, halfway between the two Moons, and so on. This chart is basically what the relationship between the two people would look like if it was a person and had a body. When the people in question are together, they are drawn to act more like that chart than like their own charts. If the composite is too unlike either of their charts, they will find themselves acting uncharacteristically while together. If the composite is similar to one person's chart but nothing like the other person's, generally the first individual will find that things tend to go their way in the relationship, not necessarily through any force on their part, but just through luck and circumstances. For the first situation, the prescription is for the parties to have their own lives and spend time apart as well as time together. For the second, the prescription is to be very aware of the situation and for the "favored" individual to do a lot of conscious sacrificing to make sure that the "less favored" one gets their way often enough. Ideally, of course, a composite chart will have roughly equal similarities to both charts, but as with many things in life, one often has to work with what one is given, ideal or not.

A couple can build an altar for their composite chart. (Or, if you have more than two people in the relationship, there are ways to figure a composite for that, too. Check out the appendix at the end of my book *Pagan Polyamory* if you want to know how, or check out *Planets in Composite* listed in Recommended Reading at the end of this book.) Building an altar to the composite chart can be a wonderful bonding activity, or it can show up the faultlines in the relationship. For one thing, you'll notice that with any composite chart, each person tends to be attracted to some parts of it and not others, and they tend to be the one who "runs" the things associated with their favorite planets and perhaps the ones who embody those qualities in the relationship.

For example, if Kai and Chris have a composite chart with an Aquarius Sun and a Pisces Moon, they may unconsciously divide these up between them. Let's say that Kai has three planets in air signs and the Sun in the eleventh house, and therefore is more comfortable with the Aquarius energy than Chris; this means that Kai may end up always being the one to act out the Aquarius Sun and suggest new things, drag Chris out to interesting events, and so on. Let's say that Chris happens to have a fourth-house Moon in Taurus and a couple of water-sign planets, and vibrates more closely to the composite Pisces Moon; the unspoken rule between the two of them may be that it is Chris who provides the nurturing, notices when feelings are hurt, and so forth.

However, with any composite chart, everyone involved is being pushed toward every part of it when they are together. Letting your partner act out the uncomfortable (for you) parts of it can have bad repercussions. First, it's laziness on your part. If you're going to be in a long-term relationship with this person, you'd better get used to the feel and action of those parts of the chart sooner or later, and just having them be in charge of those things can be an excuse for you to put that off indefinitely. Second, they can eventually start embodying those uncomfortable things in your eyes, and you can start reacting to them as the role you've pushed them into rather than as the person they are.

To get past this kind of psychic laziness, look at the planets in the composite chart and get a feel for how they manifest between you: "Oh, yeah, that Mercury in Aries comes out when we're constantly interrupting each other and pole-vaulting to conclusions over who might have said what!" "And that Mars in Pisces makes us do that game of 'What do you want to do?' 'I dunno, what do you want to do?'" "And that Saturn in the eleventh house makes us suspicious of going to groups together!" "Honey, that's *your* problem, you're the one who does that one. I'd like to go to groups with you." "OK, OK, I do tend to be the one who responds to that fear."

Then, after you've sorted out the chart and who has been unconsciously "assigned" which activity, you build the composite altar consciously doing the parts that are most uncomfortable to you, that you'd prefer your partner to handle. This is a way of telling your own unconscious, your partner, and the Universe at large that you are ready to take this on as a way of being closer to this person you love. Keep in mind, however, that the Universe will take you seriously.

Being in love with someone changes you, little by little. This is not necessarily a bad thing. If you can't abide the idea that someone else will rub off on you and change you, then don't ever go touching souls with someone else. (That's a legitimate path, but a pretty lonely one.) Often, we learn our best karmic lessons in relationships; our lovers are so often our best teachers (of lessons both rewarding and painful) that we may unconsciously or consciously seek out someone who embodies qualities that we find ourselves ready to learn about. Venus's wisdom on the matter seems to be this: It doesn't matter whether a relationship continues forever. It need not go on forever to be a success. If you learned something important, and you still think of your ex with fondness, and your ex thinks of you the same way, then it was a success. It's a long view of relationships, one that may span many lifetimes, and it may be impossible to perceive when you're in the midst of short-term emotional upheaval. Still, it is important to understand how Venus in her highest manifestation transforms into . . . Neptune, the planet of merging not only with each other but with the Divine, the planet of impersonal/transpersonal Cosmic Love. The idea is that until we get the Venus part right, we can't truly understand the love of the cosmos, so the lessons of Love are by no means merely mundane concerns. Besides, the Love Goddesses tend to smack anyone who belittles their gift, and I can guarantee that you don't want to be smacked by them.

7
Mars Magic
Anger Management

Mars is the planet of passion, action, decision making, and general get-up-and-go. It is also the place where anger comes from. By the very nature of Mars—and of life—you cannot have any self-protective instinct without also having the ability to rage. Adrenaline is adrenaline, and although we can control what we do with that urge, to deny its existence—or its value—is to deny our Mars, and that's an unwise thing. Those who deny or devalue their Mars energy often find themselves being passively taken advantage of, again and again . . . or they find that their Mars energy periodically bursts out in inappropriate ways, when they least expected it.

Mars anger needs to be controlled or it can destroy the wrong targets . . . but it also needs to be valued, or it will desert or mutiny. The following invocations are for doing both. Each is done in three parts; first, you acknowledge and respect your inner Mars warrior, then you speak from his or her position, and then you formally give him or her the boundaries within which he or she must function. All three parts must be completed for Mars to feel that he or she is respected and that you are worthy of respect as an honorable leader to follow.

First, start by creating an altar to your Mars sign (see chapter 15). Then stand before it and salute, holding some weapon or implement, which you then place before the altar. Speak the first section of the invocation, and then make some promise to that part of yourself as an offering. It might be eating a favorite food, or standing up for yourself in some arena, or going out and doing some energetic activity. If you don't feel a sense of satisfaction after making the offer, your internal Mars is not content with it, and you should think of something else.

Then say the second part of the invocation, letting the Mars part of you speak with your mouth, even if it gets to do nothing else but speak. Let yourself feel the pride of Mars, or the rage or frustration, as keenly as possible. You might want to have items around that you can pummel or break or shred, if you're doing this ritual in the face of a great deal of barely controlled anger. When you stop panting and wind down, sit quietly and center yourself. Tell your inner Mars, formally, that you are going to decide what to do, and that he or she is going to abide by that decision. Tell your inner Mars that as the leader and captain, you have the right to make that decision, and your Mars is honor-bound to go along with it. Then sit and meditate for a while—perhaps even a long while—and decide the best thing to do.

If you're sure that the best thing is to restrain your inner Mars entirely, speak that aloud. I suggest following this up with examples of when it would be appropriate to let Mars loose, so that Mars doesn't simply think that you're devaluing him or her and that you'd rather that your Mars energy just go away. (Keep in mind, the entire time that you are doing this ritual, that you are speaking not only to your own Mars, but through your inner Mars to the Mars energy of the cosmos.) If it is time to let your Mars act, say so. Then read the third part of the invocation, which describes the bonds and boundaries that are placed on your Mars so that their actions will not cause more damage than necessary and so that the battle will be honorably fought. As soon as possible afterward, go out and do whatever you have offered, as Mars is notoriously the most impatient of all the signs and has a penchant for immediate gratification.

INVOCATIONS FOR MARS
THROUGH THE SIGNS

MARS IN ARIES

I. I salute you, Warrior of Fire,
Herald of the Lifted Torch,
Soldier of the front lines,
Whose courage is unmatched.
First in the charge forward,
Lord of Adrenaline, Master of Fight-or-Flight,
Keeper of my survival,
I thank you for your endless task
Of pushing me forward where I fear to go.

II. I am the battering ram at the gate!
I am the irresistible force,
And I cannot be stymied!
My head is a tower of fire!
I take heart in battle, find power in struggle,
And I will defend you not out of duty,
But out of willingness and joy,
If only you will respect my ideals.

III. Go into battle, Warrior of Fire,
But these are the laws I place on you:
That you will not go armored so thick
That the pain of others is lost on you,
That you will not swing your sword
At any opponents unable to defend themselves,
And that you will ask before each swing,
"Is this the most effective thing I can do?"
And not merely choose what blow brings you the most joy.

MARS IN TAURUS

I. I salute you, Warrior of Stone,
Fist like the great club of the Dagda,
Slow to anger, yet great in devastation,
Whose thoroughness is unmatched.
You who have the power to smash mountains,
You who trample your enemies into the dust of the Earth,
Keeper of my survival,
I thank you for your endless task
Of defending my resources against those who would
*   squander them.*

II. I am the snorting bull ready to charge!
I am the immovable object
Against whom all tides crash
And who is never worn away.
I am the endless siege that will never tire,
The patient march through a hundred swamps,
The defender of boundaries and resources,
The Guardian of the Gates of Morning.

III. Go into battle, Warrior of Stone,
But these are the laws I place on you:
That you will choose carefully your battle,
And not take up the flag unquestioned,
That is simply the one you were taught to march beneath.
That you will not wait to charge until blind rage
Has seized you, and you have taken leave of your senses,
And cannot distinguish friend from foe,
Nor stop yourself until the earth is scorched.

MARS IN GEMINI

I. I salute you, Warrior of Knives,
Twin blades that sing through the air,

Flashing words like a hurricane of steel,
Whose dexterity is unmatched.
You who attack from every side
Like lightning, and then are gone like wind,
Keeper of my survival,
I thank you for your endless task
Of dancing me past the knife's edge of ruin.

II. I am the wind of a thousand blades
That pierce through the tiny chinks
In the strongest of armor!
I am the mirage that entices
And leads you into a sandstorm
That flays you skin from bone
And leaves you a dried husk
To be devoured by the circling carrion birds!

III. Go into battle, Warrior of Knives,
But these are the laws I place on you:
That you be not so in love with your constant agile
    motion
That you cannot focus, and your efforts
Are blown away and scattered on the winds.
That you do not stretch the truth so far
That it breaks, nor strike small and petty wounds
Merely to prove your cleverness and wit,
Nor give up too soon in the face of the long march.

MARS IN CANCER

I. I salute you, Warrior of the Tides,
Relentless rhythm of sea against shore,
Crashing flow that breaks and deadly ebb that sucks
    away,
Whose tidal flood is unmatched.

You whose first thought is to defend what you love
And protect the weakest and most innocent,
Keeper of my survival,
I thank you for your endless task
Of being the shield between my heart and the hard world.

II. I am the peasant crouched in the doorway,
My hands tight against my wooden staff,
Who will protect my home from the wild beasts,
Both human and animal, who would steal my peace
And destroy the circle of my heart!
I am the warrior who would die for love
Of family, of clan, of tribe; who would lay down my life
For the lives of those who depend upon me.

III. Go into battle, Warrior of the Tides,
But these are the laws I place on you:
That you do not treat those whom you love
Too differently in the arena, neither sparing them
Nor being overly cruel in your hurt and betrayal.
That you see the encroaching threat from the outside
As what it is, and not what your inner fears
Would have it be, and that you do not let those fears close
   out
Everyone who might, through no fault, harm your tender
   heart.

MARS IN LEO

I. I salute you, Warrior of the Sun,
Glorious spirit of the noonday heat,
Fierce lion roaming the desert,
Whose brilliance is unmatched.
Helmeted King and Warrior Queen,
Marshal of many troops,

Keeper of my survival,
I thank you for your endless task
Of helping me to hold my head high with personal pride.

II. I am the Ruler of Warriors,
Riding at the head of my celestial army!
My loyal forces are invincible,
And my confidence is the touchstone of my triumph!
My wrath scorches my enemies,
Withering them into dust!
None can withstand the light of the Sun
Burning away the clinging shadows of darkness!

III. Go into battle, Warrior of the Sun,
But these are the laws I place on you:
That your arrogance may not blind you
To mistakes that you might make,
That your reasons for war must not come
From wounded vanity or petulant pride,
And you must never forget that all righteous wars
Are fought for the sake of the humble.

MARS IN VIRGO

I. I salute you, Warrior of the Swarm,
Hundreds of tiny mouths that bite,
Thousands of tiny stings that torment,
Whose persistence is unmatched.
Sharp eyes that miss nothing,
Seeker and destroyer of every tiny flaw,
Keeper of my survival,
I thank you for your endless task
Of dedicating me to the labor of self-perfection.

II. I am the Virgin Warrior who stands alone,
The well-thought-out attack, aimed without hot rage
And only with the coolest and most exact precision.
I am the spear of the Amazons, aimed true
And keeping all at a safe distance.
I am the one who trains daily and nightly
For the martial form that is clean and absolute,
The consummate slash like the dance of Death.

III. Go into battle, Warrior of the Swarm,
But these are the laws I place on you:
That in your love of perfect detail
And your focus on perfectly winning the single battle
That you do not lose sight of the greater meaning
And make judgments based on the shorter view,
That you have patience with the errors of others
And do not hold them to standards beyond a mortal life,
Nor judge one an enemy only through your contempt.

MARS IN LIBRA

I. I salute you, Warrior of Chivalry,
Noble knight on the high white horse,
Carrier of the Sword of Justice,
Whose ideals are unmatched.
You who ride the quest for perfection,
You who champion those who cannot fight,
Keeper of my survival,
I thank you for your endless task
Of holding me to a greater code of honor.

II. I am the Knight of the Law
That says: There will be justice, or there will be war!
I am the Keeper of the Righteous Wrath,
The one who charges forth with the finest cause,

The servant who will be partnered only
With the most true and honorable authority!
I am the Sword in the right hand
Of She whose left hand holds the scales!

III. Go into battle, Warrior of Chivalry,
But these are the laws I place on you:
That you may not mistake beauty for right,
And miss the evil that hides beneath a fair mask.
That you act quickly and with decisive measure,
Not missing your chance while you ponder perspectives.
That you may not forget, in your quest for the cause,
That there are innocent hearts that must not be crushed
Lest the cause itself be tainted with their blood.

MARS IN SCORPIO

I. I salute you, Warrior of Ice,
Cold that freezes the foe in its tracks,
Heat like the cracks in the Earth erupting forth,
Whose extremity is unmatched.
Venom of the striking cobra,
Silent killer in the dark,
Keeper of my survival,
I thank you for the endless task
Of defending my heart against a hostile world.

II. I am the fighter whose sword is Will,
And whose shield is Deception,
Friend to intensity and extremity,
I fight only in the silence of the frozen grave,
Or the screaming heat of a berserker charge,
Implacable and relentless as the flow of lava
That takes the enemy from behind
Making them stone, making them flying ash.

III. Go into battle, Warrior of Ice,
But these are the laws I place on you:
That you do not become so obsessed
With the power of your own pain and wrath
That all must be destroyed down to the last flower,
And there may be no hope of regeneration.
That you learn compassion for the loser,
That you do not burn every bridge,
And that in the end, you learn the value of tears.

MARS IN SAGITTARIUS

I. I salute you, Warrior of the Bow,
Cavalry thundering across the plains,
Archer leaning for the far target,
Whose aim is unmatched.
Dreamer who is not afraid to run,
Star-follower whose eyes are on the horizon,
Keeper of my survival,
I thank you for the endless task
Of opening my eyes to new terrain.

II. I am the rider who cannot be caught
No matter how fast and furious the chase!
I am the arrow that shoots true,
The spear that never misses,
The stone in the sling that brings down
The greatest of arrogant giants!
I am the bolt of Truth that lays open
The choking veil of Lies!

III. Go into battle, Warrior of the Bow,
But these are the laws I place on you:
That any battle you may start
You will also see through to the finish;

That the slings of Truth that you wield
Be sent with calculation and not careless rage,
And that you study the conundrum of the ages,
Which knows that opposing truths
Can still sometimes both be true at once.

MARS IN CAPRICORN

I. I salute you, Warrior of the Mountain,
Leader of the armed camp at the summit,
Forced march of a thousand miles that never breaks,
Whose endurance is unmatched.
You who plot your strategy with skill
And always have the persistence to carry it out,
Keeper of my survival,
I thank you for the endless task
Of teaching me to compensate for my own limits.

II. I am the grim and silent force,
The one whose mind never stops plotting,
Who moves men like chess pieces
In a game played with deadly seriousness.
I am the cold one, the warrior of winter,
The far-reaching one whose grasp is like iron,
Who will continue through the blood-soaked snow
Long after the hotter bloods have burned out.

III. Go into battle, Warrior of the Mountain,
But these are the laws I place on you:
That you do not climb to the triumphant peak
On the trodden bodies of those who trust you
As well as those of your enemies,
That you do not let your winter cold
Chill your heart such that no love can warm it,

And that after the battle you seek out those
Whose trust can help to thaw your soul.

MARS IN AQUARIUS

I. I salute you, Warrior of the Winds,
Hurricane of spinning wildness,
Tornado that tears up the boundaries of old,
Whose command of chaos is unmatched.
You who are unafraid to reach for the newest weapon,
You who throw down the walls of convention,
Keeper of my survival,
I thank you for the endless task
Of defending my ideals to a suspicious world.

II. I am the storm cloud rising in the sky,
The lightning bolt that strikes the oak,
And brings fire to the waiting people.
I am the Blow Unexpected,
The sweeping bolt from out of nowhere,
The winds that fling the spears and arrows all awry,
The rains that wash away the walls and ditches
That were carefully laid to trap me.

III. Go into battle, Warrior of the Winds,
But these are the laws I place on you:
That your attack is not frittered away
By the forces of chaos that beset you,
That you keep your focus in the midst of the tornado,
That you do not make yourself so far detached
That people no longer have hearts and lives in your sight,
That you are able to admit your errors
And fight by the rules that have been agreed upon.

MARS IN PISCES

I. I salute you, Warrior of the Ocean,
Endless leagues of the fathomless sea,
Darkening reefs filled with floating bones,
Whose drowning depths are unmatched.
Patient song of the deadly siren
Who pulls each man down in a trance of dream,
Keeper of my survival,
I thank you for the endless task
Of protecting my bond to the All That Is.

II. I am the shark prowling the water's depths,
Unseen, waiting, waiting to strike.
I am the one who can sacrifice for years,
Seem to be merely a hapless victim,
And then slip away through the tightest grasp.
I cannot be held, any more than a fistful of salt water,
And yet the enemy will dream of me forever, weeping,
While I swim freely into the sunset.

III. Go into battle, Warrior of the Ocean,
But these are the laws I place on you:
That you give the enemy the honor of your face
At least sometimes; that you speak with words
Long before resentment boils itself to a foul stew
On the hidden fires; that you do not fear open conflict
So much that you will hide anything to avoid it,
And that you someday learn to give your word
And commitment to an honorable cause.

A free Gift or where you shine brightest

8

Jupiter Magic

Laying It On Thick

Jupiter is always the Free Gift in any chart. Your Jupiter is where you're a natural, where you have the Knack, where the Universe lets you shine. Magically, it's the kind of gift that expresses itself in "laying on" of some quality. It's like when the magician in the comic book raises his hands and cries out, "I lay (insert Quality X) on this place!" Each of the twelve different Jupiters has a different gift that can be laid on a situation, influencing it in that direction.

After each description, I give you an invocation spell for creating magically what these folks create more or less naturally. That's because we have only one Jupiter apiece, and we have to learn to artificially invoke the other eleven, should we wish to do so. If you need, say, the Jupiter in Virgo gift on a certain day, and that's not your forte, try the spell. Things that will help the spell's astrological juju:

1. Doing the spell when Jupiter is actually in Virgo, in order to bathe yourself in the nature of that transit. Since this happens only every twelve years, however, that may be difficult.

2. Doing the spell when Jupiter is making a trine or a sextile to something in Virgo. For beginning astrologers, use your computer to run the day's transits. Look for Jupiter to make a trine (usually symbolized by a triangle) or a sextile (usually symbolized by a

snowflake) to anything in Virgo. This takes some planning ahead.

3. Do the spell with someone present who has Jupiter in Virgo, and have them ceremonially lay hands on you at the end, in order to ritually pass along some of their special energy. This works no matter what's going on in the sky, as that person happens to be a living avatar of that energy, just as you are a living avatar of the energy of your own planets.

JUPITER IN ARIES

Jupiter in Aries is the laying on of courage. Sooner or later, we all come to an impasse of fear where we cannot force ourselves to go one step further. The abyss yawns beneath our feet, and no force in the Universe will convince us that we can walk across the narrow bridge and not fall in . . . except perhaps Jupiter in Aries.

People have this strange idea that courage means fearlessness. On the contrary, if you have no fear, you have no need of courage. Fearlessness in the face of danger is either a matter of incredible confidence in oneself or a complete denial or misunderstanding of the actual facts of the situation. Courage, on the other hand, is about being terrified and doing it anyway. Jupiter in Aries sees the dangers, knows that he could get hurt, and charges right in . . . because forward movement is always far preferable to cowardly retreat or to standing paralyzed until the danger comes and gets you on its own terms.

You can see this gift in the war leader who addresses his troops before an impossible battle and gets them all to run forward in a great screaming mass, because his example of courage has laid itself on all of them. You can see it in the coach of the losing team who gets his reluctant people to try once more, and maybe even win. Although winning is important to Aries, with Jupiter behind that energy, losing simply means another chance to try to win. That kind of thinking is hard for most of us, especially those who lose and then give up. Never give up, never surrender, die fighting, says Jupiter in Aries. It is the voice not just of survival, but of someone who wants to do more than just survive.

JUPITER IN ARIES SPELL
FOR THE LAYING ON OF COURAGE

Clench both fists as you say this, and then at the end, unclench them and step forward immediately, imagining yourself walking through a line of fire. If possible, hold something made of steel in your fist, and take it with you as a talisman.

I am the iron unforged
And this is the flame before me.
Iron into fire,
Fire into iron,
Fire into me,
That I may tempered be.

JUPITER IN TAURUS

Jupiter in Taurus is the laying on of value. Value is a strange quality; what one person values another finds useless. Jupiter in Taurus touches each thing that it works with, or sells, or builds, and somehow it turns to gold. Yet this Midas touch doesn't actually change the thing in question. It's just as good or bad or objectively crucial or unimportant as it would have been if it had been touched by someone with an entirely different Jupiter. It's just that the Taurus magic makes it seem more valuable in the eyes of those who see it.

This is different from the Gemini fast-talker who can bedazzle you into thinking things are not what they actually are, or the Libra salesman who can charm Alaskans into buying ice machines. Taurus really does consider these things valuable. Watch how someone with Jupiter in Taurus touches the things that they deem are of high caliber. The very motion of their hand, or their eye, says that they have assessed its worth and they are certain of it. Taurus knows more than any other sign how to possess things, and Jupiter in Taurus's first lesson in owning is: Don't bother wasting your possessiveness on things that aren't worth possessing. Cheap and expendable is not the way to go. Go for what will last out the long haul.

Somehow, after Taurus folks have laid their magic, other people take a second look at the same thing and see it differently. It isn't that they are being deceived; it's that they are seeing what's really there, under all the fluff and glitter. Taurus likes the solid rock-bottom picture. Of course, this gift can go the other way as well; if there really isn't anything of solid common-sense worth under the fluff and glitter, Jupiter in Taurus will expose it for what it is. This gift is useful for invoking when you have to consider the real practical worth of an investment of any kind, be it a car, a house, a business, or a person.

JUPITER IN TAURUS SPELL
FOR THE LAYING ON OF VALUE

Start by laying your hands on the item or person in question or on some strongly connected symbol of that item or person. Taurus is tactile energy, and this spell has to be done through touch. Recite the following, under your breath if need be.

> *Under the skin lies the flesh,*
> *And under the flesh lies the bones,*
> *And the bones may be of gold,*
> *Or the bones may be of silver,*
> *Or the bones may be of copper,*
> *Or the bones may be of iron,*
> *Or the bones may be of straw.*
> *As its bones are, so shall I see it,*
> *As its bones are, so others shall see it,*
> *Whether gold under straw or straw under gold.*

As you speak, feel the item under your hand. If any of your fingers prickle during one of the lines about bones, note which one it is. If gold, it will be worth much more in the long run than you know now. If silver, it is a good thing, but its value may fluctuate. If copper, its value is largely in its beauty. If iron, it is solid, but not of the highest value. If straw, it is useless. Whichever it is, as you speak the final lines, that will come to be what people see when they look at it. You can, by the way, lay this spell on yourself, if you think that your good qualities are generally overlooked by others.

JUPITER IN GEMINI

Jupiter in Gemini is the laying on of ingenuity. This placement usually comes with a keen and canny eye for an opportunity to do things differently, or better. Unlike Virgo, who wishes to improve things for the sake of efficiency, the Gemini Jupiter urge is to improve things because you can, because it happened to occur to you that it could be done. This is the gift of inveterate lily-gilders, who see ways to tinker with anything they come across. As it's all about pure mental facility for them, it isn't always linked to anything emotional or ethical. As a result, while under the influence of this energy, priorities can be a little skewed. Solving world peace and tinkering with the Rube Goldberg machine in the garage can seem like equally worthy ideas.

To be the ultimate problem-solver, one has to absorb a lot of small bits of information and have them on hand. It may not be necessary to know anything in depth; if you know just enough about something to know that it would be useful but deeper expertise is required, you can borrow a resident expert to do the depth work and get on with the planning. While one of the drawbacks of Jupiter in Gemini is being a dilettante, a jack-of-all-trades and master of none, this energy is great to invoke when you're faced with a complex problem requiring more handling of tiny bits of data than you feel you're up to. Borrowing this energy is like adding temporary memory banks to your astral brain, plus a faster processor. With this high-speed energy, it's not just that you look at a problem and instantly see a solution; it's that five or six solutions spin past your eyes, and you get a kind of giddy glee at the idea of all the mental gymnastics you'll have to do to figure out which one is best.

One of the talents that people with this Jupiter sometimes develop is the ability to be the Voice of Their Generation, or at least their group. Jupiter here is just as ingenious with words as with anything else—in fact, more so. People with Gemini Jupiter's high-speed brain have the perceptions turned up high, and they pick up information about the attitudes of people around them, if only the external attitudes. They then synthesize this into something coherent that can be distilled and understood by outsiders. In fact, the best use of their gift of ingenuity is to explain in words what others think cannot be explained, to speak the unspeakable, and to distill vagueness into clarity.

JUPITER IN GEMINI SPELL
FOR THE LAYING ON OF INGENUITY

This spell should be done while moving, even if it's just walking back and forth across a room. You should also have some small, brightly colored toy in your hands and be twiddling with it as you go. As this is basically a problem-solving spell, some symbol of the problem should lie in the center of the room. As you circle it, say the following, over and over again, quickly.

My mind is electric,
My eye misses nothing,
Solutions pour from my fingertips.
My hand is unerring,
My eye sees all motion,
The brightest star in the eastern sky.

JUPITER IN CANCER

Jupiter in Cancer is the laying on of a quality that can only be defined as *sanctuary*. They have the ability to make whatever space they have laid claim to seem enclosed and safe from outside disturbances. Sometimes they do this by consciously or unconsciously moving and arranging objects in the space, even simply arranging a few pillows, and then suddenly the space is as enclosed psychically as a crab's shell—sort of a Cancerian Feng Shui. Sometimes they do it by force of will alone, which is especially useful when it's someone else's space.

Cancer is the distilled force of nurturing and parenting, and the first thing that must be done to care for the child is to protect it from outside dangers. All the cooing and snuggling in the world will avail you nothing if the wild beasts break in and make off with the baby, and Cancer knows this on some level. This is a fiercely self-protective sign, as well as one that is protective of loved ones. Cancer is both the archetypal mother in the home whose overflowing breast gives endless nourishment, and the archetypal father standing in the doorway and defending the home from invaders. (This is different from the Capricorn father figure, who disciplines and teaches about the world outside, and the Capricorn mother, who instills values.) In Jupiter, which is a masculine planet, Cancer manifests through the Cancerian father energy, which guards the door and the boundaries and protects the home.

The catch is that there's no guarantee that one will be safe from the influences locked inside. Sanctuary creates a haven from what lies beyond the wall, but once you are locked in with yourself and whatever else is now enclosed with you, it's right there in your face. This gift is quite useful for therapeutic situations where someone needs to be alone with a sympathetic ear and their issues, with no anxiety-producing distractions. However, it can be a problem when you're locked in there with the Cancerian and their baggage, or your own baggage, or baggage that the two of you have created together. The Jupiter in Cancer sanctuary can feel cloistered or claustrophobic, depending on how willing you are to deal with the emotions that you cannot now avoid or ignore.

In effect, this magical sanctuary is an emotional hothouse where feelings are free to manifest and grow, irrigated with water-sign magic. Like real hothouses, the plants can sometimes develop far beyond their potential growth out in the weather, and they may perish when exposed to the cold scrutiny of the outside world. Still, for those whose feeling nature is spindly and undergrown (or battered and half-frozen by cruel circumstances) this hothouse sanctuary can be just what they need to slowly, hesitantly expand and flower.

JUPITER IN CANCER SPELL
FOR LAYING ON OF SANCTUARY

Before you start this spell, look around the room that you are in. Ask yourself what must be changed, physically, to make this place safer. It doesn't have to be anything large, like moving furniture; it can be as simple as rearranging some magazines on the table or moving a few chotchkas. Don't try to decide this rationally; let your intuition do it, entirely irrationally. Go with your first impulses, even if they seem strange. After you've done this,

stand in the center of the space and visualize that you are standing ankle deep
in a central well that nourishes everyone. Then, quietly, say the following:

> *The northern way is guarded,*
> *And the Gates of Midnight are closed to the wild beasts*
>   *that roam.*
> *The eastern way is guarded,*
> *And the Gates of Morning are closed to the whistling*
>   *winds.*
> *The southern way is guarded,*
> *And the Gates of Noon are closed to the destroying fires.*
> *The western way is guarded,*
> *And I stand at the Gates of Evening,*
> *And none shall pass into this space*
> *Save that their names be Peace,*
> *Or Security, or Serenity, or Love,*
> *Yet I do welcome the wounded*
> *To drink from the well from which these things flow.*

JUPITER IN LEO

Jupiter in Leo is the laying on of glamour, not just in the movie-star sense,
but in the faery sense. In medieval times, faeries were said to enchant
leaves into looking like gold and then trade them to hapless townsfolk
for their wares, being long gone by the time the glamour wore off and the
coins crumbled into leaves again. People with Leo Jupiters are lily-gilders,
constantly trying to make things look better than they are. If they are creative types, they can fix up ugly, shabby things—from clothes to houses—
and make them look like they're worth ten times as much, and maybe
even sell them for that. If their personal Jupiter isn't buried or afflicted,
they can lay that glamour on themselves and convince you that they are
much larger than life. (One individual we know who has Jupiter in Leo
on his ascendant is really pretty short in real life, but when you meet him,
you walk away convinced that he's at least as tall as you, if not taller, and
it's not just his regal posture.)

Leos weaves a golden glow around anything they care about, and you can be easily fooled . . . until they become ill, or depressed, or low-energy, and then suddenly everything that was so glamorous yesterday has gone back to being shabby, and you wonder what happened. It's that faery gold again. It's a great gift for artists, performers, or salespeople, as long as they don't try to use it on the people close to them, who see them when they're stumbling grumpily around the kitchen in the morning. The one problem with glamour is that when you've seen through one person's illusion a few times, that person ceases to be able to work it on you.

JUPITER IN LEO SPELL
FOR LAYING ON OF GLAMOUR

Say this while running your hands over your face and chest.

> *My hands are golden,*
> *Everything I touch becomes golden,*
> *I become golden,*
> *All shall gaze upon golden*
> *When they gaze upon me.*
> *I am wreathed in glory,*
> *I am wreathed in the morning,*
> *I am wreathed in the Sun.*

Wear something gold as a token of this spell for the next five days.

JUPITER IN VIRGO

Jupiter in Virgo is the art of laying order on things. These are the people who like to do hundreds of hours of repetitive sorting. It's not just that they're willing to do it or that they're good at it . . . they love it. It makes them happy. They can come into a place, look around, figure out everything that needs to be fixed, and then somehow do it. Not only that, but while they're around, other people find themselves neatening up, organizing, and putting things back where the Virgo Jupiter has decided that they go. They have a gift for figuring out just the right place for something. As one Virgo Jupiter explained to me, it has to be just enough out of reach, an amount corresponding to how often it's used. It has to be in a place that seems like the most natural place in the world for it to go, so that those of us with other Jupiters will instinctively remember to replace it there. When they have laid order on a place, it feels entirely comfortable that these things should go exactly here, and the organization doesn't make the place feel formal or stilted or cold, and the spell lasts for some time, even in the face of the worst slobs.

Some Virgo Jupiters have the "shamanic mechanic" gift, the sort of thing where they can merely lay hands upon a malfunctioning machine and it will behave itself. Sometimes it lasts past when they leave, and sometimes it doesn't. I remember one Virgo Jupiter who would come along behind me and look at all the digital clocks that my Pluto energy was screwing up, and reprogram them, and they would work . . . for about a week, and then I'd start to get to them again. Magically, the laying of order doesn't seem like a very exciting gift. In fact, it can look pretty mundane and modest, but that's just because you haven't seen it in action. When your room, or your desk, or your financial accounts, or your entire life is a mess, and they come through and adjust a couple of things, and all of a sudden other areas of your life start to straighten out and go right as well, you'll understand the magic of invoking the Powers of Order.

JUPITER IN VIRGO SPELL FOR
LAYING ON OF ORDER

Dedicated to Hestia

I circle my hearth from without
And I focus the work of my hands.
I circle my hearth from within
And I focus the work of my heart.
Every work of my hands
Is a victory won;
Everything that I do
Is another thing done.

JUPITER IN LIBRA

Jupiter in Libra has a dual gift. The Scales have two sides, and each side has a particular gift, but there's a catch: Jupiter in Libra can use only one gift at a time, and the two are often mutually exclusive. There's a distinct possibility, in fact, that the use of one gift will destroy the presence of the other.

One Libra gift is the laying on of justice, and the other is the laying on of harmony. When Libra lays on justice—usually with a few well-placed words, as this is an air sign—all the subtle unfairnesses bubble to the surface. Sometimes people put up with bad situations because they've convinced themselves that "this is just the way it is"; Libra's justice spell makes them suddenly sit up and decide not to take it any more. The great thing about this gift is that, after all the dust settles, things are generally fairer and more aboveboard. The problem is what kicks up all that dust. The gift of justice creates arguments. Lots of arguments. It's the way that injustices are addressed. People don't just suddenly sit up and say, "Wow, I'm going to be perfectly fair to everyone I meet today!" Jupiter in Libra's spell does make people more willing to listen and be open to someone else's perspective, but it doesn't mean that they won't have differences of opinions. In fact, it's quite fair to argue about one's differences of opinions. This means, however, that the turmoil can go on for a long time.

Jupiter in Libra's other gift is the laying on of harmony. This can be done verbally, or—since this part of the gift comes from Libra's ruler, Venus—through artfully placed decor or creation of atmosphere. When this gift is laid, people just feel as though they ought to relax and not rock the boat. They feel peaceful, or at least amiable, and willing to be easygoing and enjoy the view. It's a great gift for parties, or group entertainment, or conferences where tempers might be ruffled. However, when this gift is in full swing, people complaining about their treatment become annoyances to be smoothed over or, at worst, excised.

Libra is the sign of the Scales, which are always swinging back and forth in an attempt to balance things. People with Jupiter in Libra will swing back and forth between attempts to inflict justice and attempts to inflict harmony on their surroundings, because that's the Libra dilemma.

JUPITER IN LIBRA SPELL
FOR THE LAYING ON OF JUSTICE AND HARMONY

Stand outside in a brisk wind, with your arms outstretched to either side. Hold a long, fluttering strip of cloth or paper, or a feather, in each hand. As you finish each verse, let go of one and let it blow away, and lower that arm.

I invoke the forces of Justice,
And may the two sides of the scale
Come to balance.
Hail Dike, hail Ma'at, let it be so.
Yet if the blade of Justice must lay waste
To the peace of the realm,
This too I accept,
And I dedicate myself to being the peacemaker in turn.
I invoke the forces of Harmony,
And may the two sides of the scale
Come to balance.
Hail Irene, hail Harmonia, let it be so.
Yet if the quiet of Peace must smother the voice
That cries out for fairness,
This too I accept,
And I dedicate myself to being the sword again in turn.
And may the two sides of the scale
For the moment,
Come to balance.

JUPITER IN SCORPIO

Jupiter in Scorpio's gift is the laying on of passion. When we hear the word *passion*, we tend to think of sexual passion, and it is true that this is associated with Scorpio, and with Jupiter in Scorpio. But some Jupiter in Scorpio types are celibate, and passion still runs in their blood, because passion is much more than sex. It is that quality of absolute, intense focus on what it is that you desire. What would you starve for? For what goal would you work your fingers bloody? For what person would you crawl across broken glass? If you have nothing in your life that you have ever wanted that badly, then you've never tasted Jupiter in Scorpio's ambivalent gift.

Most people are content to go about living safe, boring lives. In fact, most people don't like the idea of Scorpio's gift of passion, until that long-term restless yearning comes upon them and they realize just how safe and empty their lives are. Perhaps they try to remedy the problem with trying to have an adventure, an Aries or Sagittarius flight from Mundania. Perhaps it helps for a little while, but then the yearning comes back. The problem is that a life that lacks passion can't be helped by fiery solutions. Fire that we can control travels along the surface of the Earth, or flies through the sky, but Scorpio is water, and water goes deep into the emotions.

Scorpio's gift is about desire. While many transcendent religions abjure desire, Paganism sees it as yet another part of the human condition. If there was no desire, no passion, no one would ever do anything beyond their own survival. All great creative works that have ever come to fruition carry the passion of their makers, the striving for some kind of ideal that might be unachievable, but which their creators have tried to reach by sheer willpower. Not to mention the fact that without passion, love and relationships would be tame indeed. What would you fight for? Jupiter in Scorpio asks. What would you bleed for? If the answer is nothing, then you are living a pale and tame half-life, and you need this spell, whether you think you do or not.

Jupiter in Scorpio Spell
for the Laying On of Passion

Get on your knees. That's where we all are when faced with our desire. Hold your hands out, empty and palm up, and say:

Something belongs in these hands,
And I do not know what it is.
A hollow lies inside me
That I have long ignored,
And now it cries to be filled.

Close your hands on air, as if grasping for something. Ask yourself what belongs in your hands, what is it that you do not yet have, what is it that you do not yet know that you want. If an answer leaps to mind, take it. If not, meditate for a while. When you have your answer—or if you already know what it is that you want—make your hands into fists, place them against your belly, and say the following:

> *No matter where you are, I will grasp you.*
> *No matter what it takes, I will have you.*
> *No matter what it costs, I will hold you.*
> *My eyes are filled with you,*
> *My heart is full of you,*
> *My will is focused on you,*
> *You will burn within me*
> *Until you lie within my grasp.*

JUPITER IN SAGITTARIUS

Jupiter in Sagittarius's gift is the laying on of hope. Here Jupiter is in its own sign, and the quality that it gives can best be described as "faith in the rightness of the future." It is that moment when you are completely at peace with the Universe and its plans for you, and you are perhaps getting the glint of some larger plan of which your pains and efforts are a small but necessary part.

To put this down as mere optimism is to do it a disservice. So is minimizing it as simply the ability to inspire enthusiasm. Optimism can be blind, or desperate, or hypocritical. Enthusiasm can be caught from another person without real understanding of what is going on, and it can burn out just as quickly. Real hope is none of these, nor does it indulge in pessimism. The essence of hope and faith is, like the secret of the Eleusinian Mysteries, to "come to Death like a bride or bridegroom"— that is, with joy and open arms and the absolute unshakeable conviction that this is the best path for you to be on. There is a calmness to it, even while it partakes of Sagittarian joie de vivre.

The laying on of hope is often discounted as a gift when things are going well. In good times, it may seem more like the work of a good coach bucking you up than anything else—and it is true that we tend to associate Jupiter in Sagittarius energy with those sorts of shallow good times. Even if we barely understand what that energy is, we think of it as good for partying and adventuring and not much else. Yet the place where this gift really comes into its own is during the bleak and barren times, when we contemplate giving up altogether. I remember when I was suffering from severe chemical depression due to a hormone imbalance, and there were days when I would wake up, stand at the top of the stairway, and seriously wonder whether I should walk on down and start the day or throw myself down them. Inevitably, like a helping hand from the Gods, a good friend with Jupiter in Sagittarius would magically call a few minutes later and give me words of hope that got me through another few hours. (Besides, the phone was in the kitchen, and I had to walk downstairs to get it.) Her answering machine message ended with "and remember, progress, not perfection." I'd sometimes call when I knew she wasn't home just to listen to her voice saying that, with such complete confidence.

I remember speaking once about anger, and how I used it as a motivating force (there's a lot of Pluto in my chart), and what was a better motivating force than that? She just shrugged and said, "Joy?" It threw me for a loop and made me think about my own motivations for many years.

Sagittarius is associated with prophecy, but I've rarely found Jupiter in Sagittarius folks to have a conscious precognitive gift—that seems more to be a function of Neptune. Instead, they cheerfully open their mouths and blurt out ridiculous things on a whim . . . which then somehow manage to be true, or come true. By this time, of course, they've moved on and forgotten it, and when you bring it up they shrug it off and say, "Well, there's nothing magical about that; it was obvious." This instinctive, childlike, almost oblivious approach to being a conduit for higher messages is very Jupiterian. Jupiter doesn't need the oracles to be somber and mysterious and vague. His voice is loud and clear and simple as a six-year-old's shout . . . and just as hopeful for joy in the future.

JUPITER IN SAGITTARIUS SPELL
FOR THE LAYING ON OF HOPE

This should ideally be done after dark or in a dark room, but it can be done at any time in a pinch. You will need a candle. You can consult chapter 15 for proper colors and symbols for the candle, and/or scratch the glyphs for Jupiter and Sagittarius into it, but the spell can also be done with a bit of birthday cake candle while sitting in a darkened bathroom and it will still work. Sitting in the dark, say:

I seek the dawning, where my goal can be seen.
I seek the horizon, where passes my path.
Through all darkness, there is a light.
Through all obstruction, there is a path.
Through all confusion, there is a way.
Through the light of my soul,
Held high like a lantern before me,
All things are possible.
(Light the candle.)
In the bottom of the tomb of despair
Burns forever one spark of light,
And here I find it within me,
Here I hold it before me,
Here I give my life to burn for its fuel.

Make sure that the candle burns for at least fifty more heartbeats. Sit quietly and count them. If it can sit somewhere and burn all the way down, so much the better.

JUPITER IN CAPRICORN

Jupiter in Capricorn's gift is the laying on of authority. This is a quality that is often confused with leadership, but it's not quite the same. Leadership is the ability to get people to willingly do what you want them to do, by whatever means works best. Authority is the ability to get people to believe that what you have to say is the most correct thing, and that what you know is the most correct information. Jupiter in Capricorn isn't so much about saying "I am *in* authority," although Capricorn certainly likes doing that. It's about saying "I am *an* authority, and you should listen to me."

This is a useful (Capricorn's key phrase is *I use*) quality to have if you need to get people to listen to you, and you don't have much in the way of Libran beauty or Leo charisma or even the Gemini ability to befuddle with fast talk. It's also useful when dealing with people who distrust such things, who have been burned by the fast and bright and charismatic, and who are more inclined to listen to someone who just seems to be exceptionally solid and sensible.

When you have Capricorn's authority energy flowing through you, it sounds like the way that you describe things is simply the most astute, credible, and prudent way to do them. No one with any common sense at all would think anything different. You come across as sane, reasonable, and practical. Part of this gift is also the ability to point out issues of grandiosity and waste that others have overlooked, and yet not sound overly critical or as if they are merely bursting the balloons of enthusiastic planners. Capricorn is the dragon who guards the resources, and utilizing Jupiter's energy here can create awareness of what the resources actually are and how to avoid squandering them.

It is the voice of the wise parent or the experienced chairman; a voice that people listen to and nod. Even if they don't agree, they will grudgingly admit that you have a point, even if your ideas are a bit too cautious and conservative for them. One other quality of this energy: it can make your most radical ideas sound sober and conservative. That may win you points if you're pitching things to people who are more cautious than you or lose them if your more radical compatriots are within hearing.

JUPITER IN CAPRICORN SPELL
FOR THE LAYING ON OF AUTHORITY

To work this spell, sit in a large chair with arms if one is around. Place objects that symbolize the area in which you are working on the floor around your feet. Sit back and survey them from a distance and say:

All that I see is under my hand,
And may my hand dispense wisdom to all.

All that I know is before my eyes,
And may my eyes see wisdom in all.
All that I am I have myself created,
And may that creation be respected by all.

JUPITER IN AQUARIUS

Jupiter in Aquarius's gift is the laying on of detachment. That's a quality that makes many people flinch when they hear it; it sounds cold and lonely, perhaps even inhuman. How can such a thing be a gift? Yet we are all human, and to be human is to be a social animal, and an emotional one too. We collide, we argue, we hurt each other, we become enmeshed in each other, we disappoint each other. The potential for drama in the human experience is enormous, and many of us never fail to make use of it. And, sometimes, that drama can lead to a worsening of the situation, not an improvement. Sometimes we get so mired in our own pain and fear and elation that we cannot see anyone, or anything, else.

The gift of Jupiter in Aquarius is the ability to step back from the human drama and see the bigger picture. It's the ability to—even temporarily—lift yourself above the quarreling masses and see how little these petty dramas matter, in the big scheme of things. From that high perspective, the evil demons intent on ruining your life become simply screwed-up people acting out their unconscious scripts over and over again, and perhaps the best thing that you can do is to refuse to engage with them and walk away. The perfect lover that you adored from afar is revealed to be just another nice person, with the same flaws as everyone else, and perhaps no better than that nice person over there who might actually be interested in you. The bad situation that felt like it was the Universe persecuting you will pass and reveal itself to be just another bad bump in the road.

The place of detachment is definitely an outsider's perspective, and it can be lonely. It can also make you feel cut off from the rest of humanity. However, humanity needs that gift. We need to be able to remember, at times, that things are not as we see them in the metaphorical six-inch space in front of our noses. The Jupiter in Aquarius gift creates the objectivity we need to be able to see as many similarities between us as differences. From a distance, we are all the same grains of sand. To really feel like one of the group, we must paradoxically see ourselves in the group from the outsider's perspective.

JUPITER IN AQUARIUS SPELL
FOR THE LAYING ON OF DETACHMENT

Breathe deeply between each two lines

I rise above the earth on which I stand
And the cries of the flesh fall away from me.
I rise above the waters that stretch far away
And the weeping of the heart falls away from me.
I rise above the fire of the Sun,
And the anger of the past falls away from me.
I rise above the wreckage of my life,
And from afar I look down upon it.
In what was chaos, I see a pattern,
There for me to grasp or leave.
In what was disaster I see hope,
There for me to build upon.
I stand outside the Universe,
And I breathe myself ready
To return to being human.

JUPITER IN PISCES

Jupiter in Pisces's gift is the laying on of empathy. That word is thrown around a lot in spiritual circles; all sorts of people claim to be "terribly empathic," to the point where it's almost as laughable as claiming to be "so sensitive." One often finds that the ones who proclaim their empathic natures the loudest are clearly oblivious to the discomfort of the person they're talking to, who may be standing there with a fixed smile or a nervous twitch. When they do try to guess what you're feeling, they tend to get it wrong. This is because what most people think of as *empathy* is either *sympathy* or simple *emotionality*.

Many individuals claim to be empathic when what they really mean is that they are emotional people who react strongly to triggering stimuli. Someone crying makes them feel bad all out of proportion to how most people will react, and they cry as well, but it's not empathy. It comes from their own issues and may have nothing to do with the exact flavor of sorrow being experienced by the crying person. In their own depth of emotion, they assume that this must be exactly what that other person is feeling, and that furthermore, they are actually feeling it from them, because their emotion triggered it.

Empathy is also not the same as being able to imagine how someone feels by imagining how you would feel in the same place. That's sympathy—"sym" means "same"—because it's you trying to see yourself in the same space as them. While that's a fine thing, it does not take you beyond your own assumptions into alien territory. You are a different person from anyone else, and your exercise in imagining being them can fail due to sheer lack of information.

Real empaths—often people who have a strong Pisces influence in their charts—are, for some strange reason, not usually the ones who are complaining about how empathic they are, hand firmly glued to forehead. They are the ones who get caught up in other people's feelings, other people's views, without even noticing it. Many of them go for years without realizing that they're doing it. They don't just imagine what it feels like to be someone else; they actually become that person in part, for a time. They may have poor boundaries and merge easily; they may unthinkingly parrot the views of others or not quite know what their own thoughts and feelings are about something. When they're away from the (usually strongly emotional) people whose feelings they absorb, they often feel empty and unanchored. Far from being tossed and turned to the point of hiding, they usually seek out people to fill them up with feelings . . . because they may not know how to have their own.

That's the dark side of it. The positive side, of course, is that most of us are not like this, but we could certainly use a dose of it now and again.

Real empathy can be a shattering experience, blowing away people's self-centered ideas about what sorts of feelings it's normal to have. Real empathy can force you to face how alien, how different from you, every other person in the Universe is. It can make you feel very alone once you come up from it. Real empathy can also blast your own worldview wide open; that moment of being able to actually apply someone else's perspective—and not in an intellectual way, but in a deep, feeling way—and to see your life through their eyes can change your life. In other words, like so many worthwhile things, it's painful, it's dangerous, and it's good for you now and again.

While this spell can be laid on oneself, it is most often laid upon another, as Pisces is the least likely to do the "it's all about me" dance. If you are laying it on yourself, you should be doing it in an extremely humble way, as Pisces is also about humility. You should be doing it because you realize that your own single perspective is limited and flawed and that the inability to step out of your own skin and really become someone else for a time is hampering your psychological and spiritual progress. You should be doing it with the understanding that it may change you in painful ways, and you should try to be at peace with that, although it's all right to be afraid. Pisces never says that you can't have fear, but the Pisces response to fear is very different from the Aries charge-ahead-with-courage. Pisces faces fear with a kind of fatalistic passivity; it's learning to be at peace with fear and with the pain that you are afraid will come, which probably will.

If this spell is to be laid on others, remember that everything you lay on someone else comes back to you, so it will affect you as well. Be sure that your motives are clear and that the spell is not done out of superiority. Consider, too, that you will be affected as well; perhaps a good thing to start your meditation with is to say to the absent (or perhaps not so absent) recipient: "I lay this upon you because I believe that you need it and that it will do you good, and I believe this because I see that also in myself, and I too need it, and it will do me good as well." That actually creates a bond of compassion (another Piscean trait) between you and the other, which is appropriate for the nature of this spell.

JUPITER IN PISCES SPELL
FOR THE LAYING ON OF EMPATHY

Start by sitting and meditating quietly for the space of at least half an hour. Then cross your hands and place them over your heart chakra. As you say the following invocation, bring them very slowly away from your chest and stretch out your arms before you, hands still crossed, until they are extended as far as possible. Then separate your hands and let them slowly move out until your arms are spread wide and your heart chakra is defenseless.

While you are speaking the words "you and you and you," picture in your mind the people you would least like to share emotions with. Pisces is all about compassion even for the most undesirable.

> *I am within my skin,*
> *I am enclosed in my own universe,*
> *But now I stretch my skin open,*
> *I widen the boundaries of my universe,*
> *I take you into my skin,*
> *And you, and you, and you;*
> *I merge inside your skin,*
> *And yours, and yours, and yours;*
> *There is no space between us,*
> *There is no time between us,*
> *There is no skin between our nerves,*
> *There is no boundary between our hearts,*
> *I am one with all.*

9
Saturn Magic
Black Stones

If Jupiter is the Freebie, Saturn is the Price You Pay for It. Although Jupiter's gifts may be given with no strings attached, since we all have a Saturn as well as a Jupiter, the bill will be rendered anyway, by the Higher Authority via the next Saturn transit. Any scientist will tell you that in this Universe, anyway, there is no such thing as a free lunch, and it all evens out in the end. Saturn transits interfere with everything. The squares and oppositions can feel like agony, and the conjunctions can be even worse. Even Saturn trines can be uncomfortable if you don't handle them properly. Saturn going over your Moon or Venus can feel like an emotional condom has just dropped over your head. Saturn impacting Mars can cause a general traffic jam in your life. Saturn going through any house can guarantee slowdowns . . . or commitments.

Sometimes it can feel as if Saturn is stalking through your houses one at a time, kicking your feet out from under you, stomping your fragile hopes, wedging his staff between your wheels, throwing monkey wrenches into your machinery, and generally creating stuckness and painful immobility wherever he goes. The archetype that we tend to think of with Saturn is the Old Man, often the dour professor who gives us an F just because he doesn't like us or the old grandpa who makes us eat our vegetables and go to bed early so that we miss the carnival, and who may beat us if he catches us sneaking out.

Although Saturn is legitimately all these things, I'd like to throw out a different image for the archetype. Imagine the Old Man as an honorable teacher who you've come to study martial arts with. As in the stories of many old masters, he may try to discourage you at first to see if you really want to learn or you're just flirting with the idea. If you hold fast in the face of insult and obvious doubt in your abilities, he will set you to doing a number of repetitive, boring, and perhaps painful exercises that may make no sense at all to you. Your attempts to get him to explain why you have to go through these awful patterns over and over will be met with a grunt and a glare, and perhaps a "Because they are necessary. You won't understand until you're further along." Your attempts to ask how long you have to go through these motions will be met with a curt "Until you get them right."

After a long period of "wax on, wax off," to quote the famous movie, he suddenly shows you why they were necessary . . . by running up and smacking you. If you have gotten them right, if you have practiced diligently and with good discipline, you will automatically meet his attack in the proper way and be able to fend it off, perhaps with only a few bruises. If you haven't, then you'll be knocked onto your ass. Is this cruelty? When you're sitting there on the ground feeling stupid or frightened or realizing that you've sprained your wrist and it will set you back a month of practice, it feels as though he's the cruelest being in the world, and you hate him.

Maybe you'll try to quit, or hide. Maybe you'll curl up in a ball, refuse to practice, and just endure blows and kicks until he gives up and goes his way. The problem is that in real life, we get sentenced to Saturn's dojo on a regular basis, whether we like it or not. In a period of twenty-nine years, he'll visit and challenge every member of our internal planetary family, including the weak and afflicted ones, and leave his calling card in every area of our lives . . . and then start all over again. If we were cowardly or lazy or undisciplined the first time, we'll have it even worse the second time around.

What you have to believe, even in the middle of confusing and frustrating periods of "wax on, wax off," even through the random sneak attacks, is that Saturn, like any sensei, honestly wants you to improve. His dojo is the School of Hard Knocks, and he does what he does because life is often difficult, and the better you are at calmly blocking what blows you can and quickly recovering from those you can't, the more likely you are to survive . . . and, more to the point for him, burn off enough karma in your lifetime that you will have a better chance of getting to wherever it is that you need to go. He's strict because you need it. We all do, whether we admit it or not. Human nature tends to laziness, and we'd rather sit around and play than do the work to earn our black belt in Living Properly.

In the dojo, if you don't practice until it's automatic, when the blow comes you'll fail and crumble. Conversely, the only way to hone your technique is to have someone hit you. And, yes, sometimes you'll end up on the mat nursing your wounds . . . and sometimes you'll manage to breathe and move and roll with the punches and land on your feet, a bit shaken but none the worse for wear. This is the way that Saturn teaches those important lessons of discipline, focus, and understanding your limits.

He's all about limits. Saturn's lesson for everyone is that by being here in a physical body (which has limits) on a highly physical plane (which has limits), you have agreed to learn about limits. You're here to learn to transcend a few of them, but most of them were not placed on you to be transcended. They were placed on you to be experienced, and acknowledged, and perhaps even appreciated. You don't beat your limits; you learn to compensate for them, work around them, and respect them. You don't beat Saturn; you negotiate with him, you compromise with him, you discipline yourself and learn from him. That's the hard lesson that every one of us needs to learn, and it's one that we keep running away from.

No matter how hard you try to create your own reality, actual reality keeps intruding . . . and it always will, because it's stronger. Changing actual reality, the one that doesn't belong to you but is shared by all of us, the one that belongs to the Higher Powers, well, that can be done, but it requires a huge amount of grubby, painful, repetitive work. All the affirmations in the world will not get your laundry done or the garden weeded or your friend's belongings moved to their new house. For that, you need to sweat. In Saturn's dojo, if you aren't sweating, you aren't getting anywhere. If it seems effortless, you're doing it wrong . . . and when you turn around, he'll be there with the stick, taking your feet out from under you.

Of all the planetary forces, Saturn—by definition—ends up being the one who gets cursed at the most. It's also the force that people have the most trouble bringing themselves to propitiate wholeheartedly. This is because they don't really respect or appreciate Saturn's lessons, and no matter how loudly they say, "Oh, yes, I know that discipline and limits are valuable," deep down they really believe that if everything that is Saturn would just go away, they could just float through life happily and with no cares, and everything would be vastly improved. Except that one of the great forces of Saturn is gravity, and although it might seem nice to think about a world with no gravity, in reality that would be a world with no atmosphere to breathe and thus no life. You'd simply go floating off into the cold airless heartless void and die.

Saturn is the force that holds down everything that is necessary; indeed, he is the force of necessity itself. Venus may bring love, but it is the Saturn force that keeps a lover around after the first flush of brain chemicals has worn off. Mars may be great motivation in the short run, but it is Saturn who keeps us going when Mars would rather get bored and go elsewhere. Mercury is brilliant, but Saturn sits down in front of the terminal every day and gets the book written. Jupiter wins you the lottery; Saturn makes sure that you pay off the IRS and don't blow the rest on junk. The Moon makes the mother love her baby, but it is Saturn that drags her out of bed even when she is ill and depressed to feed and diaper the annoying, screaming little parasite. What the other planetary forces begin, Saturn continues, and without him, we would live ephemeral, ineffective lives and never accomplish anything of worth.

It is this we have to value when we build Saturn's altars or propitiate him with remedies. If we do it with our fingers crossed, if we do it while secretly devaluing him, he will smell it and it will not work. Here's the key to ask yourself honestly when propitiating Saturn: Do I, on any level—conscious or subconscious—feel like I am *hoping to get away with something?* If so, you've missed the point, and you'd better rethink your attitude. With Saturn, you will never get away with anything. That's not the point. The point is to show your willingness to respect Saturn's work and to inconvenience yourself to show that respect.

When, for example, you check chapter 16 and discover that your problem requires giving aid to a disabled person, you must understand that they are standing in as a symbol of the Saturn force. Their physical limitation is symbolizing Saturn's ability to limit you, if he deems it necessary for you to learn something. If you react to them with any of the negative emotions that people throw at Saturn to assuage their discomfort—such as distaste, or disgust, or fear, or pity, or irritation at the object's intractability, or cheerfully patronizing behavior, or fishing for pats on the head regarding how great you are to deign to do this at all—it will backfire. You should approach them, and any stand-in for Saturn, with the attitude you approach the master in the dojo: "Tell me what needs to be done, and I will do it respectfully, without stalling or complaining or making a big deal out of my inconvenience, and I will take my contentment from the fact that I am doing the correct and useful and necessary thing."

There is a positive side to all this, though. Sometimes, when you've been good about your lessons, Saturn can suddenly hand you a gift. It likely won't be what you were expecting or what you wanted, but you can guarantee it will be what you *need*—and that it will last a good long time and be every bit worth the price that you paid for it. For instance, a trine to Saturn in your natal chart is a wonderful thing for the planet involved. It doesn't mean that planet gets to be carefree and run around like it would without a Saturn contact, but it does mean that disciplined action somehow comes easily and smoothly to that part of your nature. For example, my wife's Saturn-Uranus trine not only gives her excellent timing as a comic, it allows her to embrace being a *heyoka,* or trickster, as a spiritual path rather than as merely an excuse to mock people. The Moon-Saturn trine in our composite chart gives our marriage deep loyalty, even during rough times. And without the Saturn trine to my Mercury-Neptune conjunction, none of my books would ever have been written.

I have an astrologer friend whose Sun, Moon, and ascendant are all in the same signs as mine, and her ascendant is close enough that we tend to get transits going through our houses simultaneously. We can compare and contrast—"How's Mars in the third treating you? I'm feeling argumentative"—and see how the same planets affect different people. When Saturn went into my fourth house, the house of home and family, I was married and living in suburbia, and she was in college. She ended up with two years of rootlessness and wandering; not wonderful, but not bad either. I ended up with a premature, sickly infant whose need for constant care uprooted our entire routine and killed our social life for over a year; we did nothing but work and stay home with the baby. Then Saturn went into our fifth house, the house of romance, creativity, and children. She embarked on a series of whirlwind affairs that always ended in painful breakups (but it looked more interesting than my life from where I was standing), and she kept having unsuccessful attempts at pregnancy. I ended up divorced, single-parenting a severely learning-disabled child while my ex fled to California for a high-paying corporate job, but I did teach myself to play guitar and write songs in order to eke out a living as a street musician to support my child.

When Saturn passed into our mutual sixth houses, we both lost our jobs and fled the city. I ended up living in solitude in the woods for a while, with only my daughter for company, and my health problems assaulted me (sixth house is health). I broke my knees three times and had trouble with congenital skeletal deformities (it was in Capricorn, which rules knees and bones). She went through many bad part-time jobs and bad housing problems, and she had her own health issues, but her romantic situation stabilized. Then Saturn went into our seventh house, the partnership house. She, for whom being partnered and in a relationship had always been crucial and important, broke up with her long-term boyfriend and couldn't seem to get another. She spent most of that period celibate, lonely, frustrated, and depressed. Toward the end, she realized that she was supposed to be learning about being alone, but it was a hard lesson for her to swallow.

As for me, I'd been braced for the worst, although I felt that I could handle monastic aloneness . . . after all, I was the one who loudly proclaimed his independence, who didn't want to rely on anyone, who stood alone. No problem. My health problems, however, continued to get worse. And then Saturn pulled the trick I didn't expect: he sent me a wife. A woman came into my life who was, finally, right for me, and she was willing to help me through the difficult health period ahead . . . but she was a Saturn-ruled Capricorn, and she wanted commitment. So while my friend moped alone, I got married . . . and had to learn to get comfortable with being dependent on someone else. Both Saturn lessons, custom-designed for our individual areas of stubbornness.

SIMPLE SATURN RITUALS

This chapter on Saturn magic is somewhat more thorough and complex than many of the other planetary chapters, and that is because Saturn is more likely to cause someone distress than any other planet. Clients come to me more often with Saturn problems than any others. That's why you will find invocations for Saturn not only through the planets but through the signs. It's not that the other planets don't affect our houses—they do—but it seems especially necessary to track Saturn's trail through the areas of our life.

To do these rituals, dress formally and kneel on the ground or floor. (Saturn/Capricorn rules the knees.) Combine the invocation for the sign with the invocation for the house, and speak them. Then do the activity specified for Saturn in that sign and house in chapter 16. This is especially important; Saturn wants to see some useful and concrete action out of you. He cannot be pushed around by mere desires.

INVOCATIONS FOR SATURN
THROUGH THE SIGNS

SATURN IN ARIES

Grandfather, I kneel before you
To learn the hard lesson of honor.
For it is not enough to be a warrior

And to lash out in anger or glee;
There must also be rules of honor
That bind me to an unyielding code,
Even if my spirit cries out against this bondage
And wishes to strike where it will.
Teach me the hard road of honor,
Grandfather who makes no move impulsively,
That I may not win my battles only to lose my soul.

Saturn in Taurus

Grandfather, I kneel before you
To learn the hard lesson of rootlessness,
Being cast adrift when every fiber of your being
Longs to make a place where every morning's sun
Rises on the same kind of day.
Teach me that rootedness must be worked for,
A prize to be earned and not a gift to be given,
Grandfather who digs his place in the dirt
Shovelful by shovelful, valuing every scoop of soil,
With my sweat pouring down to fertilize the earth.

Saturn in Gemini

Grandfather, I kneel before you
To learn the hard lesson of division,
That mind and heart will always battle,
Save for the rare and perfect moments of harmony,
And these shall pass, leaving me torn again.
Teach me that neither mind nor heart
Is better; that I must give each its turn
Lest I make an enemy of half of my own self.
Grandfather who clears away lies and confusion
With the sharpness of the scalpel blade,
Let me be clean of my own illusions.

SATURN IN CANCER

Grandmother, I kneel before you
To learn the hard lesson of nurturing
When your spirit cries out against it.
Teach me to care for my responsibilities,
Even those that require my love,
When my heart urges me to run away,
Like the mother dragged from her sickbed
To care for the child she can barely love.
Teach me this kind of determination,
Grandmother whose love is tough and hard,
That I may not fail in my care merely through
*   lack of feeling.*

SATURN IN LEO

Grandfather, I kneel before you
To learn the hard lesson of brightness,
That while it lights the world,
Can do nothing greater than to cast a shadow
As great as its own flaming light.
Teach me that I cannot live only in light
Nor only in shadow, but that I must value both
And learn humility and my own lack of specialness.
Grandfather whose shadow envelops me,
Teach me to see beyond light and shadow,
That I might come to know that all things
Will still exist without them.

SATURN IN VIRGO

Grandmother, I kneel before you
To learn the hard lesson of compassion.
For the world is full of imperfections;
I count them daily, I see them everywhere,
They torment me at every turn,

And the worst of them lie in the hearts of others,
And the worst of all of these lie within my own.
Teach me to have compassion for the faults of others
That I may forgive myself for my own lack
Of perfection, and thus strive with a clean soul.
Grandmother Virgin whose patient hand counts all things,
Free me from the tyranny of numbered sins.

SATURN IN LIBRA

Grandfather, I kneel before you
To learn the hard lesson of propriety.
For people cannot live without Law,
Though they might like to think so
And though I will admit that laws chafe me as well.
Teach me how to ride the social rules
To get what I need; teach me how
I may disguise myself and use them
Without overmuch cramping of my soul,
For even the most confining have their value
In keeping our selfishness from harming each other,
O Grandfather who is the Rule of Law.

SATURN IN SCORPIO

Grandmother, I kneel before you
To learn the hard lesson of self-control,
To cage the impulse that would leap forward unchecked,
To contain my passions, to leash my feelings
And prevent them from action, yet not cease
To experience them, though they must needs be shackled.
Teach me to value that which can never be expressed
Lest others be harmed, and love it anyway.
Grandmother who is at home with longing,
Bless these hungers of mine
And keep others safe from their ravening jaws.

SATURN IN SAGITTARIUS

Grandfather, I kneel to you
To learn the hard lesson of finding God within.
Though the others take comfort in their dogma,
Their doctrine, their liturgy, none of these
Will do for me; I must find it myself or not at all,
And only once I have found the divine circle on my own
May I read the works of others and know
That I have, once again, reinvented the wheel,
And yet it must be this way for the burning of my soul.
Grandfather who holds the lantern in the dark,
Teach me that though my path be filled with thorns
It is the only one I can, with conscience, travel.

SATURN IN CAPRICORN

Grandfather, I kneel to you
To learn the hard lesson of duty,
For duty is my lot during this time.
Teach me to love and honor boundaries
And even obstacles, for they may be
The boundaries of others in disguise.
Teach me to value commitment over feeling,
For feelings may change and bend with the wind,
And leave hapless charges in the lurch,
But duty never bends, and never fails the ones
Who depend upon its timely rescue.
Grandfather who is as dependable as the stony earth,
May others come to rely upon my strong and solid soul.

SATURN IN AQUARIUS

Grandfather, I kneel to you
To learn the hard lesson of entropy,
That no matter how far I look ahead,
I will not be able to complete my life's task,

And yet neither am I permitted to lay it down.
Teach me that no matter how the misunderstanding
Of other minds may impede me,
I may not forget that all that I do
Is for the good of those very souls
Whom I would sweep aside as ignorant chaff.
Grandfather whose vision is cold and clear,
Teach me to value the ones for whom I strive
Even when they frustrate my striving itself.

SATURN IN PISCES

Grandmother, I kneel before you
To learn the hard lesson of letting go.
For the strength of my desire confines me,
And taints my relationship with everything I long for.
Teach me that in order to get what I desire
I must first resign myself to never having it,
Letting go of it entirely with no secret hopes,
And only then can I come to it cleanly
When it comes to me like a gift unlooked-for.
Grandmother whose wisdom is like the ocean's depths,
Teach me to value this nothingness
That in my weightlessness I may float into Oneness.

INVOCATIONS FOR SATURN THROUGH THE HOUSES

SATURN IN THE FIRST HOUSE

Grandmother, I kneel before you
To learn the hard lesson of the eyes of others.
Teach me how I am seen by others,
For better or for worse,
Without the film of my own views.
Teach me how to alter myself in those eyes,

Even if I must hide parts of myself,
So that when the time of Necessity is nigh
I may be able to survive.

SATURN IN THE SECOND HOUSE

Grandmother, I kneel before you
To learn the hard lesson of the empty hands,
The valued belongings that fall away or do not satisfy.
Teach me that I own nothing save my own flesh,
My own heart, my own thoughts,
And that anything that can be taken from me
May well be, and that I should not place my trust in that
     gold.
Teach me instead that this poverty is a gift,
That to have is riches, but to be able to do without
Is power, and gives freedom in the end.

SATURN IN THE THIRD HOUSE

Grandmother, I kneel before you
To learn the lesson of the foreign tongue,
To learn how alien the tongue of all people
Is to my own mind, lest I fall into laziness
And think them all copies of myself.
Teach me the pain of knowing that others
Do not understand my words, lest I shape them
Into a form that is foreign to myself,
And yet they must be so shaped to be understood.
Grandmother who is at home with silence,
Teach me the game of the razor's edge.

SATURN IN THE FOURTH HOUSE

Grandfather, I kneel before you
To learn the hard lesson of the poison inheritance,
The patterns passed down from parent to child,

The vicious cycles, the shattered family,
The invisible wounds that no one speaks of
But that dog you like chains from childhood on.
Teach me that the only way to break these chains
Is to both value them and cast them aside,
As one loves parents and hates abuse both equally.
Teach me that freedom cannot be had without mourning,
That I might walk clean and sorrowful in the world.

SATURN IN THE FIFTH HOUSE

Grandmother, I kneel before you
To learn the hard lesson of the window glass,
The barrier I press myself against to see all the others
Living with joy, with romance, with fun and games
That I cannot join in; to see the children laughing
And playing in a circle that is not for me.
Teach me that there is still hope in a life
Where every moment of happiness
Must be earned with aching toil,
Teach me that these gems of joy will be valued
All the more for their rarity,
O Grandmother who trudges on, mile after mile
And never lets such a thing as the weight of sorrow
Stop her footsteps in the graying rain.

SATURN IN THE SIXTH HOUSE

Grandfather, I kneel before you
To learn the hard lesson of organization.
For the details pile up and overwhelm me,
The many tiny things that I must remember
And sort one from another; they mesh and blend
And I fall headlong into confusion.
Teach me the patterns, the repetition,
The patience in the face of workload panic,

The ability to work each step and finish the task.
Grandfather who sees that every nail is in place,
Help me to clear my own cluttered mind
That I might mend the broken works of others.

SATURN IN THE SEVENTH HOUSE

Grandmother, I kneel before you
To learn the hard lesson of aloneness
In the face of the urge for pairing.
For I cannot be satisfied with any partner
Simply for the sake of having one; I must not settle
For less than the right relationship,
Even if that means I die cold and alone.
Teach me that the Universe gives you what you settle for,
And I must hold to a higher standard.
Teach me that aloneness is preferable
To a compromise of the heart,
Grandmother who walks in the shadow of solitude
Help me to be the best partner to myself
That I might not sell my heart for less.

SATURN IN THE EIGHTH HOUSE

Grandfather, I kneel before you
To learn the hard lesson of transformation,
The rebirth that is hard, not a joyous birth,
The one that makes you twist, writhe,
And despair of being done with,
That demands to dance fully with you
And will not take passivity for an answer.
Teach me the traditions of those who have transformed
  before me
That I might learn a discipline for my survival
And that I might have some control over my final form.
Grandfather who carves away all that is not needful,

Teach me that this painful shape-shifting
Is the prologue to a form that can better serve my tribe.

SATURN IN THE NINTH HOUSE

Grandmother, I kneel before you
To learn the hard lesson of confinement.
My soul longs to travel the carefree road
And seek only the horizon, but for this time
That path must be put aside, and the world
Of the inside must be of more value.
Teach me to set my mind flying
Instead of my body; help me to break through
Obstacles of vision rather than thickets of thorns,
And show me that there is more value in inner travel.
Grandmother whose quilt is spread over the patchwork
*   land,*
Let me fly over your hills with the power of my mind.

SATURN IN THE TENTH HOUSE

Grandmother, I kneel before you
To learn the hard lesson of ignominy.
I crave the applause and respect of thousands,
Yet all my toil brings me no closer
To the top of the mountain where the great ones,
The beautiful ones, the respected ones, live.
Teach me that there is honor in being a peasant,
That ambition is nothing if it crushes those under you
In your steep climb, and that it is far better
To rule a hovel honorably than a kingdom poorly.
Grandmother who is the maker of kings,
Teach me that by refusing me your gift for this time
You give me time to make myself more worthy of it.

SATURN IN THE ELEVENTH HOUSE

Grandmother, I kneel before you
To learn the hard lesson of being an alien.
No group is perfect for me; each tribe
Shows my differences with them, and I despair
Of ever finding the place where all are my kin.
Teach me that this very place of solitude
And isolation gives me perspective,
A point of view that is valuable
Even to those next to whom I feel so alien.
Grandmother who understands the lonely bird
Who flies crying upon the wind,
Teach me to love my alien eyes.

SATURN IN THE TWELFTH HOUSE

Grandfather, I kneel before you
To learn the hard lesson of the loneliest place,
The prison where you are locked away
From your self, your soul, your deep places
And these depths must be coaxed, cajoled, implored,
And earned only with hard work.
Teach me that those dark places are worth the work,
The pain, the striving, that I may not give up
And live a shallow life, and never know myself.
Grandfather who is the Guardian of the Gate of the
    Underworld
Let me remember that beyond my own locked doors
Lies the greatest treasure I have ever owned.

SATURN AND BLACK STONES

Although chapter 15, Planetary Altars, contains stones for every planet and sign combination, explaining every one of them here would require another book. However, Saturn being the earthiest and most rocklike of planets, he seemed to want me to talk about his rocks in this chapter, so I will discuss the black stones that seem to have affiliations with this sign.

Black is not a color of evil and negativity; it is a color of great power. This is why witches, judges, clergy, and those who want to be taken seriously wear black. Carrying the black stone for Sun, Moon, and ascendant signs will help you to deal with the entrenched bad habits each sign has a tendency to become mired in.

Carrying the black stone for the sign of your Saturn may be less comfortable. In fact, especially if you are under thirty, you may be somewhat repelled by its energy. This may be because you are still dealing with the painful issues of your natal Saturn. At the age of twenty-nine, we all endure the Saturn return, the point where Saturn returns to where it was when you were born. This is often the point when people "grow up" and realize they aren't kids anymore. The black stone for your Saturn sign may begin to feel more comfortable, or even draw you, at this time.

When you are having a Saturn transit—Saturn aspecting some natal planet in your chart—you might find that a black stone for that sign may help you feel more able to cope with the restrictive, disciplinarian energies permeating that aspect of your life. Holding it while reciting the proper invocation will charge it with intent, and then you can carry it with you to aid in your struggles.

Saturn in Aries—Black Diamond

Aries, the symbolic infant of the zodiac, is ruled by Mars, the warrior planet, which mythologically protects and shields the infant. This is reminiscent of the Kouretes of matriarchal times—warriors who protected the infant Sun god when his destruction was threatened by doing a shield dance around him. The real job of Mars is not offense but defense—and to defend the part of yourself that is most vulnerable, you need a hard shield. Aries' major stone is the diamond, primal carbon, hardest of all gemstones, and Aries' Saturn stone is the black diamond. Unlike gem-quality diamonds, black diamonds are more likely to be used for practical purposes than glitter, such as drill bits and saw edges. To protect himself, Aries has to learn to be a little practical about his fierce idealism and to shrug off criticism not through blindness to the feelings of others, but from the knowledge that his ideals are well grounded in reality.

Saturn in Taurus—Star Diopside

Taurus is the sign most likely to get itself stuck in a rut of doing things the same old comfortable way forever. Taurus doesn't chase stars, yet Taurus's black stone is the star diopside, the lovely star glowing against the night sky. What does the star symbolize? Hope. And you'll find that a Taurus in a rut is a Taurus who has lost hope. In truth, the misty dreamers tend to drift off the chase long before they've actually caught the star, which takes patience and endurance—qualities a Taurus has in abundance. To Tauruses who have lost their way, the star may guide them home, which is where all good quests end anyway. At least, all good Taurus ones.

Saturn in Gemini—Black Tourmaline

Black tourmaline, also called schorl, is the Gemini stone for negativity. Working with the stone will disclose the Gemini-like quality of tourmaline and its penchant for polarity. Every Gemini has two sides, who may or may not be in agreement on anything. Often, the main difference between the two sides may be the introvert/extrovert quality of each. It is not unusual for a Gemini to foist all the negative qualities off on one facet, believing the other is "all good." We are not, however, so divided in our souls. Each part of us has good and bad qualities. The black tourmaline, which brings up and balances the negativity of both poles, will bring this home to Geminis and help them to admit to and deal with both their duality and their wholeness.

Saturn in Cancer—Boji Stone

Cancer is the sign of nurturing, of both parent and child. Wherever you have Cancer, there you want to be both of those, at the same time or by turns. Cancer's stone is the pyritic concretion, a round little rock resembling the breasts that Cancer rules. They give out great amounts of healing energies, but only if you give them great amounts of love and affection. If you take charge of a pyritic concretion, carry it around often. Put it under your pillow. Rub it between your fingers. Cancers have a tendency to be so busy nurturing everyone else that they forget their own needs. Holding a well-loved pyritic concretion is an unconditional way to get some of that warm healing energy back, especially when feeling tired and drained.

Saturn in Leo—Jet

Leo's Sun stone is amber, and Leo's Saturn stone is jet, to which amber is symbolically "married"—in a partnership symbolizing day and night. In ancient times, jet was sacred to Cybele, the Middle Eastern goddess whose symbol was the lioness. Jet is a fossilized resin, and like amber, it holds electricity when rubbed. It is a wonderful stone for energy storage, which Leos need and won't admit to needing. All that shining and performing and being queenly is tiring. Often Leos won't go out if they're feeling less than physically perfect, thinking that no one will like them if they're not spewing out that warm sunny energy every minute. Warm, dark jet will help keep them feeling energetic and happier about themselves.

Saturn in Virgo—Morion

Virgos are the misunderstood perfectionists of this world. They fear chaos and disorder, be it physical, mental, or emotional (and usually they may focus on only one of these), and they are harder on themselves than anyone else. The black stone for Virgo is morion, or smoky quartz. This gentle, soothing stone calms hyperstrung Virgo nerves, helps them stay centered even as they suppose the world is crumbling around them, and helps them turn inactive criticism into practical action. Morion is superb for gently activating and grounding the root chakra, important for Virgos, who are often nervous and uncomfortable about body-oriented root chakra activities. It will help them deal with their fears of sensuality and bodily surrender to sensation; it will also keep their quick, bright, whirling minds from absorbing too much too fast and manifesting the tense nervousness that comes from mental indigestion.

Saturn in Libra—Black Opal

Libra's two greatest faults are bound up with Libra's two greatest gifts. One is indecision, coming from the Libran ability to see two sides to every conflict. The other is unhealthy overdependence on one's partner, a common difficulty when one is as partnership oriented as the average Libra. Libras lost in low-self-esteem-land will depend desperately on their partner for self-definition and identity, either losing themselves in the partner's identity or attempting to remake the partner's individuality over in their own ideal image. Since the stone of partnership is the opal, Libra's black stone is the black opal, the stone of mirroring. Using black opal is like using a dark mirror; it will reflect yourself back as you, warts and good points, not what others think of you. It will also show you a true mirror of your partners. This is a good stone to give to anyone who is bound up in a painful and abusive relationship and cannot seem to leave or to someone who is in denial as to how bad the relationship really is. Black opal will also mirror back what Libras are really thinking, not just the other side of someone else's argument, and so allow them to make up their minds with more ease and grace.

Saturn in Scorpio—Black Onyx

Scorpio's black stone, the black onyx, was in ancient times thought to have a demon living in it. This will ring true for many Scorpio-types who struggles with their own inner demons—power, control, intensity, jealousy, repression, rage. It is a stone of transformation, akin to the Death card in the Tarot deck, which symbolizes the ending of the old and the heralding of rebirth. Catharsis is a necessary part of the Scorpio experience; people with strong Scorpio influences in their chart (or strong Pluto aspects) will be sucked into the bottomless pit and be forced to rebirth themselves at least once in their lives, and probably more than once. Black onyx shows you your fears so that you may face them. Black onyx shows you your monsters, not so that you may destroy them or cast them out, but so you can see them clearly, find out what they want, what they're willing to settle for, how they got that way, and how to heal them to whatever extent is possible.

Saturn in Sagittarius—Staurolite

Sagittarius' black stone is the Faery Cross, called staurolite by geologists. It is usually found in the shape of crosses, although sometimes it appears as runes or other straight-line forms. The Faery Cross was used as a talisman of safety on journeys for hundreds of years, and as such it is a Sagittarian stone. Safety, of course, implies that journeys are dangerous, and for much of the history of humankind, they were. From weather to brigands to wild animals to sinking ships, those who journeyed not only beyond their village but beyond their country were risking their lives with every trip. Today fewer dangers lurk for physical journeys, but internal journeys—the kind that expand your mind and change your world—are still fraught with danger. Since Saturn in Sagittarius is a confining aspect that discourages external travel and encourages internal exploration, the Faery Cross is the perfect talisman for these more perilous quests.

Saturn in Capricorn—Obsidian

Obsidian goes back to the earliest ancestors. Many of the first stone tools were flaked out of this sharp black stone, which made itself not only useful but vital to the survival of our forebears. As the tool of the Elders, it is sacred to the eternally practical Grandfather of Grandfathers, Saturn in Capricorn. As a volcanic glass, it is linked to Capricornian mountains, whose stolid and stony surface hide molten depths. As the tool to begin all tools, its "toolness"—even in a nontool shape—gives Saturn in Capricorn an extra push in that area of usefulness. Obsidian can show you how best to find the right tool for the task before you and how to use it to its best effect. As the Ancestor Stone, obsidian comes with all the accumulated practical wisdom of Saturn, the Old Man who helped the Elders survive to create us.

Saturn in Aquarius—Black Marble

Of all the stones associated with artistic sculpture, marble holds the crown. While human beings have sculpted in granite, basalt, sandstone, and anything else they could get a chisel into, when one thinks of sculpting as the height of inspiration, it is marble that comes to mind. While it exists in many colors, black marble is the Saturn in Aquarius stone, symbolizing the flight of inspiration frozen in the medium of solid rock. A talisman of black marble can be carried by those with Saturn in Aquarius issues in order to make one's inspiration concrete. It also reminds the Aquarian soul who despairs of making a difference in the world that one's creations do live on, if one manages to finish them. "I saw the figure in the stone, and then I cut away everything that was not the figure," said Michelangelo about carving in marble. This is a truth Aquarians need to learn to make manifest their dreams.

Saturn in Pisces—Black Pearl

The white pearl, created at the bottom of the sea, is the stone for the Pisces Moon. The black pearl, on the other hand, was created from the selfsame oysters, but something went wrong in the process—a flaw, a bit of mineral staining, some indigestion on the part of the creature. This difficulty creates a stone even rarer than the white pearl of the Moon, showing that the color of struggle makes something more valuable. Since Pisces is a particularly difficult place to have Saturn, and those with this placement strongly aspected tend to have a great deal of inevitable struggle in their lives, the message of the black pearl is important: that turmoil and pain can create something beautiful, but that even the accomplishment of that pain will fade and merge back into the All that created it, as pearls again dissolve in salt water. Both are difficult truths, and both are part of the experience of Saturn in Pisces.

10
Uranus Magic
Changing the World

People rarely invoke the power of Uranus into their personal lives. It can be done, but Uranus is connected, among other things, to one's place in society. The social fabric of humanity is always in flux, even when it seems to stay the same for hundreds or thousands of years. It may fluctuate widely or narrowly, but it is never entirely static. We live and breathe in that flux, whether we like it or not, and it affects us . . . and we have the power to affect it, too, in small ways. That's what Uranus is about—affecting yourself by affecting the world.

If this sounds convoluted, think of it this way, using nonmagical action: If, say, you want to change people's minds about resource waste, you could start a recycling drive and recruit people to it. You would have to set the example and be the person who does the most to recycle and prevent waste in their personal life, and the people who are in it with you would share their tips and discoveries. As a spokesperson, you'd have to learn enough about the facts and statistics to be able to educate others correctly. In the process you would learn far more about it than if you'd just made it a personal hobby of your own. If your movement got successful enough that local statutes were passed, some people might rebel and you'd find yourself switched from the position of supporting the minority cause to supporting the Man. That alone can open your horizons to new perspectives, especially around society itself and where you fit into it. The conflict might even trigger an identity crisis, or alteration.

That's Uranus's way of changing from the outside in, from the larger picture to the smaller one. Neptune works from the cosmos down, and Pluto from the underworld up, but both of those pass through the individual's inner being. Uranus works from the group consciousness down, through whatever channels it can. Therefore, every Uranus spell comes with a caveat: Don't be a hypocrite. There is nothing that trickster Uranus loves to boot in the tail more than a hypocrite. If you do a spell to change some larger aspect of society, be assured that issues regarding your dedication to this cause will be waiting for you right around the corner . . . if not immediately, then at your very next Uranus transit. It's as if Uranus likes to test you a little, to make sure if you really meant it, and above all really understood it and all its implications, good and bad . . . or if you were just mouthing words because you thought that they sounded like a good idea.

Actually, that's caveat number two: Don't idealize your cause or look through it with rose-colored glasses. Uranus is the planet of revolutions, and no revolution has yet occurred without the deaths of innocent bystanders, from the American to the French to the sexual. Uranus is aware of this contradiction. As the planet of lightning, Uranus knows that change is always destructive, at least in the sense of destroying what has been or potentials that will never now come to fruition. And where there's destruction, people get hurt . . . and people getting hurt is still no excuse for failure to embrace change. When you plan how you'll fight for your cause, remember to spend some time thinking about all the possible casualties . . . because they might just be the subject of the Uranus test waiting around the corner for you.

A Uranus spell to change the world should be a group activity, not just something that you do yourself. This is because the implementation of the spell will be an activity requiring the hands and minds of many people, and you are part of that greater society. To do the spell yourself is to act from a place apart from all other people, and Uranus won't have that. You can be part of the group, or you can rebel and be the antihero, but your actions are still in relation to the group. To be entirely apart is the province of Pluto. Uranus wants to see you working with or against people, not on your own. (If you're casting yourself as the rebel in this spell, find other rebels who agree with you and work with them. You are never entirely alone in any worthy protest. If you're really the only person in the entire human race who thinks a certain way, then your ideas have no hope of being achieved. Work on making them more accessible to the rest of us first.)

A personal Uranus spell can be done alone, but it's better if you find other people to help actually cast it on you. That's because a personal Uranus spell will have a direct impact on how you are seen by others. There's no Uranus effect that does not change your relation to the outside world, and your place in it, if only by altering your attitude and presentation. Because of this, all the personal Uranus spells involve others, the more the merrier.

Disclaimer: The following list does not enumerate all the possible causes in the world. Far from it. I'm sure that I probably missed your pet crusade, whatever that might be. I'm also sure that if you've gotten this far in the book, you can likely figure out which flavor of Uranus should be called upon to handle it. This list is merely to give you some ideas.

URANUS IN ARIES

Possible causes: Veterans' rights. Reforming the military. Fairness in professional sports. Antiracist civil rights work. Hate crimes prevention. Any action where there may be direct confrontation and violence.

INVOCATION TO URANUS IN ARIES
To be said while lighting a fire.

Lightning strikes!
It sets the land aflame
Like a brushfire that tears
Across all it comes upon.
Let this change be like that fire,
Destroying that which is no longer useful,

Firing up enthusiasm for the new day.
Hail to the fire of change,
And may it sweep away all hesitation.

URANUS IN TAURUS

Possible causes: Organic farming. Supporting small family farms. Community supported agriculture (CSA). Saving heirloom livestock. Sustainable forestry. Alternative sustainable building methods. Affordable housing and shelter for the poor, including homeless shelters.

INVOCATION TO URANUS IN TAURUS

To be spoken while striking the earth with a great stick.

Lightning strikes!
It stirs the sleeping earth-spirit,
And rains strange water down upon the soil,
Fertilizing it with unusual seed
That will grow into incredible fruit
In its own time and season,
To feed minds into safely opening.
Hail to the season of new growth,
And may it blossom into the harvest of change.

URANUS IN GEMINI

Possible causes: Free speech. Anticensorship. Rooting out phone taps and surveillance. Honesty in journalism. Truth in advertising. Freedom of the media. The Internet and its growing subcultures. Cheap or free public transport. Bilingualism. Literacy movements.

INVOCATION TO URANUS IN GEMINI

To be shouted into the wind.

Lightning strikes!
It blows the roiling storm clouds

Until they sweep across the land
In a great tornado of change.
The stagnant air is swept away
In one great blast of wind,
Cool and clear and fresh with new ideas.
Hail to the winds of change,
And may they blow through every mind in our path.

URANUS IN CANCER

Possible causes: Homeschooling. Home birth. Midwifery. Breastfeeding. Alternative parenting styles. Parents' rights. Child abuse, of any kind. Care of pregnant women. Domestic violence. Feeding the poor, including soup kitchens.

INVOCATION TO URANUS IN CANCER
To be spoken into a pool or bowl of water or shouted at the ocean.

Lightning strikes!
The surface of the sea is energized,
Particles form and reform,
And life emerges for the first time
In the watery depths of time.
This is our origin, our history,
And may history be repeated in the ocean of the mind!
Hail to the new life crawling up onto the shore,
Born of the force of Necessity.

URANUS IN LEO

Possible causes: Teen rights. Street theater for any cause. Music and performance copyright issues. Alternative energy methods, such as solar and geothermal. Issues of looksism and appearance prejudice. Fat politics. The right to self-expression. Body-modification rights.

INVOCATION TO URANUS IN LEO

To be said into a bonfire.

Lightning strikes!
The tree bursts into flames,
The tribe gathers around it, adding fuel,
And it becomes the center of their life.
The flame burns and warms when the Sun is down,
As these new ideas may warm hearts,
As these changes may burn away all that would
    extinguish us.
Hail to the flame of the Sun,
And may it light up every new day.

URANUS IN VIRGO

Possible causes: Protecting and cleaning up the environment—anything ecological. Healthy, natural foods. Saving heirloom seeds and trees. Urban gardening. Honest food and drug labeling. Health care reform. Alternative medicine and healing forms. Medical research. Genetic engineering.

INVOCATION TO URANUS IN VIRGO

To be said while letting sand run through your fingers.

Lightning strikes!
It shatters the great thing into tiny fragments
That must be reassembled by hand,
Bit by bit, piece by piece,
And as they are put back together,
Let them be different, let them be improved,
Let them be perfected, let that which is useless dribble
    away.
Hail to the work of mending
And the generation of a new and better time.

URANUS IN LIBRA

Possible causes: Justice-system reform. Transforming laws. Legal aid for all. Fighting for the underdog. Right to marriage for sexual minorities. Alternative relationship counseling. Antitorture reform. Amnesty International and similar organizations. Death penalty issues.

INVOCATION TO URANUS IN LIBRA

To be sung into the wind.

Lightning strikes!
The gentle breezes are swirled
Into a great wind of indignation
And righteous anger that sweeps the land.
Let the blinders be blown from the eyes of all
That the multitudes may perceive justice
And a great cry for fairness may go forth.
Hail to the stroke of gentleness
That, when necessary, can wield the sword.

URANUS IN SCORPIO

Possible causes: Sexual freedom. Legalization of sex work. Free access to pornography. Age of consent issues. Sex education. Legalization of drugs. Anti-drug wars. Right to die and euthanasia movement. Abortion. Green burial.

INVOCATION TO URANUS IN SCORPIO

To be spoken into the steam rising from a boiling cauldron or pot.

Lightning strikes!
The swamp boils with its energy,
And new things rise up from the wetlands,
Things of power, things of instinct,
Whose instinct is to change the landscape from below.
We tunnel under the earth beneath their feet,
And change their world before they are aware of it.

Hail to the subtle changes that take place
Smoothly and quietly in the depths of the mind.

URANUS IN SAGITTARIUS

Possible causes: Immigration reform. Exploitation of immigrants. Aid to refugees. Aid to victims of natural disasters. Movements against religious fanaticism and religious oppression. Recognition of minority religions. Personal-theology movements. Freedom to travel over national borders.

INVOCATION TO URANUS IN SAGITTARIUS

To be spoken while holding a lantern or candle high in the dark.

Lightning strikes!
It lights up the spreading sky,
And for one moment we can see everything,
For one moment the dark is put to flight,
And all its terrors are shown to be nothing.
Let the light of these words, these concepts
Illuminate the last corners of closedness, of darkness.
Hail to the conquering beacon
That lights the way to tomorrow.

URANUS IN CAPRICORN

Possible causes: Free trade. Corporate responsibility. Labor unions. Fair pay among company ranks. Merit-based hiring and promotion. Honesty and fairness in government. Election reform. Manners for children; anti-rudeness movements. Senior citizen rights. Elder abuse.

INVOCATION TO URANUS IN CAPRICORN

To be spoken to a stone.

Lightning strikes!
It shakes the mountain to its core,
And the boulders come tumbling down.

The roads are demolished, to be made again
In a new and better spiral to the top,
And all the underground wealth is laid open
To be shared with all who merit it.
Hail to the heaving mountains
That become the backbone of the world.

URANUS IN AQUARIUS

Possible causes: Free information exchange, especially over computers and the Internet. Artificial intelligence. The right to scientific research, even if controversial. Space travel and colonization. Gay, lesbian, bisexual, and transgender rights. Polyamory rights.

INVOCATION TO URANUS IN AQUARIUS

To be spoken while creating static electricity with your hands, hair, or clothing.

Lightning strikes!
It strikes where it will,
Not where we would have it,
And it sets the very air to tingling!
We are electrified with its presence,
And should we survive the strike,
Our world will have made a radical change.
Hail to the very spirit of lightning itself,
Opening the confusion of our minds to the ultimate
*   possibilities.*

URANUS IN PISCES

Possible causes: Peace and antiwar movements. Drunk driving prevention. AA and its related groups. Rights for the mentally ill. Institution reform. Alternative mental health methods. Disability rights. Disability research. Prison reform. Ecology of the oceans. Fair fishing rights.

INVOCATION TO URANUS IN PISCES

To be whispered into a large seashell.

Lightning strikes!
It energizes the depths of the ocean,
Where at first no one can see a change,
But the great wave gathers its strength,
Mile after mile as it approaches land,
Until, from nowhere, the wall of water hits,
And all is swept away and must be rebuilt.
Hail to the power of the waters
That wash clean our collective soul.

11
Neptune Magic
Lifting the Veil

Throughout the thousands of years that human beings have created magical practices, one type of magic stands out above all as ubiquitous: divination. Every culture has some form of it, if only remaining in folk practice, superstition, and games. Indeed, once it has been relegated to the latter status, people for whom it is not acceptable to believe in divination (like most modern Western people) can play with it without being accused of heresy or foolishness. They can even openly pretend to believe in it, while giving the impression that this pretense is just affected for the sake of having fun, and this attitude can obscure their actual belief in it. That's why people have card-reading "psychics" in for parties.

Secretly, everyone would like to know the future, even if they are skeptical about traditional fortune-telling. The entire stock market, after all, is predicated on guessing the future. Yet even with the many sorts of "scientific" methods of prediction, when you get past the present moment, things are still misty or vague or changeable. Yes, the Sun will still rise tomorrow—but will you see it from your porch or somewhere else? Like all things Neptunian, divination gives both amazing insights and frustrating ambiguities.

In this chapter on Neptune magic, we'll profile twelve types of divination that reflect the energies of the twelve signs. Telling the future can be an activity unto itself, or it can be used in conjunction with a spell, perhaps beforehand to get an idea of whether the goal is worthy or practical, or afterward to see if the spell is likely to have worked. In any case, it makes sense that if you are working magic with a proliferation of certain sign, planet, and house energies, heralding or following it up with a divination form that shares those energies is consistent and appropriate. To that end, here is a list of divinatory methods appropriate to sign energies. To coordinate them with planets and houses, use rulerships.

The divination method for Aries is pyromancy, or divining with fire. Pyromancy comes in several forms, all of them useful and most of them intertwined in folk practice. One form consists of simply staring into the flames and seeing what figures appear in your mind or doing the same thing with the smoke. Other more active (and thus more Aries) methods include lighting a candle or bonfire while asking your question, and then watching the action of the flame to get your answer. Small, bright, steady flames mean small successes; large, bright, steady flames mean large successes. Dim flames are a disappointment; constantly flickering flames mean wavering fortune that could go either way; sparking means danger; and twisting means unseen enemies. Flames that lean to the side should be checked for direction; they might lean toward a person who will prove to be important, or indicate a direction in which to go, or point toward the querent, in which case a major change will come to them due to this magic working. A flame that goes out by itself, or refuses to stay lit, is a definite No.

Still another form of pyromancy involves throwing things into the fire—such as alcohol or objects that might explode—and seeing how the fire reacts, or throwing in objects and seeing what effect the fire has on them—are they barely scathed, are they burned up entirely, or do they crack or char in interesting and interpretable patterns? Some of these forms of pyromancy can end up being dangerous, especially the ones where shrapnel might be shot out of the fire at the onlookers, which Aries of course finds highly exciting.

The divination method for Taurus is the runic alphabet of the old Norse, Germanic, and Saxon tribes. The runes are ancient, earthy, drawing on the daily work of ancestral lives, symbols that echo the original Indo-Europeans. They are usually carved onto wood, stone, clay, or bone. Their symbols are wonderfully concrete and physical—fire, water, ice, animals, trees, physical objects—and their meanings strongly practical.

The most basic readings consist of three runes drawn to form a sentence; no air-sign verbosity here. There are different versions of the runes, but they all begin with Fehu or Feoh, the rune of cattle, which symbolizes wealth, a true calling-card of Taurus. And, true to form, the Pagan folk most drawn to runes are those who worship the Norse, Germanic, and Saxon gods, and their practices tend to be extremely practical, conservative, and even hidebound in some cases.

The divination method for Gemini, the sign of books and words and communication, is bibliomancy. This simple method consists of picking a book at random off a shelf, opening it at random and placing your finger down on the page without looking, and then interpreting the results to see how they relate to your question. If you can't figure out the relevance, you can grab another book and get a second opinion, and a third. This ends up requiring a lot of interpreting of turns of phrase, something that Gemini loves.

The divination method for Cancer is tasseography, or tea leaf reading. It seems appropriate to assign watery, nurturing Cancer, which rules the stomach, a divining method that can also double as a warm cup of medicinal or simply comforting tea. Tasseography consists of pouring unstrained tea (Chinese or herbal) into a cup, swirling it around so that the plant matter sticks to the sides, carefully drinking off the liquid, and interpreting the shapes formed by the remaining bits. Interpretation tends to be highly subjective and intuitive, which is right up Cancer's lunar alley, and all the "traditional" shapes tend to be simple household objects rather than grandiose concepts. Even the association with mysterious but inviting dark females in exotic draperies is lunar in nature.

For regal and performance-oriented Leo, we've chosen the Celtic Ogham system as an appropriate method. In ancient Celtic society, Ogham was reserved for the upper classes; it was the soothsaying method of the educated (and somewhat haughty, if history is to be believed) druids rather than of the peasant classes. Ogham is showy and colorful, with many lists of associated trees, birds, animals, colors, hand gestures, months, and letters. It is also associated with many Celtic myths, of which most feature kings, queens, and great warriors.

Two divination methods seem to partake of Virgo energy. The first is numerology, which is the art of symbolizing anything with strings of numbers. It requires huge amounts of detailed calculations, which convey the symbolic numbers in words, names, dates, times, and dimensions. Drums, and their precise rhythms, are also ruled by Virgo, and so is drum divination. This involves taking a ring or other small object belonging to the querent and placing it onto a frame drum whose skin is patterned with symbols. A rhythm is tapped onto the skin from below, causing the ring to skitter across the surface, and when the rhythm is completed, the position of the ring determines the answer. This method has been used most often by tribal shamans, who tend to work the most with drum magic.

Libra's divination method is the Tarot. Every Tarot deck is, in addition to being a divining method, a work of art—or more specifically, seventy-eight works of art. Today, more Tarot decks are on the market than ever before, and many if not most of them were created by artists who wanted a chance to combine spiritual symbolism with aesthetic beauty. In fact, Tarot decks have become an art form unto themselves, which is appropriate to the sign ruled by Venus and associated with the archetype of the Artist. Tarot is highly visual, as befits an air sign, and intellectually complex, with multiple meanings for each picture. Two of its Major Arcana cards are the Lovers and Justice; it is the only method that so clearly shows the two faces of Libra.

Scorpionic divination methods, with one exception, all seem to come under the heading of a practice that I jokingly refer to as "pestering the Dead." They include the necromantic practices of calling up the dead to ask their advice and the (sometimes shamanic, sometimes spiritualist) practice of contacting minor spirits in general. Séances and Ouija boards come under this group, as do various forms of questioning animal or plant spirits. While some people may enjoy and even be good at these things, they are beyond the reach of most people, and there are ethical questions for some of them (an argument that Scorpio enjoys). Since one of the Scorpionic gifts is sensing energy and moving it around, I will suggest dowsing as an alternate Scorpio practice. Dowsing is most widely known as a way to find underground ley lines and water channels (and Scorpio instinctively likes finding hidden underworld things), but it can also be used to dowse between options that are written down or symbolized by specific items.

In ancient times, one of the most famous sorts of divination was that of consulting divine oracles. These were individuals who would go into trance states and speak with the voice of Deity to answer questions. Where Scorpio's milieu is pestering the dead, this method of divination could be conceived of as pestering the Gods and Goddesses (who are quite capable of taking care of Themselves, and who will answer or not as they choose), and it belongs to Sagittarius, the sign of religion. As with spirit contact, oracle practice—while extremely accurate when you can get a skilled one—cannot be learned by most people and thus is difficult to come by.

As Sagittarius's ruler, Jupiter, is also the patron of gambling, alternate Sagittarian methods would be divination with playing cards (cartomancy) or dice (cleromancy). The latter, while it seems frivolous, goes back to ancestral times, when dice made from the bones of sacrificial victims were rolled to choose the next victim. The recreational aspect did not come in until much later, and even today playing with dice is referred to as "rolling the bones," which reminds us that this, too, was a religious practice. Thus Jupiter's different sides are represented here as well.

The augury method best suited for Capricorn is the I Ching. Capricorn loves things that are antique, established, and respected, and the I Ching is thousands of years old, possibly the oldest known divination form of its complexity. It is strongly concerned with hierarchy—each of the lines of the hexagram is dedicated to a different social class—and one of its underlying themes is that by obeying and finding harmony within the social order, one finds harmony with the mandate of heaven—a very Capricornian ideal. While it can be consulted by anyone, its ideal querent is addressed by titles that can be variously translated as "the Superior Man," or "the young noble," or "the worthy student," giving advice that helps the aspiring social climber rise in the ranks with wisdom, clemency, and good judgment. The centuries of accrued Confucian commentary only strengthens the conservative, philosophical Capricorn flavor.

Aquarius, as a sign, is less concerned with static symbol systems and more concerned with the inspiration of the moment, and so the augury method for Aquarius is that most unstructured of divinings, the interpretation of omens. For thousands of years, people have asked their question and then just wandered out the door, confident that the Powers That Be would send them an omen in short order. Sometimes it was supposed to be the first thing one saw, or the first thing said by the person that you meet on the road, or the way the weather changed, or just the most intense experience of the day. The reading of omens was spontaneous rather than a set, formal soothsaying. Although some people took their omens to professionals to interpret, the more likely situation was interpretation by the individuals themselves, who might have no training in divination, reflecting the Aquarius sense of populism. It requires imagination, intuition, and a willingness to see the Universe as a connected web where all things reflect each other if you just know where to look. To try this, just ask your question and walk out the door. If you trip over the doorstep, that's a bad omen. If an envelope in your mailbox says, "You May Have Already Won . . ." it will be an unlikely gamble. If it's a bill, perhaps more consequences will be coming due than you expect. If the neighbor who you haven't seen in weeks hails you cheerfully and tells you that his cancer is in remission, that's a very good omen, but suggests striking while the moment is still positive . . . and so on.

The Pisces form of divination is scrying, which involves staring at some fluctuating surface and letting shapes form in front of your eyes or in your mind. This is probably the "softest" and most intuitive of all the arts of augury, and while it has been done with many different mediums—earth, sand, fire, moving tree branches, egg white, vodka— it is still most often done with water or with mirrors, which symbolize water. Scrying, more than any other divining form, requires that you open your mind to the All That Is and tap into something greater than yourself. It also tends to work for those who have a knack; people either do it naturally or have to struggle, and some cannot seem to get the hang of it no matter what they do. This is in contrast to Tarot or bibliomancy or other systems based more on images or symbols, where even if you have some difficulty interpreting the results, at least you are guaranteed to get some. To scry, one has to remain relaxed and very psychically open, and a certain amount of "merging with the All" is involved. Being open and merging is a very Piscean quality, and one that other energies may find it hard to master.

12
Pluto Magic
Into the Darkness

Pluto is serious power. This is the planet of the transformative experience. Sometimes that can be like a larva going into a cocoon and coming out a butterfly. Sometimes it's like being ripped apart into pieces and put back together differently. Even in the case of the apparently peaceful caterpillar transformation, keep in mind that the caterpillar has to be asleep for the whole thing . . . because if it was conscious, it would hurt. Usually, with us human beings, we have to do it awake and painfully.

The power of Pluto is the magic of last resort. You don't start propitiating this planet because a few little things went wrong, or you're bored with your life, or you want something badly. You kneel before the power of Pluto when your entire life is crashing down around you, when everything that you are and were is falling to pieces, when there is literally nothing left to lose. If you have never been to a place like this in your life, be happy. If you never go there, you may die knowing that you lived a charmed and protected life, and you'll never have to bother with propitiating the planet of darkness and ruthlessness.

Of course, Pluto won't put things back the way they were. That's not his job. What you're asking for is a little mercy and a little guidance . . . to be able to navigate this storm with your sanity reasonably intact. When you go before Pluto, you must already have accepted that life as you have known it is over and that a new life is beginning. Whether that new life will be better or worse, well, that's something that can be negotiated. But the actual change is nonnegotiable.

When clients show up with an affliction by the outer planets, Pluto is second only to Saturn in the frequency of being the culprit. While a Saturn affliction feels like stuckness, or obstacles, or repeatedly banging your head against a brick wall, Pluto feels more like being dragged willy-nilly toward an untested and perhaps frightening goal, heedless of any thornbushes and rocks and mud that you have to slam through. It can also feel like something is deliberately setting out to destroy you, and there's a truth to that. Whenever Pluto aspects some part of your life, he demands a sacrifice. Some part of you needs to be dragged to the stone altar and have its throat slit. Ideally, it will be a part of you that you don't need any more, that is holding up your growth, that needs to be set free.

With Saturn, the offering is always work . . . but Pluto will change you whether you agree to work or not. What Pluto asks for is even harder. It's trust . . . in the face of pain and fear and despair. It's trust that you will be better for all this suffering. It's the willingness to be open to the surgeon's knife, cutting away the rot. Make no mistake, Pluto will open you up anyway, with or without your consent. It's you who will benefit from being able to trust him. He'll get his pound of flesh either way. If he is aspecting your Venus, all those misconceptions about love will be painfully excised, perhaps by a nasty breakup. If he is messing with your Moon, be prepared to have your face rubbed in every negative pattern left over from childhood . . . and if he should go over your Sun, all Gods help you, because your very core identity will be smashed and rebuilt from scratch. We are all different people when Pluto gets done with us.

Like the affirmations for Saturn, these Pluto invocations are mantras to survive the transit. I suggest doing them sitting in a dark place, just before you go forth to do whatever remedy is appropriate for the sign and house. Remember, while you do the remedy, you are basically forging a deal with Death. You don't break a deal with Death, not if you want to survive even remotely intact. Try to summon as much humility as possible during the work that you do in aiding Pluto.

INVOCATIONS FOR PLUTO
THROUGH THE SIGNS

PLUTO IN ARIES

I lay myself before Death
And offer up as sacrifice
The part of me that is named Fear.
I understand that my fears must be faced empty-handed,
Torn out, offered up, worn down with my bleeding flesh,
Even though it leaves me weak as an infant.
May I someday come once again to the challenge of living
With a clean spirit to face it.

PLUTO IN TAURUS

I lay myself before Death
And offer up as sacrifice
The part of me that is named Greed.
I understand that I must live, for a time,
Without having, and learn to find security
In the surety of empty hands.
May I someday come once again into riches
With a clean spirit to value them.

PLUTO IN GEMINI

I lay myself before Death
And offer up as sacrifice
The part of me that is named Duality.
I understand that the dark and light within me
Will no longer live in separate rooms, to be let out
One at a time or not at all; all doors will be opened
And I must make peace between them.
May I someday come once again to contradictions
With a clean spirit to stand between them.

PLUTO IN CANCER

I lay myself before Death
And offer up as sacrifice
The part of me that is named Defenses.
I understand that I must be stripped naked,
Vulnerable, exposed, trusting to the Universe
That the Gods will care for me as their own child.
May I someday come again to be my own protector
With a clean spirit to shield myself.

PLUTO IN LEO

I lay myself before Death
And offer up as sacrifice
The part of me that is named Entitlement.
I understand that for now I must be a mediocrity,
That I must learn what it is to be no one special,
A mere face in the crowd, and yet find joy therein.
May I someday come once again to the spotlight
With a clean spirit to appreciate it.

PLUTO IN VIRGO

I lay myself before Death
And offer up as sacrifice
The part of me that is named Wastefulness.
I understand that nothing will be wasted
During Death's time in my body;
Not my pain, not my despair, not even my tears—
All will be put to use in the lessoning.
May I someday come once again to generosity
With a clean spirit to give forth.

PLUTO IN LIBRA

I lay myself before Death
And offer up as sacrifice

The part of me that is named Judging.
I accept that whenever I place myself
Above another, I will be shown my flaws
As in a twisted mirror, and grovel before my
*   imperfections.*
May I someday come once again to balance
With a clean spirit to dance with others.

PLUTO IN SCORPIO

I lay myself before Death
And offer up as sacrifice
The part of me that is named Implacable.
I accept that whenever I strike from the place
Of black and white, I will fall and be humbled
In grayness, until I learn the ways of mercy.
May I someday come once again to power
With a clean spirit to wield it.

PLUTO IN SAGITTARIUS

I lay myself before Death
And offer up as sacrifice
The part of me that is named Righteousness.
I understand that this thing I name Truth
Will be overturned, and I must face many truths,
Some contradictory, and mine no better than others.
May I someday come into enlightenment
With a clean spirit to pass it on.

PLUTO IN CAPRICORN

I lay myself before Death
And offer up as sacrifice
The part of me that is named Ambition.
I understand that for now I must live lowly,
Without hope of respect in the eyes of strangers

And those who look on to judge me.
May I someday come once again to the great climb
With a clean spirit to pursue it.

PLUTO IN AQUARIUS

I lay myself before Death
And offer up as sacrifice
The part of me that is named Genius.
I understand that for now I will be just another fool
Who must follow the Rules like all the other fools,
Who gets no special leeway due to brilliance.
May I someday come once again to inspiration
With a clean spirit to follow it.

PLUTO IN PISCES

I lay myself before Death
And offer up as sacrifice
The part of me that is named Helplessness.
I understand that I must learn
That whatever disaster strikes me,
If I can change my attitude to embrace it,
Then nothing else will matter.
May I someday come once again into peace
With a clean spirit to embrace it.

PLUTO IN THE FIRST HOUSE

I lay myself before Death
And offer up as sacrifice
The part of my life that is my Mask.
I accept that the way I have learned to act
When the eyes of others are watching
Must be shed like a snakeskin, heedless of scrutiny.
May I someday come once again into a face
That more cleanly resembles who I am.

PLUTO IN THE SECOND HOUSE

I lay myself before Death
And offer up as sacrifice
The part of my life that is Worth.
I accept that what I value now will have no value
In the hard time to come, and I must find
New jewels among that which is cast off
By those with shorter sight and disdainful minds.
May I someday come once again into treasure
With a clean spirit to measure it.

PLUTO IN THE THIRD HOUSE

I lay myself before Death
And offer up as sacrifice
The part of my life that is Lies.
I accept that for this time, all twisty words
Will trip and stumble, will tie up my tongue,
And I may be left plain-voiced or silenced
Until nothing is left in me but truths.
May I someday come once again into eloquence,
With a clean spirit to speak through it.

PLUTO IN THE FOURTH HOUSE

I lay myself before Death
And offer up as sacrifice
The part of my life that is Sanctuary.
I accept that for this time, the only peaceful place
I will have to rest must be hard-earned,
And often I will wander homeless in the cold.
May I someday come into my true home
With a clean spirit to inhabit it.

PLUTO IN THE FIFTH HOUSE

I lay myself before Death
And offer up as sacrifice
The part of my life that is Frivolity.
I accept that for this time, I must be humbled,
Grinding and ground down, working with no respite,
And that pleasure must be put aside for Duty.
May I someday come once again into joyfulness
With a clean spirit to revel in it.

PLUTO IN THE SIXTH HOUSE

I lay myself before Death
And offer up as sacrifice
The part of my life that is Ableness.
I accept that for this time, my body
Must be treated with care, and even then may fail me
In order to teach me my limitations.
May I someday come once again into health
With a clean spirit to care for it.

PLUTO IN THE SEVENTH HOUSE

I lay myself before Death
And offer up as sacrifice
The part of my life that is Projection.
No lover will give me my identity,
Or live anything for me; I must live it myself,
Be my own Other, until I am whole.
May I someday come once again into partnership
With a clean spirit to offer in love.

PLUTO IN THE EIGHTH HOUSE

I lay myself before Death
And offer up as sacrifice
The part of my life that is Certainty.

I understand that for a time, I must live on the raw edge,
As if Death might take me any day,
And I cannot die well if I have not lived well.
May I someday come once again to solid ground
With a clean spirit to build my life anew.

PLUTO IN THE NINTH HOUSE

I lay myself before Death
And offer up as sacrifice
The part of my life that is Flight.
I accept that my feet will be weighted down,
Staying slow and heavy though I yearn to flee away,
For there is no demon that I can outrun
And facing them here is as good as anywhere else.
May I someday come once again to the road
With a clean spirit to see the horizon.

PLUTO IN THE TENTH HOUSE

I lay myself before Death
And offer up as sacrifice
The part of my life that is Reputation.
I accept that I must be seen doing rightly,
Even though it will earn me scorn and contempt
From those whose approval I crave.
May I someday come once again into influence
With a clean spirit to guide my decisions.

PLUTO IN THE ELEVENTH HOUSE

I lay myself before Death
And offer up as sacrifice
The part of my life that is Belonging.
I accept that for a time, I shall be the outcast,
Outsider, lonely one who has no tribe,
Who looks, with yearning eyes, on the celebrating people.

May I someday come once again into community
With a clean spirit to join it.

PLUTO IN THE TWELFTH HOUSE

I lay myself before Death
And offer up as sacrifice
The part of my life that is Hidden.
For all things must come forth from my darkness,
Even the ugly, the angry, the pathetic, the disturbing,
And I must somehow learn to love and feed them all,
Lest they feed on me and eat my soul.
May I someday come once again into the light
With a clean spirit open to its radiance.

PART THREE

Magical Prescriptions

*Tools, Holidays,
Altars, and Practices*

13

The Astrology
of Magical Tools

M odern Pagans, witches, and magicians use a variety of traditional implements to focus, aid, and strengthen our magical workings. Astrologically, each of these traditional Western implements links itself to a particular sign. If you are doing magical work around a specific sign, it's useful to use the tools that it's "hooked up" to. That doesn't mean that you can't use other tools as well, but much of magic works on the principle of affinities, and it can make your spellwork more efficient.

This chapter discusses the traditional magical tools that have an affinity for each sign. Just because you don't have any planet in a particular sign doesn't mean that you can't use a specific tool. We all partake of all the sign energies, eventually. It does mean, however, that when doing a spell for one type of sign energy, certain tools will help you make a better connection.

The magical tools of Aries are the sword (or spear) and the torch. Aries is cardinal fire, the blaze that leaps forward like a brushfire and wants to be in the lead. Not for him a tiny candle or a stationary campfire. You can use tiki torches or just a stick with the end set on fire. (If you use accelerant, use only a little, and douse only the fire end and not the handle end.) All large weapons used to cast and defend the circle, such as swords and spears, come under the domain of the Mars-ruled sign. To pick them up is to take on the role of the sacred warrior, if only for a moment.

The magical tools of Taurus are the horn and the cord. In the past, drinking horns were passed ritually at feasts and ceremonies, filled with mead or ale or wine. It was a symbol of hospitality, a way for the leader to show his generosity and wealth, and a way for the people to bond with each other. The last of the mead was usually poured out on the earth as a libation to the Gods. Earthy Taurus resonates to this tool and also to any horns mounted on headdresses, regardless of what animal they came from.

Cords are used for knot magic; as one pulls the knot tight, one binds one's will and intentions. One says, "I have this now; it is bound to me." No one says "I have" as strongly as Taurus, and no one is quite so good at possessing things. The knotted cord holds the magic tight and safe, and Taurus is an expert at holding.

The tools of Gemini are the small knife and the censer. Unlike the warrior's sword, the knife is an air symbol. It cuts things apart and analyzes them; it is as sharp and quick as a Gemini mind and tongue. Whether you call it an athame or a bolline or just "my knife," whether it is a fancy dagger or a jackknife whisked out of the back pocket, it is the tool of this first air sign. Traditionally, the athame was a double-edged blade, which is appropriate for the sign of the Twins. In addition to the knife, Gemini has an affinity for the censer, which brings scent to the air in the form of clouds of burning smoke. Smell is the physical sense associated with the element of air, and incense both clouds and purifies. Gemini's dark and light sides are capable of doing both.

The tools of Cancer are the chalice and the rattle. As a sign associated with nurturing, Cancer is the open cup that gives of itself to others. Cancer is also a sign associated with birthing and the Mother, and it is the water-filled womb that the chalice symbolizes. The rattle is traditionally made of dried gourds, a contained round space filled with the voices of the seeds that are the gourd's fossilized children, and thus also a womb symbol. In some cultures the rattle is a wooden container filled with beans, which are a symbol of life.

The tools of Leo are the bonfire and the wand. A bonfire can be any stationary fire bigger than a candle, from a small fire laid in a bucket or hibachi to a huge bonfire. Either way, the idea is that it is big enough to give warmth as well as light, and people cluster around it. It's part of Leo's solar energy to be the center of attention and draw in the admirers. Leo's wand can be made of wood or metal; it is a conduit for focusing energy and directing it toward a goal. The wand is a fire tool, like the Tarot suit of wands; it is also reminiscent of the king's sceptre.

The tools of Virgo are the drum and the bag of herbs. Virgo resonates to precision and rhythm, and these are the qualities necessary to be a good drummer. In some countries, master drummers must study for decades, learning hundreds of complex rhythms and their effect on the human body and the Universe. A drum can be the steady backbeat, hardly noticed yet keeping everyone else in time, or it can be the complicated front rhythm that must be hit perfectly and precisely. Both are Virgo skills. The drum is also usually made of wood and animal skin, two earthy materials.

Virgo's other affinity is for the magical realm of herbs. Unlike a staff that you merely cut from a tree or a stone that you pick up, herbs must be grown deliberately with a good deal of organization and toil on the part of the gardener. Even if they are wild-grown herbs, they must be hunted down, and discriminating decisions must made as to how much to take and how much to leave. (The only instrument that requires such toil to get its materials is the skin of the drum, which is usually made from domestic livestock.) Then their meanings and uses must be learned, one by one, perhaps by trial and error. This is the domain of the sign that loves to work and classify.

The tools of Libra are the fan and the poppet. Fans are used ritually to invoke the element of air and to blow Gemini's mental smoke to the places that it needs to go. They are also associated, in the mind of any Westerner who has read the story of Cinderella, with elegant balls where beautiful princesses meet their handsome princes, appropriate for this airy sign of romance and marriage. Poppets are dolls used the world over for many purposes, but the most common seems to be that of love spells. Stuffed with the right substances and marked with the proper sigils, they are bound together with ribbons, and the caster hopes for love to come. Even the more sinister uses for poppets—vengeance—are Libra-ruled in their own way, as the usual reason for such a last resort is that the caster feels unfairly served in some way and believes this is the only option for justice.

The tools of Scorpio are the cauldron and the ring. This is the sign of transformation, and the bubbling cauldron transforms separate items into stew or potions, usually under high pressure and violent turbulence (also Scorpio traits). Scorpio is a water sign, but its affinity lies with water at its extremes—ice and boiling steam—and the cauldron transforms water into the latter. The magical ring resonates with the image of the enchanter creating the perfect enspelled object to be worn on the body. Rings symbolize power, and also vows, both appropriate for this Pluto-ruled sign. Rings are also circles, which suggests the cycle of transformation again and reminds Scorpio that what goes around comes around.

The tools of Sagittarius are the candle and the staff. As the sign of the seeker, Sagittarius looks for truth and sheds its light on the world; *better to light a candle than curse the darkness* could have been coined for this optimistic, yearning sign. Truth may be only a tiny light in the shadow, but it is still Truth. The staff was originally an aid for wanderers on long journeys, so the traveler's staff rightly belongs to this sign of travel. It is also the tool held up to the sky to storm the heavens, something that Sagittarius sometimes has to do in its search for wisdom.

The tools of Capricorn are stones and salt. Both are dug out of the bowels of the Earth; both have many different uses. "I use" is the Capricorn motto, and its tools must be multipurpose and not wasteful. Salt purifies, drives away ghosts, keeps water clean, soaks wounds, and is essential to cooking. Stones of all sorts can be used for jewelry, buildings, ashtrays . . . and, of course, magical and energy work. They are hard and enduring, lasting longer than a human lifetime, which are traits Capricorn values.

The tools of Aquarius are the lamp, or lantern, and the bell. Lanterns (and their descendants, oil lamps) are the sigil of the scholar, reading books late into the night. In medieval times, most people were illiterate, lived an agricultural lifestyle, and rose and slept with the Sun. The few who had reason to stay up late and read were the intellectuals of society, those who were not like the rest of the unwashed masses. The lantern eventually became the magical symbol of enlightenment, as it is shown held up in the hand of the Tarot Hermit. Bells clear and purify the air with their piercing sound, carried on the invisible sound-wave ocean. This association with sound waves is one clue to the mystery of why this air sign is the Water Bearer.

The tools of Pisces are the glass ball and the mirror. When we think of glass balls, we picture the fortuneteller's heavy rock crystal ball in which visions are seen, but for most hedge-witches, such a valuable item was out of their reach. Hollow glass sea floats, or even more commonly glass bottles of water, were used for professional scrying by the average granny witch. Ruled by Neptune (who has an affinity for glass, the solid that is actually a very slow-moving liquid), this oceanic sign is linked to the altered states that make scrying possible. The mirror has long been used as a symbol of both the sea and the soul, and it is used for magics that have to do with searching and changing one's inner self, as is appropriate for this sign of introspection.

For an astrological tool-blessing ritual—assuming you have at least one of each of the tools associated with the twelve signs—you can lay the tools out in a circle, with each direction of the clock-hour for one sign. Anoint them, one at a time, with appropriate oils (see chapter 15). Stand in the center and picture yourself standing in the center of the Universe, with the twelve zodiacal energies around you like the strands of a web. Visualize the strands linking via the signs to your tools, binding themselves to you and to those energies. Then, starting with the Aries tool, say the following invocation, one line to each sign's tool or tools:

> *Blessed be by the power of all beginnings.*
> *Blessed be by the power of all that is valued.*
> *Blessed be by the power of all that is spoken.*
> *Blessed be by the power of kin and tribe.*
> *Blessed be by the power of all that rules.*
> *Blessed be by the power of all that labors.*
> *Blessed be by the power of all that bonds together.*
> *Blessed be by the power of all that desires.*
> *Blessed be by the power of all insight.*
> *Blessed be by the power of all aspiration.*
> *Blessed be by the power of all inspiration.*
> *Blessed be by the power of all that believes.*

14
The Astrology
of Pagan Holidays

Most modern Neo-Pagans use, or are at least familiar with, the Celtic solar calendar of eight holidays. These include the solstices and equinoxes (the quarter days), and the four days exactly between each one (the cross-quarter days). While the number 8 may not seem to have much to do with astrology (which tends to run on the number 12), in actuality the eight holidays are placed in a way that gives them strong associations with the Sun's path through the zodiacal signs.

SAMHAIN

The Neo-Pagan year tends to end on Samhain, which falls on October 31/November 1. In some traditions, this is also the New Year; in others, there is a "dead" period between Samhain and Yule, and the year proper begins on Yule. At any rate, during Samhain the Sun is in Scorpio, the sign of intensity, which is ruled by Pluto, the planet of death and transformation, named for the Lord of the Underworld. It is no accident that Samhain is the holiday of honoring the ancestors and the beloved dead, and it is the day when the Land of the Dead is closest to our own.

SCORPIO INVOCATION FOR SAMHAIN

Desert's child of the scorching heat,
Bearing each night of barren cold,

179

Springing from the core of the Earth,
Underground water running beneath,
Darkest cave of mysteries,
You whose gift is Desire,
Bless us with the ability
To follow our true passions
And to start over again from the beginning
When the burning comes.
By the power of all that transforms,
You challenge us
To forever stoke the inner flame.
May we go forth with lust for life.

YULE—THE WINTER SOLSTICE

The next holiday, Yule, is the time of the Winter Solstice. The two figures who appear again and again, all over European and even modern American Christmas iconography, are the Holly King of abundance and the cold white Snow Queen. The Holly King wears such faces as Santa Claus, St. Nicholas, the Russian Frost King, and even the Sun Child. No matter what his face, however, he represents abundance and generosity, the feeling that there is enough of everything to go around. He is always laden with gifts, and he comes with heaping feasts and a glow of joy and light.

On the other hand, the Snow Queen is a different figure altogether. Although she sometimes brings gifts (as when she shows her self as Befana, the old woman who is the gift-giver for parts of Italy), she is more usually associated with the dangers of winter. If you do not get enough from the Holly King, the myths seem to say, the Snow Queen will leave you a frozen heap on the sidewalk. She is both alluring and cruel, the embodiment of the rigors of nature. Winter is a hard time, especially in far northern areas of Europe. People die. If there is not enough abundance from the rest of the year, a lot of people die. This is her brutally straightforward message.

The Feast of Yule is a time of almost desperate merrymaking. We tend to blame this on modern commercialism, but the ancient Romans commented on it as well during their Saturnalia, with complaints of overspending and post-holiday depression, so it seems to be more a product of the long nights and short days causing general low-grade depression, as well as the fear of the incoming winter. Astrologically, this is the time when the Sun passes from Sagittarius into Capricorn. Put a different way, this is the time when the Sun passes from a fiery masculine sign ruled by benevolent Jupiter, the planet of abundance, into an earthy feminine sign ruled by Saturn, the planet of cold limits and crystallization. The two characters in the annual Yule extravaganza are excellent avatars of Jupiter and Saturn, and the entire feeling of the holiday reflects this innate knowledge: that we are moving from the time of warmth and plenty into the time of bitter cold and hunger. Even those of us who live modern first-world lives with middle- to upper-class incomes, who don't need to worry about hunger, remember this on a deep level, because our ancestors knew it too . . . and because the cosmos reflects that energy at this time.

SAGITTARIUS-CAPRICORN INVOCATION FOR YULE

Archer born of fire,
Spirit of seeking,
Eyes on the horizon,
Mystical centaur whose gift is Clear Sight,
Bless us with the ability
To see truth in all its forms,
Wherever it is found
And wherever it may hide,
Even in its ugliest disguise,
And to speak it aloud without fear of censure.
By the power of all insight,
You challenge us never to falter in our trust.
May we all go forth in great adventure.
And now your time in the Sun is passing,
And you yield your place to the cold nights

Of the child of Saturn, the chained god.
Climber of the highest mountain,
Goat whose strength does not give in,
Who is a friend to hardship and endurance,
Whose gift is Persistence,
Bless us with the ability
To keep going even when the way is hard,
Even when all hope seems to be lost,
Even when there is no light on the horizon.
Even in the utter darkness,
Never let us lose sight of our goals.
By the power of all aspiration,
You challenge us to help each other
Achieve what we have yearned for.
May we all go forth in unswerving loyalty
And keep each other safe throughout the winter.

IMBOLC

The next holiday on the Wheel of the Year was called Imbolc by the Celts, Oimelc by the Saxons, and Candlemas by the Catholic Church. It was also known as St. Brigid's Day, after a saint who was the barely concealed canonized version of the popular Celtic goddess Brigid or Brid. The modern holiday of Imbolc is a fire festival, a light festival, a time of a hundred candles. This has much to do with its development in the northern parts of Europe, where winters were harsh and early February was a time of propitiating the gods of fire and light to ensure survival. While this may not seem very Aquarian, there are still hints of that sign behind the trappings.

First, the defining factor of Imbolc in northern Europe is the weather, particularly erratic, unpredictable, harsh weather—storms that could sweep through and bury the roads, deep freezes that could kill, sudden thaws that could cause snowmelt and flooding. We tend to forget, in our modern cerebral ideas about elemental symbolism, that air is the most unpredictable element of all and that Aquarius, ruled by lightning-strike Uranus, has a strong affinity for storms and generally inclement weather. On the other hand, one of the traditional symbols of Aquarius is the light of knowledge, and the thousand candles of this holiday remind us of that point.

Brigid, the goddess who is associated most with Imbolc, is a highly creative figure of inspiration. Her five faces include the smith and crafts-woman, the poet and inventor of alphabets, the warrior, the prophetess, and the goddess of sovereignty. She is not a nurturing mother goddess; indeed, she is sometimes shown as blowing hot and cold by turns, much like volatile, intellectual Aquarius.

AQUARIUS INVOCATION FOR IMBOLC

Bearer of the heavenly waters
Of knowledge and inspiration,
The ebb and flow of the Apsu,
Dipped from the Milky Way,
Neither man nor woman,
Looking ahead in time,
Whose gift is Newness,
Bless us with the ability
To be ready for the future
And all it may bring
And to welcome rather than fear changes.
By the power of all inspiration,
You challenge us
To be open to new things,
And never to give in to stagnation.
May we all go forth in wonder.

EOSTRE—THE SPRING EQUINOX

The spring equinox was referred to as Eostre by the Celts and Ostara by the Saxons after the goddess of spring. It is the time when the winter is ending and the new growth is springing up, and astrologically it is the time of changing from Pisces to Aries.

The twelve signs of the zodiac have often been associated with stages of life, from infancy to adolescence to the various stages of adulthood and their values. As last and most passive sign, Pisces rules the advanced part of old age, when one is dependent on others to do things for you, and the biggest job you have is preparing for death. We tend to ignore this stage of life in our culture or pretend that it will never happen to us, but the Universe points it out with stark bleakness in the astrological life stages. Pisces is ruled by Neptune, which is strongly associated with spirituality, and this is the time of life when one is getting ready to let go of the physical and go onward. It is followed again by Aries, the sign of infancy, showing the circular motion of souls as they reincarnate. Death follows life and rebirth follows death in this worldview, turning in a never-ending cycle.

It's not difficult to see Pisces and Aries in the turning of winter to spring. Aries is the most rampantly enthusiastic of signs, and the sheer breadth and motion of spring growth is Martially aggressive in its own way. As a fire sign, Aries represents the warming of the soil and the lengthening of days. Winter is a time of contemplation, and spring is a time of turning to outdoor activity—a Neptune to Mars transformation.

PISCES-ARIES INVOCATION FOR OSTARA

Glimmer in the deepest waters,
Dweller in water salty as tears,
Sacrificed and sacrificing,
Neptune's elusive child,
Bathed in obscuring mystery,
Whose gift is Faith,
Bless us with the ability
To step beyond ourselves
And learn compassion for all beings.
By the power of all believing,
You challenge us to remember always

That we are part of a destiny
Much greater than ourselves,
One in the Many and Many in the One.
May we go forth always in hope.
And now your time in the Sun is passing,
And you yield the Earth to the fire of Mars's child
And the warmth of the spring.
Infant of the springtime,
Warrior of the long spear
And the short temper,
Ram who protects his flock,
Fiery torch of First Light,
Whose gift is Bravery,
Bless us with the courage
To do what we know is right,
And never to walk ashamed.
By the power of all beginnings,
You challenge us to defend each other from attack,
Abuse, scorn, and mistreatment,
Even if it endangers our own bodies and spirits.
May we all go forth in courageous innocence.

BELTANE

Beltane is the time of the lush green—the color of Taurus—and its avatar, the Green Man, made of foliage. The Green Man is a very Taurus figure; he is usually some sort of living tree, appropriate for the slowest and most rooted of signs. Beltane is the great fertility festival of the year, and Taurus's feminine side is the cow-eyed goddess who gives forth milk and babies, the horned Earth Mother. Furthering the bovine imagery, the ancient Saxons called the month of May *Thrimilchimonath,* or Three Milk Month, because this was the time of year when the cattle had birthed their calves, and the cows were so full of milk that it was necessary to milk them three times a day.

Taurus is a highly sexual and sensual sign, and the symbol of Beltane is the Maypole thrust into the ground, a blatant image of divine phallus and vagina in sacred intercourse. Some modern Pagans have tried to suggest other symbolism for the Maypole—an electrical connector from Earth to sky or a symbol of upspringing inspiration—largely because they are uncomfortable with the sexual-penetration imagery as a public rite. It is all those things as well. However, no matter what else is suggested, for most people the Maypole will primarily be a giant phallus in the Earth's vagina, and that's that. It's a Taurus way of looking at it—simple, straightforward, and extremely physical.

TAURUS INVOCATION FOR BELTANE

Great Bull of the North,
Lover of the green fields,
Sturdy as bedrock,
Ox who pulls the plow,
Friend of the peasant worker,
Whose gift is Strength,
Bless us with the ability
To endure anything without crumbling,
And never break no matter how heavy the burden.
By the power of all that is valued,
You challenge us to be constant and enduring
In our commitments,
Never allowing Time to wear away our vows.
May we go forth in wealth of our own making.

THE SUMMER SOLSTICE

The Summer Solstice is, of course, associated more with the Sun than anything else. These days, it tends to be little more than a solar holiday, and much of the rich symbolism of former solstice rituals has been lost or is unused due to unfamiliarity. However, looking at the ancient symbolism and cast of characters of this holiday can yield some interesting astrological knowledge.

First, there is the fight between the Oak King and the Holly King. Various scholars have held forth on the battle between these two rivals, which is repeated on a dimmer scale at Yule, when the two switch places again. Many and sundry deities have been associated with these two tree gods, but in the end it hardly matters. They have little in the way of personality except for what is laid onto them by different cultural myths; by themselves they have only one thing in common: they are opposites. The Oak King and the Holly King are warring opposites locked in an eternal embrace that is also an eternal battle. One slays the other with a sword (the symbol of air, and both reason and violence) and assumes his crown, and the slain brother's soul goes into the womb of the Mother Goddess, who chooses the victor as her consort. In six months, the child born of her womb will be grown, will challenge his brother/father with a different sword, and will defeat the incumbent and take his place. Few myths so simply lay out the eternal contradiction that is Gemini.

And what of the other character in the story, the Mother Goddess who watches, weeps, and yet does not interfere? She is the same goddess who was the May Queen at Beltane and who was then courted by yet another sacrificial king, the Green Man, whose head is lopped off so that we may have food and firewood and homes. At the Summer Solstice she is pregnant with the Green Man's child or the Holly King's child (there is a great deal of overlap among the tree kings and their earlier avatar, the Green Man). June is thought of as a time of weddings, the formal pairing-up after the lasciviousness of Beltane, but in our post-Christian era of prenuptial chastity, we forget that in ancient times many June brides were expected to be pregnant at the wedding; if they weren't, it might mean that one or the other was infertile and thus possibly inferior marriage material.

The pregnant Mother Goddess of the Summer Solstice, standing in the backdrop to the fight of the kings, is the influence of maternal Cancer moving in on dying Gemini. Each of the high holidays has a sacred food associated with it (as well as a taboo food), and the sacred food most associated with this season is fruit. June sees the strawberry harvest, which moves into the thorned berries a couple of weeks later, and so on. This was the month of the first fruit of the year, also a ripening Mother Goddess symbol. From the Summer Solstice on, the agricultural emphasis begins to change from growth to harvesting, from feeding the Earth to feeding the people, another Cancerian image. In some cultures, such as the Afro-Caribbean Yoruba faiths, the Summer Solstice is the celebration of Yemaya/Iemanja, the maternal sea goddess, and altars to her are laid in the sand at the edge of the tide and carried away by the sea that night.

GEMINI-CANCER INVOCATION FOR THE SUMMER SOLSTICE

Light twin of daytime,
Dark twin of night,
Speaker, writer, storyteller, and rider of the wind,
Quicksilver child of Mercury whose gift is Thought,
Bless us with the ability
To think sharply as a razor,
And to separate the True from the False.
By the power of all that is spoken,
You challenge us not to underestimate
The power of Mind.
May we all go forth in clarity.
And now that your time in the Sun is passing,
We welcome into its golden rays
The child of his consort, the lunar goddess.
Child of the changing Moon,
Dweller between earth and sea,
Dancer of the ebb and flow,
Mother whose breasts flow with life,
Loving fountain of karuna,
Whose gift is Feeling,
Bless us with the ability
To know our own hearts
And to gather our loved ones
About our hearth in love and safety.
By the power of kin and tribe,

You challenge us
To build each other a safe home
And to help each other to work through
The scars and heartaches of our childhoods.
May we all go forth in sanctuary.

LAMMAS

When astrologers talk about the archetypes of Leo—the King, the Star, the Performer, the Golden One—they often fail to notice that all of these characters were once the main player in ancient rites of human sacrifice. In the theater of archaic religion, kings were once sacred kings, offered up for the survival of their people. There is debate as to whether he is the waning Sun, or the scythed grain, or the slaughtered animal, but it doesn't matter, as all are true. The Golden One was born to be cut down, whether we call him Lugh, or Baldur, or Adonis, or Ing, or Frey, or John Barleycorn, or any of the other gods and spirits who wear that shining crown that marks them as He Who Must Die That All May Live.

Today, as we have passed from the Age of Pisces/Virgo to the Age of Aquarius/Leo, our cultural icons have changed from Christ and the Virgin Mother to the Scientist and the Rock Star. In democratic America, the archetypes of royalty have been filled by performers—actors, models, and especially musicians. Our Lughs and Baldurs are figures like John Lennon, Jim Morrison, Jimi Hendrix, Kurt Cobain, and Jerry Garcia (himself a Leo who died very close to Lammas). They live bright, larger-than-life existences, claim the adoration of thousands, and then conveniently die between performances rather than deteriorating in nursing homes. We revere the archetype even when we don't know why we're doing it, but this is the essential hidden mystery of Leo: the golden mask marks you out as special, sacred, above the people . . . and marks you also as a sacrifice to them.

Not all stars go down this road, of course—and today, in these slightly more gender-equal times, we are as likely to have sacrificial queens like Marilyn Monroe as kings—but it seems that we, as a people, need to have a sacred king die every so often to feed our hunger and propitiate old gods who most of us barely recognize. This is the story of Lammas, the holiday of John Barleycorn, the second funeral of the year. That which dies in its youth at Summer Solstice (Gemini is the Child and Cancer the Adolescent) dies at the height of its powers at Lammas, a carefully chosen death that comes with all the adulation of an avatar of the Sun. Leo's holiday reminds us that solar light can shine through someone, but it can also consume them.

LEO INVOCATION FOR LAMMAS

Great Golden King of Summer,
Bonfire whose warmth draws us near,
Sun whose light is the source of Life,
You who draws the trees upward in joy,
You who burns with radiance,
Whose gift is Will,
Bless us with the ability
To act on our joy
And to bare our souls without fear.
By the power of all that rules,
You challenge us
To gain yet more confidence,
And yet never belittle another's spirit.
May we all go forth in assurance.

THE AUTUMNAL EQUINOX—MABON

The autumnal equinox is a most misunderstood holiday. The Celts called it Mabon; the Greeks had it as the time of their Eleusinian Mysteries. It is the time of the main bulk of the harvest, when everything is coming ripe and must be processed. For our ancestors, food processing was a gargantuan job and one on which their lives depended. The food must not only be grown, tended, and cut down, but enough of it must be preserved to keep the whole community through the winter. There would be times ahead when nothing would grow; only the stores would keep the people alive. If enough had not been stored, someone would not make it to spring.

The Greek goddess most associated with food storage was Hestia, the elderly virgin goddess of the hearth. Under her name Hestia Tamia, or Hestia of the Pantry, she was in charge of accounting for every grain of food that was stored and of judging how much should be kept for next year's seed. In the North, the solitary Germanic goddess Holda held a similar position; she was in charge of householding, stockpiling, and spinning—clothing was also dependent on what was taken in from the fields, such as flax. These goddesses of household accounting are classic Virgo figures, and they were honored every year during the height of the harvest season.

Another name for the autumn equinox was the Reckoning Day, in the sense that by the time you were that far through the harvest, you had a good idea of whether you were going to have enough to get by. At this point in the year, if you've screwed up, there was no going back. Everything had to be weighed, and measured, and judged as to whether you would have enough to sell, to lend, or to be generous that winter. We tend to think of Libra in terms of its Venus side, its penchant for beauty and relationships, and we often ignore the side of that sign that is the Judge, the scale in which things are weighed and reckoned. The passage from Virgo to Libra is the sacred accounting being laid into the hands of the judge who will decide your fate. It is the moment of truth, the bell that tolls, because in forty days the land will walk with the dead again at Samhain, and all accounts must be tallied and evaluated before then.

VIRGO-LIBRA INVOCATION FOR MABON

Lady who harvests the grain of thought
With the sickle of discrimination,
Lady who works alone
And understands solitude,
Lady whose center is untouched,
Whose gift is Mending,

Bless us with the ability to work hard
At the greatest of tasks,
The Repair of the World,
And to see divine will
In all the tiniest details.
By the power of all that labors,
You challenge us to perfection.
May we go forth in purity.
And now that your time in the Sun is passing,
You yield the cropped fields of your harvest
To the Judge with his ruthless Scales.
There are two sides to every scale,
The side of beauty and what is loved,
The side of fairness and what is just,
And it is a life's work
To bring the two together.
You whose gift is Balance,
Bless us with harmony in every debate
And help us see our views
Through the eyes of others.
By the power of all that bonds together,
You challenge us
To listen as much as we speak,
To speak as much as we listen,
To go back and forth in the dance of I and Thou.
May we all go forth in equality.

Did you reap your life's own bounty,
Or did you cut your hopes instead?
Remember that in forty days
This land walks with the Dead,
Did you count each blessing and each fear
For next year's vital seeds,
Did you cut down what was ripe to go

And plow the rest beneath?
Are you doomed to have to borrow,
Do you have enough to lend?
Are you safely bound within the ties
Of family and friends?
Did you preserve each perfect memory
And hoard them safe away,
Or did they all slip through your fingers
And empty-handed you come to the Reckoning Day . . .
Did you waste your life away?
Can you measure out your light and dark
And weigh your soul in the balance of night and day?
The price we have to pay,
The summer yields her golden crown
As the leaves come down at the end of the Reckoning
 Day . . .
 —FROM "RECKONING DAY," A MABON SONG
 by RAVEN KALDERA

15
Planetary Altars

Why make an altar for your personal planets or, for that matter, for the ones currently going through the sky? For the same reason that you'd honor any powerful forces that move through you and affect you. Even if you don't believe in any divine forces, doing the kind of tactile-sensual exercises that are described in this book can bring you to a deeper and more functional relationship with certain parts of yourself—or with those parts of the cosmic current that are washing over you. If Pluto is aspecting some part of your chart and producing heavy effects, propitiating the force of astrological Pluto as if it were a god can be surprisingly useful. If nothing else, it can trigger the part of your deep unconscious that connects to the collective unconscious, helping you to better understand this force of nature.

I've seen it do more than that, though. As a deist, and as someone who does work magic, I've seen that when you build altars to any deities—or forces—that have arrived in your backyard, they frequently soften their blows. It's as if propitiating and honoring them touches some deep groove in the Universe, and your slide through their spotlight becomes significantly easier. It doesn't really matter whether you believe in them or not; just acting as if you do believe can make change manifest.

These are lists of suggestions for magical altars that can be set up for honoring planetary aspects. There are two sorts of aspects that you're likely to be dealing with here—the ones already in your natal chart and the ones formed between your chart and the circling planets in real time.

The ones in your chart are like a snapshot, a moment of the cosmic clock captured forever on the medium of your soul. They're set in stone, and they don't move in relation to each other. If you have Mars square Venus, they will always be squared until you die and reincarnate and take breath once again. If your Moon is in Cancer, it will always be in Cancer. For making an altar to a single planet in your chart, just refer to that planet's listing. For natal aspects—two planets in your chart aspecting each other, like the aforementioned Venus and Mars, you'll have to be a little more imaginative, because the altar should be a blended mix of the two, and you'll have to work out the details with your own intuition.

For example, if you've got Mars in Virgo squared to Venus in Sagittarius, and you'd like to build an altar for these two parts of yourself—perhaps to bring them together and get them a little more in tune with each other so that they can, say, agree on a lover—you'd first compare and contrast the two different altar ideas. Mars in Virgo is a reddish brown color, and Venus in Sagittarius is apricot colored, so you could have two altar cloths, one laid over the other, or find a printed cloth or paper that combined both. Mars in Virgo suggests drums or small delicate tools, and Venus in Sagittarius suggests items from other cultures that you find to be romantic, so a drum or small tool from one of those cultures would be ideal. Jewelry that incorporates both their stones, or incense or a mojo bag that incorporates both their herbs, would also be appropriate. If the herbs in question are edible and nonpoisonous, making and drinking a tea of them works well, as does sprinkling the herbs around something symbolizing the problem . . . for example, in this case, a symbol of love.

If you want your altar to symbolize a transiting planet that's rolling over one of your natal planets, you can combine their energies as above, or you can gather separate piles of stuff on the same altar. Whichever you choose, the transiting planet should dominate the altar, as its energies are stronger. The actual moving being is more powerful than the snapshot of the being. If you like, speak to that planet using the voice of your contacted natal planet. For example, if Mars in Cancer is going over your Moon, you could speak from the part of yourself that is most Moon—your emotions, your inner child or inner parent, your vulnerable point—and say something like

"Please, great Mars in Cancer, Warrior who protects the home and family, you of the unbreakable shield, cautious one who understands strategy, you who lead from behind . . . please have mercy on my most vulnerable side. Teach my Moon how and when to defend herself, and show her when she should withdraw rather than be taken advantage of. Please do not merely provoke her into exploding a dozen times a day and frittering her energy away in petty irritations. Be kind and patient with her, and I will honor you during your passage through my life."

You can also get a jump-start on a transit by building a planetary altar to it just before it starts or at the very beginning of the transit. This works not only for transits that you fear will be painful or difficult (such as Saturn or Pluto steamrolling over one of your planets) but also for transits that might be very good (such as Jupiter or Venus dancing over your natal chart). For example, if you were going to have your Jupiter return—the time, approximately every twelve years, when Jupiter returns to the point where it was when you were born—and you wanted to petition the Powers That Be for an extra-special time, you could create a Jupiter altar laden with the symbols of your natal Jupiter sign. If Venus in Gemini was going to trine your Mars in Libra, and you could really use some hot romance, then a Gemini Venus/ Libra Mars altar would be in order.

You can also build an altar for the planet and sign of an important event. If you've chosen the perfect wedding day, you might want to create a good-luck altar that represented the chart for that day (say, Sun in Cancer, Moon in Libra, Venus in Leo, and so on). If you have a painful family dinner coming up, check the sign that the Moon will be in and put together an offering to the Moon in that sign, asking her to be easy on you and facilitate compassion and understanding.

The following information is an all-purpose list of astrological correlations that can be used for building altars, or making mojo bags, or creating any other kind of spell. Yes, this does not cover all the trees and herbs that could possibly be grown, but I had to stop this book somewhere. Also be warned that not all the astrological associations of the trees and herbs listed here are the traditional ones listed by Nicholas Culpeper and other medieval astrologer-herbalists. Some are more intuitive, reflecting a magical rather than a medicinal essence of the plant. Some planets were not discovered in medieval times, and many of the plants and trees were unknown to medieval herbalists. Because of this, expect some associations to be quite nontraditional. If any of them don't work for you, feel free to use something else.

Keep in mind that an "altar" can be as large or small as you want; it can be a square foot on a bookshelf somewhere, or a collage poster on a wall, or a huge table set up in your garage. It can have any arrangement of stuff on it, as aesthetic or unaesthetic as you prefer. You don't have to use all—or, for that matter, any—of the items listed; if you can think of better ones, go right ahead. These are presented for aid and inspiration.

Sun in Aries

COLOR: Bright warm red

ANIMAL: Bighorn sheep

STONE: Yellow diamond

HERBS: Cumin, millet

TREE: Holly

ITEMS: Red candles, figures of heroes and mythical warriors, swords, knives, spears, pictures of daredevil stunts and acrobatic dancers and children running and jumping, the number 1

Sun in Taurus

COLOR: Bright yellow green

ANIMAL: Cattle

STONE: Moss agate

HERBS: Oregano, wheat

TREE: Oak

ITEMS: Green candles, agricultural implements, bricks, pottery, sheaves of wheat, vegetable seeds, cowhorns, money, a handwritten list of your values and priorities

Sun in Gemini

COLOR: Light turquoise

ANIMAL: Sparrow

STONE: Lapis lazuli

HERB: Thymes of all kinds

TREE: Aspen

ITEMS: Two of everything listed here—knives, feathers, pens or pencils, pictures or figures of birds flying or birds' wings, books of jokes, games, witty sayings or other clever things

Sun in Cancer

COLOR: Silvery beige

ANIMAL: Crab

STONE: Mother-of-pearl

HERBS: Chamomile, rice

TREE: Beech

ITEMS: Crabs, shells, seawater, seaweed, family albums and photos (especially of your childhood home), pictures of country cottages and gardens, a picture of your favorite childhood Christmas present, things made by you as a child or by your children, children's food dishes, comfort food

Sun in Leo

COLOR: Golden yellow

ANIMAL: Lion

STONE: Amber

HERBS: Sunflower, marigold

TREE: Cedar

ITEMS: Crowns, thrones, puppets, small theaters, yellow candles, cloth of gold, brass statuary, a golden chalice of mead, pictures of flashy rock stars

Sun in Virgo

COLOR: Warm medium brown

ANIMAL: Bee

STONE: Sardonyx

HERBS: Chicory, rye

TREE: Birch

ITEMS: Crafts that require detail work, sheaves of wheat, seeds, grain, figures of maidens, small Zen gardens with perfectly raked sand circles, clean white cloth, starkly pure artwork, work gloves, tools, wood that you have sanded smooth by hand

Sun in Libra

COLOR: Warm medium pink

ANIMAL: Heron

STONE: Rutilated quartz

HERBS: Meadowsweet, apothecary rose

TREE: Apple

ITEMS: Scales, law books, pictures of famous movie lawyers and courtroom scenes, articles about famous court cases, flowers, candy, wholesome but sweet foods, gourmet food arranged gracefully, figures and pictures of dancers, brightly colored autumn leaves or pictures thereof, pictures of the Sun shining on flowers

Sun in Scorpio

COLOR: Medium wine red

ANIMAL: Eagle

STONE: Purple onyx

HERBS: Winter savory, oats

TREE: Blackthorn

ITEMS: Fossils, bones, boiling water belching steam, ice cubes, ice sculpture, pictures of hot springs and Arctic wastes, pictures of the midnight Sun, pictures of the desert Sun, figures of scorpions, figures of flying eagles, scalpels, anatomy diagrams, tapes of low throbbing music, a bowl of sand

Sun in Sagittarius

COLOR: Bright golden orange

ANIMAL: Horse

STONE: Azurite

HERBS: Onion, buckwheat

TREE: Alder

ITEMS: A bow and quiver of arrows, photos of faithful pets, pictures and figures of horses, figures of the Sun from foreign cultures, photos of the Sun over other countries, brochures for college campuses, a public library card, a model or picture of a brightly painted van or RV, decorative fabric or paper with a hunting or fishing theme, anything tie-dyed

Sun in Capricorn

COLOR: Warm reddish black

ANIMAL: Goat

STONE: Garnet

HERBS: Arnica, amaranth

TREE: Pine

ITEMS: Pictures of the Sun shining over mountain ranges next to pictures of the Sun shining over a cityscape, pictures of people looking sharp in business attire, pictures of people in uniform, any piece of an actual work uniform, a good briefcase, a leather binder, a sign saying "Responsibility," shoes with cleats, large rocks piled up, a rock hammer, an heirloom from a beloved grandfather

Sun in Aquarius

COLOR: Medium purple

ANIMAL: Albatross

STONE: Chrysanthemum stone

HERBS: Calendula, quinoa

TREE: Spindle tree

ITEMS: A globe, stacks of world atlases, printouts of your web page, printouts of your friends' web pages, a CB radio, science gadgetry, brochures for interest groups, brochures for humanitarian groups, books and articles and pictures on spaceflight, pictures of the Sun shining on the Earth from space, tapes of world beat music, chains of paper dolls

Sun in Pisces

COLOR: Medium teal blue

ANIMAL: Salmon

STONE: Pink coral

HERBS: Rosemary, barley

TREE: Ash

ITEMS: Fish (real or otherwise), shells, coral, salt water, white wine or beer, pictures of the Sun rising or setting over the ocean, pictures of Christ and/or saints and/or John Barleycorn, figures that represent compassion (for instance, Buddha or Mother Theresa), figures of open hands

Moon in Aries

COLOR: Medium magenta

ANIMAL: Domestic sheep

STONE: White diamond

HERBS: Tarragon, peony

TREE: Fir

ITEMS: Pictures of fireworks and firecrackers against the Moon, a red and white bandana, a bright red model car, red spicy food (especially quick snack food), a picture of a child swinging high on a swing or climbing a tree or running wildly, a hula hoop, a cup-and-ball game, a spinning top, a baseball

Moon in Taurus

COLOR: Gray green

ANIMAL: Water buffalo

STONE: Jade

HERBS: Cowslip, wild strawberry

TREE: Elm

ITEMS: Pictures of homey kitchens and living rooms, fresh-baked bread, potato soup, a jug of cream, fabrics with soft textures (silk, velvet, flannel), flowered pillows, kitchen items with cows, bunches of culinary herbs, pictures of beautiful cottage herb gardens, pictures of a house silhouetted against the Moon

Moon in Gemini

COLOR: Silvery blue

ANIMAL: Mockingbird

STONE: Labradorite

HERBS: Wintergreen, eucalyptus leaf

TREE: Eucalyptus

ITEMS: Bells, a penny whistle, a wooden flute, dark-and-light twin dolls, opposite-color child's mittens or gloves, origami paper birds, beautiful glass marbles, pen pal letters, stacks of favorite children's storybooks, light puffy crunchy snack food, pictures of the Moon shining through clouds and tree branches

Moon in Cancer

COLOR: Medium silver gray

ANIMAL: Manatee

STONE: Moonstone

HERBS: Motherwort, field poppy

TREE: Willow

ITEMS: Silver crescent or round Moon figures, round white marbles, shells, seawater, seaweed, glass sea floats, toys for babies or young children, figures of mothers and babies, items that belonged to your mother or you as a baby, old quilts, comfort foods, soft white food such as rice or custard, pictures of the Moon shining over the beach

Moon in Leo

COLOR: Iridescent gold

ANIMAL: Cat

STONE: Yellow calcite

HERBS: Saffron, hawthorn berry

TREE: Hawthorn

ITEMS: Golden Moon figures, Sun-Moon combination figures, cat figurines, pictures of house cats, soft furs, children's masks and costumes, programs from school plays or dance recitals, children's plastic crowns, honey, yellow foods such as saffron rice, round yellow fruits and vegetables

Moon in Virgo

COLOR: Silvery brown

ANIMAL: Luna moth

STONE: Aragonite

HERBS: Primrose, chaste tree berry

TREE: Chaste tree

ITEMS: Household broom, pots and pans; child's toy kitchen items; child's craft kits; figures of maidens; silver-sprayed wheat sheaf; flour; cornstarch; whole-grain bread; fresh vegetables; pictures of small, clean, neat apartments; pictures of the Moon shining over an open field

Moon in Libra

COLOR: Rose pink

ANIMAL: Duck

STONE: Opal

HERBS: Sweet Annie, dame's rocket

TREE: Peach

ITEMS: A bathroom or kitchen scale, boy and girl dolls holding hands, pictures of children learning to dance together, books on how to teach children to play fairly, pink ruffled clothing, sweet foods, sugar, tapes and CDs of calm peaceful music, pictures of the Moon shining over a beautiful cityscape

Moon in Scorpio

COLOR: Cranberry red

ANIMALS: Domestic pig, wild boar

STONE: White onyx

HERBS: Mugwort, licorice

TREE: Acacia

ITEMS: Smooth mysterious stones, black and white marbles, a black disk for the dark Moon, black and white candles, a children's book of secret codes, a diary with a lock, small sealed glass bottles of water, raw meat, rare steak, pigs' feet, pictures of the Moon shining over a graveyard

Moon in Sagittarius

COLOR: Terra-cotta, like clay

ANIMAL: Deer

STONE: Sphalerite

HERBS: Shallot, jewelweed

TREE: Rowan

ITEMS: Hunter camouflage, stag horns, deer figurines, a child's bow and arrows, favorite foreign/ethnic food, souvenirs from a childhood vacation trip, pictures of recreational vehicles or mobile homes or hippie traveling vans, books of children's traveling adventures, pictures of the Moon shining over the road

Moon in Capricorn

COLOR: Grayed black

ANIMAL: Dog

STONE: Selenite

HERBS: Myrrh, patchouli

TREE: Lemon

ITEMS: Coffee cups, canned food, gingham fabric, an heirloom from a beloved grandmother, pictures of perfect rural farms, pictures of farm animals, oatmeal, potatoes, beets, carrots, parsnips, a rotating chart of house chores, pictures of children dressed as somber adults, child dolls dressed as somber adults, books that refer to housewives as home executives, pictures of the Moon over a mountain

Moon in Aquarius

COLOR: Lavender gray

ANIMAL: Monkey

STONE: Sugilite

HERBS: Marsh mallow, houseleek

TREE: Olive

ITEMS: Alien dolls, toy spaceships, a toy microscope, science toys, children's science books, a school science textbook, a picture of children playing while one child stands aside and left out, children's computer and video games, toy robots in children's doll clothing, shiny silver fabric, pictures of the Moon shot from space

Moon in Pisces

COLOR: Medium blue gray

ANIMAL: Dolphin

STONE: Pearl

HERBS: Evening primrose, dulse

TREE: Grapevine

ITEMS: Fish curved into a crescent Moon, pearls, water lilies, figures of mermaids, salt water, white wine, books of heroes and heroines who sacrificed themselves for the good of humanity, books about parents who sacrificed for their children, pictures of women dressed in white, pictures of the Moon shining on the sea

Mercury in Aries

COLOR: Light peach pink

ANIMAL: Hawk

STONE: Fulgurite

HERBS: Fenugreek, ginger mint

TREE: Cinchona

ITEMS: A sledge, a welder, a welder's mask, a soldering iron, solder, books on how to achieve your goals, a tape of confidence-building pep talk, an exercise video

Mercury in Taurus

COLOR: Pale green

ANIMAL: Pigeon

STONE: Green fluorite

HERBS: Bee balm, slippery elm bark

TREE: Slippery elm

ITEMS: A hammer, nails, an anvil, books on how to build things, Legos, an erector set, specific instructions on how to do something with big illustrations

Mercury in Gemini

COLOR: Blue white

ANIMAL: Parrot

STONE: Clear fluorite

HERBS: Spearmint, lemongrass

TREE: Palm

ITEMS: A chisel, books on any subject as long as they are varied, letters, computer printouts of e-mails, lists written in shorthand, telephones and telephone books, tapes of talk radio shows

Mercury in Cancer

COLOR: Gray white

ANIMAL: Sandpiper

STONE: Unakite

HERBS: Chervil, bayberry

TREE: Quince

ITEMS: Fancy or high-tech cooking utensils, cookbooks (especially ones with glossy colorful pictures), books on child psychology, your inner child's most interesting toy

Mercury in Leo

COLOR: Pale yellow

ANIMAL: Peacock

STONE: Yellow fluorite

HERBS: St. John's wort, orange mint

TREE: Tree of Heaven

ITEMS: A battery charger; high-watt lightbulbs; a book on theatrical lighting, props, or makeup; a picture of someone in the spotlight; books on increasing creativity; books on doing creative things

Mercury in Virgo

COLOR: Eggshell beige

ANIMAL: Woodpecker

STONE: Blue fluorite

HERBS: Caraway, Corsican mint

TREE: Locust (carob)

ITEMS: A power drill, an electric sander, sandpaper, books and articles on how to repair and maintain things, books on health and medicine, small craft kits, a small drum

Mercury in Libra

COLOR: Very pale pink

ANIMAL: Nightingale

STONE: Pink fluorite

HERBS: Marjoram, apple mint

TREE: Linden

ITEMS: A carpenter's level, an air compressor, air tools, books on law, books on social justice, books on beauty tips, books on fashion and/or modeling

Mercury in Scorpio

COLOR: Light mauve pink

ANIMALS: Raven, crow

STONE: Purple fluorite

HERBS: Anise, agastache

TREE: Ginkgo

ITEMS: A scalpel, a pipe wrench, books on anatomy and surgery, books on psychology and psychiatry, books on how to read people and figure them out

Mercury in Sagittarius

COLOR: Very light peach

ANIMAL: Seagull

STONE: Orange fluorite

HERBS: Mustard seed, betony

TREE: Juniper

ITEMS: A saw, a crowbar, a primitive tool from a strange culture, travel advertisements, a college course catalog, books on travel, books on radical honesty, adventure stories

Mercury in Capricorn

COLOR: Pale gray

ANIMAL: Cuckoo

STONE: Cavansite

HERBS: Dill, dittany of Crete

TREE: Spruce

ITEMS: A screwdriver, screws, books on how to start your own business, books on how to impress people, pictures of wealthy and powerful people who aren't beautiful and artificial, pictures of mountains

Mercury in Aquarius

COLOR: Palest lavender

ANIMAL: Starling

STONE: Kyanite

HERBS: Peppermint, sesame

TREE: Jujube

ITEMS: A multimeter; a microscope; ultraviolet lightbulbs; electronic equipment; books on artificial intelligence, parapsychology, or radical politics; books on educating your young child

Mercury in Pisces

COLOR: Palest aqua

ANIMAL: Kestrel

STONE: Zebra stone

HERB: Sweet cicely, calamint

TREES: Mimosa

ITEMS: A fishhook, fishing line, a lathe, a net, books of poetry, books on dream interpretation, a bottle of seltzer water, a pipe for smoking

Venus in Aries

COLOR: Pale red

ANIMAL: Cock

STONE: Carnelian

HERBS: Ginger, ground ivy

TREE: Grapefruit

ITEMS: Cock feathers; massage oil with a hot, spicy scent; heart-shaped Red Hots; a small toy pistol; scarlet satin lingerie; a cigarette lighter; a sparkler; tiny firecrackers; red roses; a glass of red wine

Venus in Taurus

COLOR: Mint green

ANIMAL: Bear

STONE: Aventurine

HERBS: Sweet woodruff, orris root

TREE: Sugar maple

ITEMS: Teddy bears hugging each other, soft blankets and sweaters, maple syrup, maple sugar, pancakes, potpourri, pictures of quaint homey cottages, paired coffee mugs, pink roses, massage oil scented with flowers

Venus in Gemini

COLOR: Baby blue

ANIMAL: Butterfly

STONE: Pink tourmaline

HERBS: Lemon verbena, speedwell

TREE: Blueberry

ITEMS: Butterflies, china figurines (especially of children dancing), clasped hands, double weddings, twined hearts, love letters, long colored ribbons hung in the wind, massage oil with a brisk, clean scent

Venus in Cancer

COLOR: Silvery pink

ANIMAL: Sea otter

STONE: Rose quartz

HERBS: Southernwood, lady's mantle

TREE: Apricot

ITEMS: A pretty child's doll, a china tea set, books on cooking romantic dinners, pictures of happy couples holding babies, a picture of a romantic bed and breakfast in a quaint flowered cottage, seashells from a romantic beach, white roses, massage oil with a vanilla scent

Venus in Leo

COLOR: Light golden yellow

ANIMAL: Lynx

STONE: Citrine

HERBS: Heliotrope, scented geranium

TREE: Orange

ITEMS: A teen doll dressed in a glamourous sequined outfit, sexy lingerie in metallic lamé, brochures or programs for expensive theatrical productions, a dance-floor glitterball, a big heart-shaped box of chocolates, a bunch of long-stemmed yellow roses, massage oil with a citrus scent

Venus in Virgo

COLOR: Light warm tan

ANIMAL: Dragonfly

STONE: Marcasite

HERBS: Lemon balm, melilot

TREE: Honey locust

ITEMS: Mug of hot tea, clean-scented soaps, a bunch of cottage posies picked from a garden, dolls or pictures of women in Victorian undergarments, pictures of couples working together in a garden or doing construction, massage oil with the scent of tree woods

Venus in Libra

COLOR: Baby pink

ANIMAL: Dove

STONE: Bixbite

HERBS: Basil, jasmine

TREE: Cherry

ITEMS: Pink sugar candy or cookies, heart-shaped food, pink roses, the top tier of a wedding cake, a wedding invitation, a list of traditional anniversary gifts, actual anniversary gifts, books on making marriage more romantic, dolls in romantic clothing, massage oil scented with flowers

Venus in Scorpio

COLOR: Light fuschia

ANIMAL: Weasel

STONE: Muscovite

HERBS: Coriander, summer savory

TREE: Pawpaw

ITEMS: Blackberry or raspberry wine, dark red roses, books on sex magic, books on Tantra, books on sexual psychology, controversial pornography, black lace, black silk gloves, many fine chains, massage oil scented with musk, Obsession perfume

Venus in Sagittarius

COLOR: Apricot

ANIMAL: Magpie

STONE: Lodestone

HERBS: Cinnamon, clove

TREE: Pear

ITEMS: Peach wine, exotic tropical fruits, a tropical beach hat, pictures of cruise ships, exotic jewelry, pictures of couples on romantic foreign getaways, pictures of couples driving together in sporty cars, massage oil with a light spicy scent

Venus in Capricorn

COLOR: Light gray

ANIMAL: Fox

STONE: Kunzite

HERBS: Vervain, vetiver

TREE: Lime

ITEMS: Expensive wine, expensive liqueurs, filet mignon, lacy ferns, pictures of couples in expensive restaurants, a black silk slip, a sensible cotton nightgown, a Victorian romance novel, Victorian courting advice, a fan, silk gloves, a brochure for a mountain-climbing tour for couples, massage oil with a piney scent

Venus in Aquarius

COLOR: Light lavender

ANIMAL: Frog

STONE: Spinel

HERBS: Elecampane, stevia

TREE: Persimmon

ITEMS: Tamarind juice, white roses dyed strange colors with food coloring, futuristic or abstract-looking pornography, romantic science fiction stories, books on alternative relationships, stories of activist couples, clear plastic high heels, sexy plastic clothing, two toy robots hugging

Venus in Pisces

COLOR: Light aqua

ANIMAL: Goldfish

STONE: Herkimer diamond

HERBS: Sweet violet, love-in-a-mist

TREE: Plum

ITEMS: A bottle of sea water, a glass of plum wine, paintings of plum blossoms, Japanese geisha dolls, mermaid dolls, lavender roses, violets, books on sexual healing, books on codependency, white lace lingerie, pictures of saints, massage oil with a salty-floral scent

Mars in Aries

COLOR: Scarlet

ANIMAL: Wolverine

STONE: Tiger iron

HERBS: Cayenne, blessed thistle

TREE: Prickly ash

ITEMS: A torch and a spear

Mars in Taurus

COLOR: Bright green

ANIMAL: Buffalo

STONE: Bull's eye

HERBS: Horseradish, skirret

TREE: Red maple

ITEMS: A big wooden club, an ax, and a shovel

Mars in Gemini

COLOR: Sky blue

ANIMAL: Falcon

STONE: Orange tourmaline

HERBS: Fennel, eyebright

TREE: Poplar

ITEMS: A wide selection of small knives, scalpels, and pens interspersed with each other

Mars in Cancer

COLOR: Metallic silver

ANIMAL: Lobster

STONE: Amazonite

HERBS: Milk thistle, wild yam

TREE: Papaya

ITEMS: Crab and lobster claws, a model of a lobster trap, and a sign that says "Beware of Dog"

Mars in Leo

COLOR: Blazing yellow

ANIMAL: Leopard

STONE: Tiger eye

HERBS: Turmeric, safflower

TREE: Blood orange

ITEMS: A big fancy sword with a crown on the hilt and a big fancy flag

Mars in Virgo

COLOR: Rusty reddish brown

ANIMAL: Ant

STONE: Red jasper

HERBS: Horehound, sorrel

TREE: Guelder rose

ITEMS: A wide selection of both tools and weapons (any kind) sorted neatly into piles and categories, and a paper scroll that lists and cross-references them, handwritten in the neatest possible calligraphy

Mars in Libra

COLOR: Hot pink

ANIMAL: Swan

STONE: Fire opal

HERBS: Borage, gentian

TREE: Crab apple

ITEMS: A sword-shaped letter opener crossed with a plumed pen and a picture of a white-armored knight

Mars in Scorpio

COLOR: Blazing crimson

ANIMAL: Rat

STONE: Sulfur

HERBS: Garlic, Alexanders

TREE: Date palm

ITEMS: Scary-looking toothed knives, a small and easily hidden stiletto, and the figure of a black-armored knight

Mars in Sagittarius

COLOR: Safety orange

ANIMAL: Elk

STONE: Chrysocolla

HERBS: Galangal, centaury

TREE: Horse Chestnut

ITEMS: A crossbow, an exotic weapon of some primitive tribe, and pamphlets advertising trips to dangerous places

Mars in Capricorn

COLOR: Shiny black

ANIMAL: Wolf

STONE: Bloodstone

HERBS: Black pepper, cotton thistle

TREE: Mahogany

ITEMS: A shiny handgun (real or fake), a book of strategy such as *The Book of Five Rings* or *The Art of War,* and mountain-climbing equipment

Mars in Aquarius

COLOR: Bright purple

ANIMAL: Hyena

STONE: Hawk's eye

HERBS: Nasturtium, fuller's teasel

TREE: Camphor

ITEMS: A shiny plastic ray gun, a model of a missile, a model of a science-fiction battle spaceship, and the picture of a mushroom cloud

Mars in Pisces

COLOR: Bright blue

ANIMAL: Barracuda

STONE: White coral

HERBS: Hops, watercress

TREE: Cornelian cherry

ITEMS: A net and trident, a small submarine, a diver aquarium figurine, scuba equipment, the jaw of a toothed fish

Jupiter in Aries

COLOR: Ruby red

ANIMALS: Gazelle and other types of antelope

STONE: Ruby

HERBS: Angelica, sainfoin

TREE: White walnut

ITEMS: A military general's cap, many toy soldiers in impressive uniforms lined up in row upon row, a flag of victory, biographies of brave heroes, pictures of Olympic athletes, large medals, the names of everyone who broke the four-minute mile

Jupiter in Taurus

COLOR: Deep emerald green

ANIMAL: Elephant

STONE: Emerald

HERBS: Aloe vera, good king henry

TREE: Hickory

ITEMS: Piles of faux gold and jewels like a dragon's hoard, fine antique musical instruments, the figure of an elephant, rich velvet cloth, and a comfortable fisherman's cap for contrast

Jupiter in Gemini

COLOR: Clear medium turquoise

ANIMAL: Robin

STONE: Sodalite

HERBS: Clary sage, coltsfoot

TREE: Brazil nut

ITEMS: A reporter's hat with "Press" in the hatband, an unabridged dictionary, the Yellow Pages for a large city, advertising for any product that reeks of Madison Avenue, advertising for advertising agencies, testimonials, books on how to talk anyone into anything

Jupiter in Cancer

COLOR: Ivory

ANIMAL: Blue whale

STONE: Nephrite

HERBS: Vanilla, pineapple sage

TREE: Coconut

ITEMS: Many small, happy, smiling dolls looking like an ideal family; a picture or model of a big beautiful ancestral home; gourmet food on expensive china; a model bankbook with a comfortable balance written in; obituaries for beloved parents

Jupiter in Leo

COLOR: Amber

ANIMAL: Cougar

STONE: Golden beryl

HERBS: Bay, fo-ti

TREE: Chestnut

ITEMS: A jeweled crown, a sceptre, pictures of movie stars and royalty (and their huge houses, castles, rich lifestyles, etc.), expensive gourmet food, gold jewelry, fabric with large and splashy Sun designs, articles about rich people giving huge amounts of money to charity, brochures and programs from lavish theatrical productions

Jupiter in Virgo

COLOR: Honey brown

ANIMAL: Scarab

STONE: Vandanite

HERBS: Garden sage, soapwort

TREE: Pecan

ITEMS: A miner's hard hat with a light in front, the ruffled cap of a high-class maid or the cap of a high-class chauffeur, pictures of elaborate herb gardens, an accounting book with neatly tallied high-money figures, well-polished expensive silver

Jupiter in Libra

COLOR: Deep rose

ANIMAL: Crane

STONE: Rose beryl

HERBS: Lavender, clove pink

TREE: Honeysuckle

ITEMS: An elegant flowered hat with a floating veil, an elaborately decorated cake, pictures of famous high-class models and actresses, the menu to an expensive restaurant, pictures of elegant weddings, pictures of famous couples with good long marriages, articles about justice prevailing in high courts, leather-bound law books

Jupiter in Scorpio

COLOR: Deep garnet red

ANIMAL: Snake

STONE: Peridot

HERBS: Hyssop, echinacea

TREE: Black walnut

ITEMS: A classic detective's fedora, expensive cigars, figures of Egyptian mummies, figures of Egyptian gods, tomb paintings, labyrinths, rubbings of elaborate tombstones, a small model of a shiny black hearse, an elaborate antique hookah, expensive wine goblets

Jupiter in Sagittarius

COLOR: Royal purple

ANIMAL: Kingfisher

STONE: Turquoise

HERBS: Yarrow, cinquefoil

TREE: Almond

ITEMS: A safari hat, an ethnic mask, brochures for expensive foreign tours and cruises, brochures for expensive Ivy League colleges, pictures of large elaborate places of worship, leather-bound books of history or foreign culture or religion or philosophy, expensive imported foreign food

Jupiter in Capricorn

COLOR: Iron gray

ANIMAL: Beaver

STONE: Cinnabar

HERBS: Comfrey, ashwagandha

TREE: Piñon pine

ITEMS: An elegant top hat, white gloves, pictures of large executive desks, expensive pens, monogrammed linens, pictures or models of limousines, pictures of the tops of skyscrapers, fancy certificates displaying earned credentials, photos of high society (especially Victorian high society), articles about millionaires, the stock market page of the paper

Jupiter in Aquarius

COLOR: Medium amethyst

ANIMAL: Gorilla

STONE: Amethyst

HERBS: Purple sage, astragalus

TREE: Banyan

ITEMS: A space helmet, computer equipment, computer books, photos of Einstein, quotes from Einstein, Mensa brochures, books on the history of unions, books on the history of social work, brochures from large humanitarian organizations, articles about everyday life in the possible near future, articles about shiny new scientific developments, tapes of music made for humanitarian fund-raisers

Jupiter in Pisces

COLOR: Sapphire blue

ANIMAL: Tuna

STONE: Sapphire

HERBS: Diviner's sage, sea holly

TREE: Hazel

ITEMS: A Renaissance minstrel's plumed velvet hat, sea salt, a large valuable nautilus shell, coconut milk, a crown made of fishes, a figure of a crowned mermaid or triton, books of poetry by the great masters, biographies of great spiritual leaders, articles on doctors who sacrificed themselves in third-world countries, Christ figures

Saturn in Aries

COLOR: Dark grayish red

ANIMAL: Rabbit

STONE: Black diamond

HERBS: Valerian, bloodroot

TREE: Larch

ITEMS: Broken weapons, a cracked shield, burned-out matches, an empty lighter, broken candles, pictures of slain medieval crusaders, a picture of a cowering child, books of "true confessions," books about overcoming fears, articles about damaged athletes

Saturn in Taurus

COLOR: Very dark evergreen

ANIMAL: Aurochs

STONE: Star diopside

HERBS: Parsley, mayapple

TREE: Sequoia

ITEMS: An empty wallet, ragged clothing, books and articles on homeless people, pictures of refugees, books and articles on poverty, pictures of beggars, an empty begging bowl, books on surviving bankruptcy, budgeting ledgers

Saturn in Gemini

COLOR: Navy blue

ANIMAL: Stork

STONE: Black tourmaline

HERBS: Mullein, pleurisy root

TREE: Coca

ITEMS: Shredded magazines, children's books with ripped-out pages, books on learning disabilities, broken phones, tangled phone wire, toy cars with no wheels, toy planes with no wings, a poorly written alphabet, an unfinished letter full of misspellings

Saturn in Cancer

COLOR: Dark charcoal gray

ANIMAL: Sea elephant

STONE: Pyritic Concretion

HERBS: Rue, pennyroyal

TREE: Black mulberry

ITEMS: Books on healing dysfunctional families, items that bring up painful childhood memories, abortion information, a picture of a child's tombstone, broken dolls and toys, bland food, cut-up family photos

Saturn in Leo

COLOR: Dun yellow

ANIMAL: Salamander

STONE: Jet

HERBS: Mistletoe, foxglove

TREE: Bitter orange

ITEMS: Burned-out light bulbs, dead Christmas tree lights, Barbie dolls missing their heads or bodies, articles about stars who committed suicide or overdosed, "Where are they now?" articles about famous has-beens, portraits of tyrants and dictators, cracked sunglasses

Saturn in Virgo

COLOR: Very dark brown

ANIMAL: Praying mantis

STONE: Smoky quartz

HERBS: Skullcap, monkshood

TREE: Nux vomica

ITEMS: Empty or discarded accounting ledgers, a broken calculator, crumpled grocery lists, watches, annoying alarm clocks, egg timers, extremely nutritious but completely unappetizing high-fiber health food, a monastic liturgy

Saturn in Libra

COLOR: Dark pinkish brown

ANIMAL: Vulture

STONE: Black opal

HERBS: Myrtle, oleander

TREE: Medlar

ITEMS: Wilted dead flowers, shabby or broken decorative trinkets, stilted Victorian manuals of manners, accounts of nasty divorces, happy-couple pictures torn in two, newspaper articles about injustice, lawyer bills, Amnesty International pamphlets

Saturn in Scorpio

COLOR: Very dark burgundy

ANIMAL: Scorpion

STONE: Black onyx

HERBS: Shepherd's purse, poison hemlock

TREE: Sycamore

ITEMS: Symbols of obsession, anatomical pictures of reproductive organs, pornography that makes you uncomfortable, psychiatric medications, skulls and death's heads, coffins

Saturn in Sagittarius

COLOR: Dark orange brown

ANIMAL: Squirrel

STONE: Staurolite

HERBS: Leek, hellebore

TREE: Yew

ITEMS: Worn-out shoes, model boxcars, college exam papers, crutches, fundamentalist religious literature (any faith), stories of religious conversion, old and forbidding religious icons, stories of runaway nuns, stories of runaway teenagers

Saturn in Capricorn

COLOR: Black

ANIMAL: Jackal

STONE: Obsidian

HERBS: Boneset, pokeberry

TREE: Bristlecone pine

ITEMS: Photos of disliked family members, a sign saying "DUTY," alarm clocks, kitchen timers, pictures of old battered cars, pictures of rows of corporate drones in cubicles, name tags or uniform pieces from dead-end wage slave jobs, check stubs with meager pay, articles about abused elders or abuse in retirement homes

Saturn in Aquarius

COLOR: Very dark purple

ANIMAL: Orangutan

STONE: Black marble

HERBS: Lobelia, asafoetida

TREE: Cherimoya

ITEMS: Pictures of people standing alone in the rain, anarchist symbols, articles about political terrorism, articles about world hunger, pictures of starving people in third-world countries, biographies of despised geniuses who died ignored, a sign saying "YOU ARE OUT," mindless corporate advertising with glaze-eyed smiling people, articles about union busting, articles about scientific research gone bad

Saturn in Pisces

COLOR: Blue black

ANIMAL: Shark

STONE: Black pearl

HERBS: Calamus, belladonna

TREE: Buckthorn

ITEMS: Broken sea floats, torn fishing nets, fish traps, anchors, broken ships, books about mental illness, symbols of karmic debts, pictures of the Lakota Sun Dance or the Hindu Kavandi ceremony or any people suspended by hooks in their flesh, paintings by Van Gogh or Edvard Munch

Uranus in Aries

COLOR: Neon red

ANIMAL: Grasshopper

STONE: Zoesite

HERBS: Nettles, ephedra

TREE: Calamondin

ITEMS: Red Hots candy, joy buzzers, pictures and models of high-tech warrior robots or futuristic war weapons, models of fast planes and futuristic motorcycles and cars, science fiction stories or movies about exploring new frontiers, a plastic ray gun

Uranus in Taurus

COLOR: Neon green

ANIMAL: Tortoise

STONE: Hematite

HERBS: Tormentil, burdock

TREE: Silver maple

ITEMS: Catalogs and products from businesses that are especially unusual or politically correct, unusual grains, unusual vegetables, examples of unusual architecture and ultramodern buildings, modern farm equipment, articles about genetically engineered agriculture

Uranus in Gemini

COLOR: Electric blue

ANIMAL: Hummingbird

STONE: Rubellite tourmaline

HERBS: Feverfew, kava kava

TREE: Kumquat

ITEMS: A propeller beanie; bright, plastic, modern-looking, fiddle-with toys; articles about future cell phones; chat room transcripts; a model of a modern wind turbine; juggler's beanbags and pins; performance throwing knives

Uranus in Cancer

COLOR: Bright white

ANIMAL: Seal

STONE: Chrysoprase

HERBS: Raspberry leaf, curry plant

TREE: Pineapple

ITEMS: A robot doll in a diaper, robot pet toys, a model family SUV or RV, an infant carrysack, books on modern childrearing, pictures of kids using computers, books on new high-tech ways of educating children, books on rebellious children, books on rewriting the religion of your birth, high-tech kitchen gadgets

Uranus in Leo

COLOR: Neon yellow

ANIMAL: Cheetah

STONE: Sunstone

HERBS: Dandelion, catnip

TREE: Cassia

ITEMS: Crazy bright neon clothing, weird-looking shoes, mismatched bright socks, oddly colored hair dye, glittery iridescent makeup, pictures of strange-looking rock stars, pictures of comedians, books on how to tell jokes

Uranus in Virgo

COLOR: Bright tawny

ANIMAL: Wasp

STONE: Goldstone

HERBS: Cardamom, herb Robert

TREE: Neem

ITEMS: Books on the energy centers of the body, books on interesting new health fads, books on alternative medicine, herbal tinctures, herb capsules, diet foods (especially with high-tech ingredients), all-natural toothpaste, all-natural cleaning products

Uranus in Libra

COLOR: Neon pink

ANIMAL: Pheasant

STONE: Lepidolite

HERBS: Lovage, rhubarb

TREE: Chokecherry

ITEMS: Books on alternatives to marriage, pictures of alternative families, stories of justice obtained by unusual means, valentines combined into bizarre modern-art sculpture, upside-down hearts and crazy flowers

Uranus in Scorpio

COLOR: Neon magenta

ANIMAL: Lizard

STONE: Brown-striped onyx

HERBS: Black cohosh, viper's bugloss

TREE: Black haw

ITEMS: A trowel, a sifter, bizarre pornography, futuristic pornography, books of kinky sex acts, detective stories, a detective's fedora with strange things tucked into the brim, books about new and unusual psychological theories, stories about modern forensics

Uranus in Sagittarius

COLOR: Neon orange

ANIMAL: Mouse

STONE: Howlite

HERBS: Egyptian onion, chickweed

TREE: Tangerine

ITEMS: Protest posters on sticks for picketers, activist slogans or stickers or articles, buttons with radical slangy sayings, brochures for avant-garde schools, pictures of modern churches with unusual architecture, books on radical honesty, books on radical modern philosophy

Uranus in Capricorn

COLOR: Steel gray

ANIMAL: Coyote

STONE: Basalt

HERBS: Agrimony, dock

TREE: Ebony

ITEMS: Pictures and articles on high-tech prosthetics and wheelchairs, articles on extending life and abolishing old age, biographies of entrepreneurs in unusual businesses, brochures for new and unusual businesses, pictures of elderly people doing sports or t'ai chi or running marathons, science-fiction views of corporate life

Uranus in Aquarius

COLOR: Neon purple

ANIMAL: Chimpanzee

STONE: Man-made artificial stones

HERBS: Tansy, saw palmetto

TREE: Rubber tree

ITEMS: Techno-junk, the more high-tech the better, especially Rube Goldberg machines or cutting-edge stuff

Uranus in Pisces

COLOR: Neon blue

ANIMAL: Sea horse

STONE: Dolomite

HERBS: Salad burnet, datura

TREE: Loquat

ITEMS: A scuba mask, swim fins, photos of unusual fish, pictures of coelacanths, pictures of chameleons, books with stories of escape from prisons, a children's Cinderella story, real-life Cinderella stories

Neptune in Aries

COLOR: Deep violet red

ANIMAL: Cockatrice

STONE: Blue diamond

HERBS: Ginseng, toloache

TREE: Pepper

ITEMS: Cigarettes, tiki torches, candelabra, national flags, the words of national anthems, books about the glories of battle, books extolling courage under fire, books about mythic heroes, pictures of heroes being awarded medals, pictures of Olympic medalists

Neptune in Taurus

COLOR: Malachite green

ANIMAL: Babylonian winged bull

STONE: Granite

HERBS: Joe-pye weed, kudzu

TREE: Norway maple

ITEMS: Green Man faces, leaves, vines, acorns, Monopoly money, faery gold, books about get-rich-quick schemes, castles made of sand, castles made of clouds, pictures of the perfect home, pictures of trees and vines choking buildings, sugar food with little food value, diet food with little food value

Neptune in Gemini

COLOR: Medium blue violet

ANIMAL: Winged faery

STONE: Green tourmaline

HERBS: Balm of Gilead, California poppy

TREE: Pistachio

ITEMS: Caterpillars, chrysalises, wind chimes, pinwheels, spinny wind toys, pens and pencils with strange erasers, books on automatic writing, pictures of conjoined twins, pictures of flower faeries, pictures of evil faeries, a glass knife

Neptune in Cancer

COLOR: Light blue gray

ANIMAL: Mermaid

STONE: Rhodochrosite

HERBS: Wormwood, goat's rue

TREE: Manna Ash

ITEMS: Fishing nets, model fishing boats, clamshells, canned seafood, the recipe for your favorite childhood dish made by Mom, pictures smiling, perfect families of the 1950s, books on spiritual healing of wounds, books on healing your inner child, poems about your inner child

Neptune in Leo

COLOR: Light yellow green

ANIMAL: Gryphon

STONE: Topaz

HERBS: Goldenseal, morning glory

TREE: Laurel

ITEMS: Glittering stars of all sizes, a spotlight, camera equipment, idealized crowned lion figurines, glossy idealized photos of stars and models, books about movie stars being discovered, books about mythic or faery-tale royalty, poems about kingship

Neptune in Virgo

COLOR: Light lavender brown

ANIMAL: Unicorn

STONE: Charoite

HERBS: Solomon's seal, avens

TREE: Tamarack

ITEMS: Magical botanical floor washes; magical soaps; a scrub brush; all-natural detergent; books on yoga and energy healing; books on meditation for health; pictures of monks and nuns from all world traditions; the Benedictine Rule; the Buddhist Precepts; a small bed of nails; books of saints, miracles, and fakirs

Neptune in Libra

COLOR: Lavender pink

ANIMAL: Siren

STONE: Celestite

HERBS: Holy basil, passionflower

TREE: Ylang-ylang

ITEMS: Flowers, hearts of semiprecious stones, valentines from your internal ideal dream lover, how-to books for healing a marriage, magazine pictures of romantic getaways and embracing perfect couples, pictures of beautiful people

Neptune in Scorpio

COLOR: Deep maroon

ANIMAL: Manticore

STONE: Serpentine

HERBS: Yohimbe, hemp

TREE: Catalpa

ITEMS: Grateful Dead paraphernalia, books on drugs and drug culture and spiritual drug use, grapes, thyrsus, jug of wine, books on Tantra, books on sex magic and spiritual sex, a sign saying "BODY = TEMPLE," statues of Hindu gods, psychedelic rock tapes

Neptune in Sagittarius

COLOR: Dark red orange

ANIMAL: Pegasus

STONE: Cuprite

HERBS: Chives, nutmeg

TREE: Banana

ITEMS: Smiley-face buttons, "Don't Worry, Be Happy" buttons, soap bubbles, pictures of stars on the horizon, pictures of gypsy wagons, books on Romany magic, books on gurus and disciples, books on cults, pictures of smiling cult members, a mirror covered in chiffon, an arrow labeled "TRUTH"

Neptune in Capricorn

COLOR: Midnight blue

ANIMAL: Dragon

STONE: Trilobite

HERBS: Costmary, cranesbill

TREE: Norfolk Island pine

ITEMS: Photos or portraits of honored ancestors, bowls of musky incense, votive candles, modest white and black veils, mortician tools, pamphlets from funeral parlors, 19th-century books of utopias, brochures of idyllic-looking retirement communities

Neptune in Aquarius

COLOR: Deep violet blue

ANIMAL: Roc

STONE: Moldavite

HERBS: Sweetgrass, ololiuqui

TREE: Bodhi

ITEMS: Psychedelic pictures, books on mind expansion (with or without chemical help), lava lamps and other mesmerizing many-colored moving knickknacks, books on idealistic philosophies, crystals of any sort, tinfoil hats, small UFOs

Neptune in Pisces

COLOR: Deep sea blue

ANIMAL: Sea serpent

STONE: Clear quartz

HERBS: Purslane, opium poppy

TREE: Beach plum

ITEMS: A fishtank crowded with all the little fantasy figurines—castles, divers, rainbows, and so on—with a background of swirly colors, filled with salt water and bright tropical fish

Pluto in Aries

COLOR: Fiery crimson

ANIMAL: Rhinoceros

STONE: Zircon

HERBS: Smallage, ayahuasca

TREE: Tea tree

ITEMS: Red-stained white cloth, guns (real or fake), a black-painted spear, fake grenades, articles about police corruption, articles about police-department internal affairs workers, articles about military corruption, photos of bloody battlefields, pictures of third-world dictators

Pluto in Taurus

COLOR: Dark moss green

ANIMAL: Hippopotamus

STONE: Green jasper

HERBS: Celandine, uva ursi

TREE: Hemlock

ITEMS: Moss, earth, stones dug up from underground, pictures of mine shafts, tree roots, pictures of trees uprooted by a storm, a model bulldozer, pictures of buildings being demolished, tapes of dramatic orchestral music, raw lumps of copper, raw unpolished stones

Pluto in Gemini

COLOR: Dark blue gray

ANIMAL: Goose

STONE: Tourmalinated quartz

HERBS: Bistort, fly agaric

TREE: Sandalwood

ITEMS: Artificial fingernails, books on handwriting analysis, surgery scalpels, X-ACTO knives, cameras, eyeballs, disembodied hands, books about witnesses to crimes, books about combat journalism, a sign saying "WITNESS PROTECTION"

Pluto in Cancer

COLOR: Dark purple gray

ANIMAL: Orca

STONE: Asbestos

HERBS: Lady's bedstraw, trillium

TREE: White mulberry

ITEMS: Photos of killer whales feeding, photos of dead whales cut up, pictures of animals and plants from the bottom of the sea, dried shells and claws of crustaceans, books and articles on child sexual abuse and emotional incest, pictures of devouring Mother Goddesses, a ruler for smacking a child's palms or a birch rod for beating students

Pluto in Leo

COLOR: Deep orange yellow

ANIMAL: Tiger

STONE: Cat's eye

HERBS: Frankincense, lion's tail

TREE: Magnolia

ITEMS: Portraits of famous historical monarchs with great power, a crown with black stones, tiger fur, books about the divine right of kings, photos of world leaders, photos of rock stars being worshipped by their fans, photos of famous actors being worshipped by their fans, fan letters to the Gods and Goddesses, photos of people worshipping famous dead people

Pluto in Virgo

COLOR: Dark russet brown

ANIMAL: Spider

STONE: Leopard jasper

HERBS: Witch hazel, elderberry

TREE: Elder

ITEMS: Clean bleached bones, lye soap, medicated soap, bleach, a hypodermic needle, sterile packaged medical instruments, anything hermetically sealed, Egyptian linen bandages, preservative spices, herbal tinctures, abortifacient herbs, an enema bag, pictures of corpse-devouring insects and worms, books on drastic alternative healing methods

Pluto in Libra

COLOR: Dark purple brown

ANIMAL: Owl

STONE: Iolite

HERBS: Columbine, damiana

TREE: Tamarisk

ITEMS: A black widow spider symbol, articles about or empty or full bottles of tranquilizers or mood stabilizers, books on power struggles in marriage, books and articles about spouse murderers, two empty wineglasses, pictures of models dressed in black, husband-and-wife bondage pornography

Pluto in Scorpio

COLOR: Deep blood red

ANIMAL: Cobra

STONE: Chiastolite

HERBS: Dragon's blood, mandrake

TREE: Pomegranate

ITEMS: A pressure cooker, a steaming mug of dark tea, black candles, a black leather coat, night vision goggles, blood, a bullwhip, chains, a devotional picture of Kali the Destroyer, tapes of heavy metal music, books on deep psychology, articles about murderers, books on anger management

Pluto in Sagittarius

COLOR: Dark orange brown

ANIMAL: Toad

STONE: Malachite

HERBS: Bittersweet, horsetail

TREE: Staghorn sumac

ITEMS: Wild animal skins, a bow and arrows for hunting, scrimshawed bones, a picture of a cornered wild animal, a Havahart trap for a large wild animal, hunting trophy heads, books about polyamory, books about travel to dangerous places, books about whistle-blowing and dangerous truth-telling

Pluto in Capricorn

COLOR: Dark purple black

ANIMALS: Alligator, crocodile

STONE: Nuumite

HERBS: Roseroot, lupine

TREE: Cypress

ITEMS: A model of a black limousine with blacked-out windows, a glass of bourbon, a black stone ashtray, expensive cigarettes, pictures of skyscrapers at night, pictures of forbidding-looking CEOs, articles about corporate corruption, a copy of Machiavelli's *The Prince*

Pluto in Aquarius

COLOR: Darkest magenta

ANIMAL: Bat

STONE: Igneous lava rock

HERBS: Pyrethrum Daisy, mezcal

TREE: Cocoa

ITEMS: Books of exotic and/or Tantric sexual practices, futuristic-looking sex toys, pictures of big cities at night, colored neon lights, pictures of mushroom clouds, plastic or metal cyborg figures, psychedelic spirals

Pluto in Pisces

COLOR: Deep violet

ANIMAL: Piranha

STONE: Alabaster

HERBS: Ivy, periwinkle

TREE: Tupelo

ITEMS: Books on deep-sea creatures, squids, and octopi; fishbones; pictures of crumbling temples and statuary, Pandora's box, undersea volcanos, and sunken ships; bags of garbage

16
Magical Prescriptions for Westerners

Some time ago, our newly forming Pagan church found itself in need of money to build a chapel. I'd been doing divinatory readings of various kinds for friends since I'd been in junior high, so I decided to use these skills to help with fund-raising. Due to my own religious restrictions, I'm not allowed to accept money for readings for my own benefit, but I can accept them on behalf of others. I set up a space in a friend's occult store one day a week and put up a sign saying that I was taking all comers, doing astrology, Tarot, runes, palmistry, Weirdin, or whatever they chose.

Most of my clients were ordinary sorts who just wanted a reading about their love lives or job situation or something like that. I expected those, and I was confident in my ability to handle them. What surprised me was the folks—often immigrants from third-world countries who spoke very little English—who expected more from a reader. They assumed that you would not only diagnose their problem but also give them some kind of magical remedy—a spell, a charm, a meditation, a ritual—to solve it. If I couldn't come up with something, they were openly disappointed. I learned, very quickly, how to think fast, combine symbolisms, choose from a spell-and-ritual buffet, and come up with a custom-made magical remedy for them. It gave me a great respect for the Vedic astrologers who do the same thing for their clients.

At the same time, I was watching Western astrologers arguing about the Vedic system of prescribing astrological remedies. Some claimed it was superstition and shouldn't be encouraged among Vedic astrologers, much less Western ones. Some claimed that it was psychologically useful and operated under the power of suggestion, which implied that it was all right to prescribe such things to benighted, ignorant brown people or particularly stupid white people, but that we educated intellectuals, of course, would have no need of such things. Some felt that it was an interesting cultural dead-end that had no use for us because, let's face it, we don't have sacred cows wandering the streets or local temples to Shiva in every town.

As a shaman and hedge-witch, I was disturbed not only by their ethnocentrism but by their attitude that anyone who believed in magic must be not just mistaken but clearly either an ignorant primitive or a delusional idiot. I looked over the lists of astrological remedies consulted by traditional Vedic astrologers, and although I didn't quite understand the cultural framework of some of them, most made a whole lot of sense. Since I am also just as polytheistic as the average Indian hill peasant, the idea of propitiating—meaning actively honoring and respecting—a deity or cosmic force in order to gain positive effects seemed quite reasonable to me.

One day while working as a reader in the occult store, I had a long chat with an Indian college student who wandered in to buy candles. We discussed the fact that astrology in the Western world is considered entirely a science, at least by astrologers. Much effort has gone into making it seem as cold and rational and scientific as possible. For other forms of divination such as scrying or palmistry, there's an assumption that the best readers have some sort of knack, like the Sight or some other psychic sensing ability. Astrology, on the other hand, is assumed to be a straightforward mathematical procedure that anyone can learn. In fact, if there is a knack that's considered useful for Western astrology, it's the left-brained ability to keep a whole lot of details straight in your head. All right, maybe you could also throw in an ability to translate things clearly for clients, if you're doing it professionally.

This contrasted with the experience of my Indian acquaintance, who had been taught that Vedic astrologers were expected to have some sort of psychic powers, if they were any good at all. Considering that the job description of Vedic astrologers includes so much magical advice, they pretty much have to be hedge-witches on top of being able to read and cast charts. In other words, they have to be just as good at the right-brained stuff as the left-brained stuff. Their clients expect more than just being told how they're screwed up or what awful things are going to happen to them; clients expect their Vedic astrologers to help them help themselves.

This was an astrological system that I could dig into . . . but there was the problem of cultural context. That led me to create the following chart, which should be comprehensive enough for any professional astrologer who wants to give remedies that any modern Westerner ought to be able to follow. It's also great for personal use; magical practitioners who need personal help during a difficult transit can find it themselves in this chart without having to pay any astrologer.

To use this chart with a computer program, just input the chart and print a list of transits, and then cross-check them with the remedies in this section. You will note that I have remedies not just for "negative" transits but also for "positive" ones; that's because you might want the option of getting the absolute best out of a positive transit. I refer to a transiting planet encountering a natal planet in a harsh, difficult way (as in squaring or opposing it) as *afflicting*. I refer to a transiting planet encountering a natal planet in a positive way (as in trining or sextiling) as *enhancing*. Remember that all conjunctions can be either positive or negative, or sometimes both at once. For conjunctions, I suggest using both the "afflicting" and the "enhancing" remedies.

To read the chart, find the transiting planet and start by making an altar of some kind, even a small one, to that planet in that sign, using the list in chapter 15. (You can also put together an altar that harmoniously combines both the transiting planet and your natal planet that's being affected.) Then check down this list to the transiting planet that's affecting you, including its sign and house—each section is listed by transiting planet—and put together the remedy. You can do one of the things or all of them; I included so many because not everyone can plant trees or get hold of rare herbs or buy expensive stones.

One note: When I use the term *to render service* to a specific person or organization, I don't mean breezing in and giving them something that you think they ought to have. I mean going humbly to them and asking, "Is there any way I can help you? What kind of help do you need?" This has to be real service, not done for an ego boost, or it won't have the desired effect.

You'll notice that the remedies for the personal and interpersonal planets—Sun through Saturn—have to do with rendering service to individuals, while the remedies for the transpersonal planets—Uranus, Neptune, and Pluto—mostly have to do with rendering service to organizations and groups. I should also add this caveat: These are only suggestions, not set in stone; if you think you can come up with something better and more appropriate to your situation, by all means go ahead.

THE REMEDIES

The Transiting Sun

Light a candle on the appropriate planetary altar.

Sun Transiting Natal Sun

AFFLICTING: Bring a symbol of the Sun with you, either the stones of the appropriate signs or at the least a talisman painted with a Sun symbol, and keep it hidden on your person, in a place where you will be very aware of it, to propitiate the Sun.

ENHANCING: Bring a symbol of the Sun with you, either the stones of the appropriate signs or at the least a talisman painted with a Sun symbol, and wear it openly to combine the energies with the most positive effect.

IN ARIES: Hike or run as far as you can physically stand . . .

IN TAURUS: Build something out of stone . . .

IN GEMINI: Write or carve words of inspiration on something . . .

IN CANCER: Play a game that you enjoyed playing as a child . . .

IN LEO: Leave something shiny and bright . . .

IN VIRGO: Clean up a mess . . .

IN LIBRA: Leave something of beauty . . .

IN SCORPIO: Search under things for hidden omens . . .

IN SAGITTARIUS: Take a long, rambling walk to see the sights . . .

IN CAPRICORN: Climb to a high place . . .

IN AQUARIUS: Bring something new and inspired . . .

IN PISCES: Recite poetry aloud . . .

IN THE FIRST HOUSE: . . . to or in front of a clothing store you like.

IN THE SECOND HOUSE: . . . in a place where wealthy people live.

IN THE THIRD HOUSE: . . . under a billboard.

IN THE FOURTH HOUSE: . . . in the neighborhood of your childhood home.

IN THE FIFTH HOUSE: . . . in a place of beauty.

IN THE SIXTH HOUSE: . . . in a place that contributes to your good health.

IN THE SEVENTH HOUSE: . . . in a romantic place where a couple could meet and tryst.

IN THE EIGHTH HOUSE: . . . in a dark, mysterious place.

IN THE NINTH HOUSE: . . . in a strange place more than a day's drive away.

IN THE TENTH HOUSE: . . . in a large corporate building.

IN THE ELEVENTH HOUSE: . . . to or at a social club or interest group center.

IN THE TWELFTH HOUSE: . . . to, in, or in front of a hospital or mental institution.

Sun Transiting Natal Moon

AFFLICTING: Wrap food offerings in yellow and gold packaging, or put Sun designs on it, or get yellow food to propitiate the Sun.

ENHANCING: Wrap food offerings in white or silver packaging, or put Moon or combined Sun-Moon symbols on it, or get white food to combine solar and lunar energies.

IN ARIES: Send food to a soldier in the military who is stationed far from home . . .

IN TAURUS: Bring food to a farmer, especially something they can't grow . . .

IN GEMINI: Give food to a writer or journalist or exchange student who is far from home . . .

IN CANCER: Give food to your mother, or someone who is like a mother to you, or if you have no one like this, someone who you feel symbolizes the most positive qualities of motherhood . . .

IN LEO: Give food to a struggling actor or musician . . .

IN VIRGO: Give food to someone who works a low-paying and invisible service job . . .

IN LIBRA: Give food to someone who frequently suffers from unjust discrimination due to their physical appearance . . .

IN SCORPIO: Give food to a sex worker . . .

IN SAGITTARIUS: Give food to a far traveler who misses home . . .

IN CAPRICORN: Give food to a small business owner who is struggling to make a project pay . . .

IN AQUARIUS: Give food to a full-time activist in a humanitarian cause . . .

IN PISCES: Give food to a homeless alcoholic or drug addict . . .

IN THE FIRST HOUSE: . . . and enclose a prayer that they may be able to get the attention they need.

IN THE SECOND HOUSE: . . . and enclose a prayer that they may gain wealth.

IN THE THIRD HOUSE: . . . and enclose a prayer that their words may ring with clarity.

IN THE FOURTH HOUSE: . . . and enclose a prayer for happiness in their (eventual) home.

IN THE FIFTH HOUSE: . . . and enclose a prayer that they may always feel free to be themselves.

IN THE SIXTH HOUSE: . . . and enclose a prayer that their hard work may reap a great harvest.

IN THE SEVENTH HOUSE: . . . and enclose a prayer that love might bless their lives.

IN THE EIGHTH HOUSE: . . . and enclose a prayer that they may walk through the dark unharmed.

IN THE NINTH HOUSE: . . . and enclose a prayer that they may find their own path and walk it with ease.

IN THE TENTH HOUSE: . . . and enclose a prayer that the world shall know their name and praise it.

IN THE ELEVENTH HOUSE: . . . and enclose a prayer that they shall have a wealth of friends.

IN THE TWELFTH HOUSE: . . . and enclose a prayer that they shall find a light in darkness.

Sun Transiting Natal Mercury

AFFLICTING: Draw a Sun symbol on the book (or magazine or other reading material) that you give out, to propitiate the Sun.

ENHANCING: Draw a Mercury symbol, or a combined Sun-Mercury symbol, on the book in order to combine their energies for greatest benefit.

IN ARIES: Give a book on courage . . .

IN TAURUS: Give a book on making money . . .

IN GEMINI: Give a book on communicating better . . .

IN CANCER: Give a cookbook . . .

IN LEO: Give a book of dramatic fiction . . .

IN VIRGO: Give a book on organizing your life . . .

IN LIBRA: Give a book on social justice . . .

IN SCORPIO: Give a detective, mystery, or horror novel . . .

IN SAGITTARIUS: Give a book on far countries or other cultures . . .

IN CAPRICORN: Give a book on getting ahead in your job . . .

IN AQUARIUS: Give a book on computers . . .

IN PISCES: Give a book of poetry . . .

IN THE FIRST HOUSE: . . . to a public figure.

IN THE SECOND HOUSE: . . . to a builder of houses.

IN THE THIRD HOUSE: . . . to a journalist or writer of nonfiction.

IN THE FOURTH HOUSE: . . . to a teacher of children.

IN THE FIFTH HOUSE: . . . to a writer of fiction.

IN THE SIXTH HOUSE: . . . to a doctor or other health professional.

IN THE SEVENTH HOUSE: . . . to a married couple.

IN THE EIGHTH HOUSE: . . . to a tax accountant.

IN THE NINTH HOUSE: . . . to a library.

IN THE TENTH HOUSE: . . . to a politician.

IN THE ELEVENTH HOUSE: . . . to a club, social group, or humanitarian nonprofit group.

IN THE TWELFTH HOUSE: . . . to someone in prison.

Sun Transiting Natal Venus

AFFLICTING: Take someone out to do an activity that strongly resonates with their identity and that their current love life stifles, prevents, or at least discourages. If possible, have them do the same for you. While doing the activity, keep a symbol of the Sun hidden, to propitiate it.

ENHANCING: Pay for, arrange, or otherwise provide for a pair of lovers to do an activity together that supports their identity and goals as a couple. Give them a Sun symbol to wear openly, in appreciation.

IN ARIES: Take them to a sporting event or on a risky adventure . . .

IN TAURUS: Take them for a massage or other sensual pleasure . . .

IN GEMINI: Take them to a book or poetry reading . . .

IN CANCER: Take them to a historical recreation park . . .

IN LEO: Take them to a theatrical production . . .

IN VIRGO: Take them on a tour of a factory . . .

IN LIBRA: Take them for a makeover or to an art museum . . .

IN SCORPIO: Take them to a dark and slightly sleazy club . . .

IN SAGITTARIUS: Take them camping in the wilderness . . .

IN CAPRICORN: Take them on a tour of a large business . . .

IN AQUARIUS: Take them to a concert of unusual music . . .

IN PISCES: Take them to a session of meditation, Reiki, or energy healing . . .

IN THE FIRST HOUSE: . . . and remind them that they are still individuals.

IN THE SECOND HOUSE: . . . and remind them that it's OK to have their own values.

IN THE THIRD HOUSE: . . . and remind them that communication is important.

IN THE FOURTH HOUSE: . . . and remind them that they still have family, regardless of blood kin.

IN THE FIFTH HOUSE: . . . and remind them that having creative fun is important.

IN THE SIXTH HOUSE: . . . and remind them that mentorship is important.

IN THE SEVENTH HOUSE: . . . and remind them that fair love leaves space for lovers to be themselves.

IN THE EIGHTH HOUSE: . . . and remind them that they still have a sexual spark.

IN THE NINTH HOUSE: . . . and remind them that their cultural framework is not the only one.

IN THE TENTH HOUSE: . . . and remind them that their life goals are still achievable.

IN THE ELEVENTH HOUSE: . . . and remind them that having and being friends is important.

IN THE TWELFTH HOUSE: . . . and remind them that their secret dreams are important.

Sun Transiting Natal Mars

AFFLICTING: Find someone whose anger or aggressive feelings are preventing them from expressing themselves properly, and take them to the event listed below. If you merely pay for the outing rather than take them, wrap the money or tickets in gold paper with red ribbons.

ENHANCING: Find someone who does some sport or physical thing that you are envious of, and take them to the event listed below. If you merely pay for the outing rather than take them, wrap the money or tickets in red paper with gold ribbons.

IN ARIES: Take them to play an aggressive physical sport with friends . . .

IN TAURUS: Take them to get a deep body-work massage . . .

IN GEMINI: Take them on a bicycle trip at high speed or a motorcycle ride . . .

IN CANCER: Take them to play rough-and-tumble games with children . . .

IN LEO: Take them dancing in a public place . . .

IN VIRGO: Take them to a drum circle . . .

IN LIBRA: Take them to see (or take part in) a debate . . .

IN SCORPIO: Take them on an endurance course . . .

IN SAGITTARIUS: Take them hiking up a mountain . . .

IN CAPRICORN: Take them to a job fair . . .

IN AQUARIUS: Take them to a protest or political rally . . .

IN PISCES: Take them to a loud concert with wild trance dancing . . .

IN THE FIRST HOUSE: . . . and encourage them to express their individuality.

IN THE SECOND HOUSE: . . . and get them to talk about what they'd do if they won the lottery.

IN THE THIRD HOUSE: . . . and get them to yell, loudly.

IN THE FOURTH HOUSE: . . . and get them to vent about whether their family supports their individuality.

IN THE FIFTH HOUSE: . . . and get them to talk about whether people appreciate them.

IN THE SIXTH HOUSE: . . . and get them to vent about being a cog for their day job.

IN THE SEVENTH HOUSE: . . . and get them to talk about whether their relationships repress them.

IN THE EIGHTH HOUSE: . . . and get them to talk about the compromises they make for their sex life.

IN THE NINTH HOUSE: . . . and get them to talk about some faraway place that they've always dreamed of visiting.

IN THE TENTH HOUSE: . . . and get them to talk about the career that would be most "them."

IN THE ELEVENTH HOUSE: . . . and get them to talk about how the groups they belong to support or repress their individuality.

IN THE TWELFTH HOUSE: . . . and get them to talk about their repressed anger.

Sun Transiting Natal Jupiter

AFFLICTING: Give a gift to someone who has given up wealth and prestige to follow the beat of their own drum. Wrap the gift in purple paper and ribbons.

ENHANCING: Give a gift to someone who has managed to earn wealth and prestige by following the beat of their own drum. Wrap the gift in purple paper and ribbons.

IN ARIES: Your gift should be very individual to them . . .

IN TAURUS: Your gift should support their physical comfort . . .

IN GEMINI: Your gift should pay their phone bill, Internet connection, or the like . . .

IN CANCER: Your gift should be of food . . .

IN LEO: Your gift should make them feel important . . .

IN VIRGO: Your gift should support their basic practical needs . . .

IN LIBRA: Your gift should beautify their world . . .

IN SCORPIO: Your gift should entice their sense of mystery . . .

IN SAGITTARIUS: Your gift should further their higher education . . .

IN CAPRICORN: Your gift should support their career goals . . .

IN AQUARIUS: Your gift should support a social group or cause that they believe in . . .

IN PISCES: Your gift should support their spiritual life . . .

IN THE FIRST HOUSE: . . . and be attached to a wish for good luck in protection.

IN THE SECOND HOUSE: . . . and be attached to a wish for financial good luck.

IN THE THIRD HOUSE: . . . and be attached to a wish for a silver tongue.

IN THE FOURTH HOUSE: . . . and be attached to a wish for good luck for their family.

IN THE FIFTH HOUSE: . . . and be attached to a wish for good luck in impressing people.

IN THE SIXTH HOUSE: . . . and be attached to a wish for rewards after hard work.

IN THE SEVENTH HOUSE: . . . and be attached to a wish for happy marriage.

IN THE EIGHTH HOUSE: . . . and be attached to a wish for a great inheritance someday.

IN THE NINTH HOUSE: . . . and be attached to a wish for safety in travel.

IN THE TENTH HOUSE: . . . and be attached to a wish for fame and fortune in the public eye.

IN THE ELEVENTH HOUSE: . . . and be attached to a wish for good fortune in friends.

IN THE TWELFTH HOUSE: . . . and be attached to a wish for open-hearted faith.

Sun Transiting Natal Saturn

AFFLICTING: Give a gift to someone who is struggling to find their identity as a human being and is having a difficult time of it.

ENHANCING: Give a gift to someone who has struggled to find their identity as a human being, has succeeded, and is a role model for you in that way.

IN ARIES: Your gift should remove an obstacle in their ability to get out and exercise . . .

IN TAURUS: Your gift should remove a small financial obstacle . . .

IN GEMINI: Your gift should remove an obstacle in their ability to make short trips . . .

IN CANCER: Your gift should remove an obstacle in keeping their house clean . . .

IN LEO: Your gift should remove an obstacle in their ability to look good . . .

IN VIRGO: Your gift should remove an obstacle in their ability to keep organized . . .

IN LIBRA: Your gift should remove an obstacle in achieving justice in an unjust situation . . .

IN SCORPIO: Your gift should remove an obstacle for their ability to express strong feelings . . .

IN SAGITTARIUS: Your gift should remove an obstacle in their ability to attend a spiritual event . . .

IN CAPRICORN: Your gift should remove an obstacle in their ability to get ahead in their job . . .

IN AQUARIUS: Your gift should remove an obstacle in their ability to attend an interest group . . .

IN PISCES: Your gift should remove an obstacle in their ability to believe in miracles . . .

IN THE FIRST HOUSE: . . . and help them feel more motivated to be active.

IN THE SECOND HOUSE: . . . and help them feel more financially secure.

IN THE THIRD HOUSE: . . . and help them feel more able to ask for what they want.

IN THE FOURTH HOUSE: . . . and help them feel happier in their home.

IN THE FIFTH HOUSE: . . . and help them feel more comfortable with taking risks.

IN THE SIXTH HOUSE: . . . and help them feel more physically healthy.

IN THE SEVENTH HOUSE: . . . and help them feel less alone.

IN THE EIGHTH HOUSE: . . . and help them feel more able to count on others for help.

IN THE NINTH HOUSE: . . . and help them feel more able to move around.

IN THE TENTH HOUSE: . . . and help them feel more motivated to succeed.

IN THE ELEVENTH HOUSE: . . . and help them feel more like part of a group.

IN THE TWELFTH HOUSE: . . . and help them feel more faith that things will turn out well.

Sun Transiting Natal Uranus

AFFLICTING: Give aid to an activist for a minority identity that is struggling to be known and heard.

ENHANCING: Give aid to an activist for a minority identity that has been a long-standing, experienced voice in our society.

IN ARIES: Your gift should help some immediate emergency . . .

IN TAURUS: Your gift should help them obtain a solid foundation for their work . . .

IN GEMINI: Your gift should help make a change in their ability to disseminate information . . .

IN CANCER: Your gift should help make a change in their ability to work from home . . .

IN LEO: Your gift should help make a change in promoting them . . .

IN VIRGO: Your gift should help make a change in how they organize the details of their work . . .

IN LIBRA: Your gift should help make a change in their ability to find useful partners . . .

IN SCORPIO: Your gift should help make a change in their ability to face emotional adversity . . .

IN SAGITTARIUS: Your gift should help make a change in their ability to dream big . . .

IN CAPRICORN: Your gift should make a change in their ability to be seen as an authority . . .

IN AQUARIUS: Your gift should go directly toward their wildest goal . . .

IN PISCES: Your gift should make a change in their resources for handling stress . . .

IN THE FIRST HOUSE: . . . regarding their public image.

IN THE SECOND HOUSE: . . . regarding financial solvency.

IN THE THIRD HOUSE: . . . regarding education about their cause.

IN THE FOURTH HOUSE: . . . regarding the ways their cause affects families.

IN THE FIFTH HOUSE: . . . regarding the ways their cause affects children.

IN THE SIXTH HOUSE: . . . regarding the ways their cause can be practically implemented.

IN THE SEVENTH HOUSE: . . . regarding the ways their cause is a natural ally of other causes.

IN THE EIGHTH HOUSE: . . . regarding financial aid from other parties.

IN THE NINTH HOUSE: . . . regarding the ways they can be heard in higher education.

IN THE TENTH HOUSE: . . . regarding the ways their cause can be a real career for them.

IN THE ELEVENTH HOUSE: . . . regarding the ways they can gain more volunteers.

IN THE TWELFTH HOUSE: . . . regarding the ways they can reach those who have no access.

Sun Transiting Natal Neptune

AFFLICTING: Give a gift to someone who has recently made a radical change in religious affiliations and who is happy and content with their choice.

ENHANCING: Give a gift to someone who is having a faithquake and struggling with the direction of their spiritual life.

IN ARIES: Give them a gift that encourages them to get out and exercise . . .

IN TAURUS: Give them a gift that aids their financial situation . . .

IN GEMINI: Give them a book that concerns their spiritual path . . .

IN CANCER: Buy or cook them a meal that reflects their spiritual values regarding food . . .

IN LEO: Take them to a performance that celebrates aspects of their spirituality . . .

IN VIRGO: Give them a gift that helps them integrate spirituality into their ordinary work life . . .

IN LIBRA: Give them a gift of something beautiful that also inspires them . . .

IN SCORPIO: Give them a gift that encourages the mystical side of their faith . . .

IN SAGITTARIUS: Give them a gift that aids their religious education . . .

IN CAPRICORN: Give them a gift that celebrates the oldest traditions of their faith . . .

IN AQUARIUS: Give them a gift that reflects new and progressive developments in their faith . . .

IN PISCES: Give them a gift that encourages them to be alone and meditate . . .

IN THE FIRST HOUSE: . . . and provides unbiased information about how their faith looks to others.

IN THE SECOND HOUSE: . . . and honors their new spiritual values.

IN THE THIRD HOUSE: . . . and furthers communication between their faith and others.

IN THE FOURTH HOUSE: . . . and helps them integrate their spirituality and their home life.

IN THE FIFTH HOUSE: . . . and helps them to think about the spirituality of Love.

IN THE SIXTH HOUSE: . . . and helps them remember that their life still has a practical side.

IN THE SEVENTH HOUSE: . . . and aids them in finding a spiritual mentor of some kind.

IN THE EIGHTH HOUSE: . . . and helps them to weather this change of life.

IN THE NINTH HOUSE: . . . and encourages them to travel somewhere important to their faith.

IN THE TENTH HOUSE: . . . and encourages them to integrate their spiritual values with their career.

IN THE ELEVENTH HOUSE: . . . and encourages them to discover other interest groups.

IN THE TWELFTH HOUSE: . . . and encourages them to commune with the Divine in their own way.

Sun Transiting Natal Pluto

ENHANCING: Give a gift to someone whose life was turned upside down, who had to start over with a new sense of identity, and who has done well for it.

AFFLICTING: Give a gift to someone whose life was turned upside down, who had to start over with a new sense of identity, and who has suffered social ostracism for it, but who has never wavered in their convictions.

IN ARIES: Give aid to a soldier who can no longer do his or her job . . .

IN TAURUS: Give aid to someone who became suddenly impoverished . . .

IN GEMINI: Give aid to someone who has suffered brain damage . . .

IN CANCER: Give aid to a child who has any of the above conditions . . .

IN LEO: Give aid to someone who has gone blind . . .

IN VIRGO: Give aid to someone who has gone deaf . . .

IN LIBRA: Give aid to someone who has been released from many years in prison . . .

IN SCORPIO: Give aid to someone who has come down with a possibly fatal illness . . .

IN SAGITTARIUS: Give aid to refugees from countries in turmoil . . .

IN CAPRICORN: Give aid to someone who has become severely physically disabled . . .

IN AQUARIUS: Give aid to someone who has undergone sex reassignment . . .

IN PISCES: Give aid to someone who has come down with chronic mental illness . . .

IN THE FIRST HOUSE: . . . and the gift should help them feel better about their appearance.

IN THE SECOND HOUSE: . . . and the gift should go toward a financial goal.

IN THE THIRD HOUSE: . . . and the gift should help them find information that they need.

IN THE FOURTH HOUSE: . . . and the gift should go toward finding or funding appropriate housing.

IN THE FIFTH HOUSE: . . . and the gift should give them some happiness.

IN THE SIXTH HOUSE: . . . and the gift should go toward medical care.

IN THE SEVENTH HOUSE: . . . and the gift should go toward a supportive mentor for them.

IN THE EIGHTH HOUSE: . . . and the gift should help them to survive despair.

IN THE NINTH HOUSE: . . . and the gift should go toward their education.

IN THE TENTH HOUSE: . . . and the gift should aid them in dealing with the government.

IN THE ELEVENTH HOUSE: . . . and the gift should help them connect with support groups or events.

IN THE TWELFTH HOUSE: . . . and the gift should go toward therapy or healing.

The Transiting Moon

Place a chalice of milk on the appropriate altar.

Moon Transiting Natal Sun

ENHANCING: Give a gift to your father, or if he is not alive or not around to know you, give a gift to someone who embodies paternal energy to you.

AFFLICTING: Give a gift to someone who is struggling to be a good father, but who sometimes fails. If this describes your father, give a gift to him.

IN ARIES: Give him a gift that encourages him to exercise . . .

IN TAURUS: Give him a gift that makes him more comfortable . . .

IN GEMINI: Give him a gift that stimulates him intellectually . . .

IN CANCER: Give him a gift that helps him spend more quality time with his kids . . .

IN LEO: Give him a gift that makes him feel like a king . . .

IN VIRGO: Give him a gift that helps him get organized . . .

IN LIBRA: Give him a gift to remedy some injustice in his life . . .

IN SCORPIO: Give him a gift of something he feels passionately intense about . . .

IN SAGITTARIUS: Give him a gift that broadens his horizons . . .

IN CAPRICORN: Give him a gift that aids his career . . .

IN AQUARIUS: Give him a gift that must be used with a group of friends . . .

IN PISCES: Give him a gift that shows how much compassion you have for him . . .

IN THE FIRST HOUSE: . . . and tell him that he is courageous not to have given up.

IN THE SECOND HOUSE: . . . and help him build something useful.

IN THE THIRD HOUSE: . . . and have a good conversation with him.

IN THE FOURTH HOUSE: . . . and do something to give him more time to be with his kids.

IN THE FIFTH HOUSE: . . . and take him to some entertainment.

IN THE SIXTH HOUSE: . . . and help him clean his house.

IN THE SEVENTH HOUSE: . . . and give him two tickets that he can use as he wishes.

IN THE EIGHTH HOUSE: . . . and let him use some resource of yours.

IN THE NINTH HOUSE: . . . and drive him somewhere.

IN THE TENTH HOUSE: . . . and give him a job reference or referral.

IN THE ELEVENTH HOUSE: . . . and spend time just being his friend.

IN THE TWELFTH HOUSE: . . . and encourage him to follow his dreams.

Moon Transiting Natal Moon

ENHANCING: Give a gift to your mother, or if she is not alive or not around to know you, give a gift to someone who embodies maternal energy to you.

AFFLICTING: Give a gift to someone who is struggling to be a good mother, but who sometimes fails. If this description fits your own mother, give her the gift.

IN ARIES: Give her a gift that encourages her to exercise . . .

IN TAURUS: Give her a gift that makes her feel physically pampered . . .

IN GEMINI: Give her a gift that stimulates her intellectually . . .

IN CANCER: Give her a gift that helps her do her mothering job . . .

IN LEO: Give her a gift that makes her feel beautiful . . .

IN VIRGO: Give her a gift that helps her get organized . . .

IN LIBRA: Give her a gift that beautifies her surroundings . . .

IN SCORPIO: Give her a gift of something that she feels passionately intense about . . .

IN SAGITTARIUS: Give her a gift that broadens her horizons . . .

IN CAPRICORN: Give her a gift that helps her in her career . . .

IN AQUARIUS: Give her a gift that must be used with a group of friends . . .

IN PISCES: Give her a gift that shows how much compassion you have for her . . .

IN THE FIRST HOUSE: . . . and tell her that she is courageous not to have given up.

IN THE SECOND HOUSE: . . . and help her build something useful.

IN THE THIRD HOUSE: . . . and have a good conversation with her.

IN THE FOURTH HOUSE: . . . and take her kids off her hands for a while.

IN THE FIFTH HOUSE: . . . and take her to some entertainment.

IN THE SIXTH HOUSE: . . . and help her clean her house.

IN THE SEVENTH HOUSE: . . . and give her two tickets that she can use as she wishes.

IN THE EIGHTH HOUSE: . . . and let her use some resource of yours.

IN THE NINTH HOUSE: . . . and drive her somewhere.

IN THE TENTH HOUSE: . . . and give her a job reference or referral.

IN THE ELEVENTH HOUSE: . . . and spend time just being her friend.

IN THE TWELFTH HOUSE: . . . and encourage her to follow her dreams.

Moon Transiting Natal Mercury

ENHANCING: Give a gift to someone who acted as a teacher in your life and whose lessons came easily and were welcomed.

AFFLICTING: Give a gift to someone who acted as a teacher in your life and whose lessons were difficult but necessary.

IN ARIES: Give a teacher who taught you about courage . . .

IN TAURUS: Give a teacher who taught you about money . . .

IN GEMINI: Give a teacher who taught you about books . . .

IN CANCER: Give a teacher who made you feel listened to . . .

IN LEO: Give a teacher who increased your self-esteem . . .

IN VIRGO: Give a teacher who taught you math or science . . .

IN LIBRA: Give a teacher who taught you about fairness . . .

IN SCORPIO: Give a teacher who made you think deeply . . .

IN SAGITTARIUS: Give a teacher who broadened your horizons . . .

IN CAPRICORN: Give a teacher who taught you job skills . . .

IN AQUARIUS: Give a teacher who made you think about the future . . .

IN PISCES: Give a teacher who was sensitive to your needs . . .

IN THE FIRST HOUSE: . . . a gift certificate to a gym or clothing store.

IN THE SECOND HOUSE: . . . a gift certificate to a department store.

IN THE THIRD HOUSE: . . . a gift certificate to a small bookstore.

IN THE FOURTH HOUSE: . . . a gift certificate to a home furnishings store.

IN THE FIFTH HOUSE: . . . a gift certificate to an arts and crafts store.

IN THE SIXTH HOUSE: . . . a gift certificate to a hardware store.

IN THE SEVENTH HOUSE: . . . a gift certificate to a place they might like to go with a partner.

IN THE EIGHTH HOUSE: . . . a gift certificate to an unusual gift store.

IN THE NINTH HOUSE: . . . a gift certificate to a large bookstore.

IN THE TENTH HOUSE: . . . a gift certificate to a store that specializes in their career.

IN THE ELEVENTH HOUSE: . . . a gift certificate to a club.

IN THE TWELFTH HOUSE: . . . a gift certificate to the movies.

Moon Transiting Natal Venus

ENHANCING: Give a gift to a happily married couple who are confirmed homebodies and whose home is a place of warmth and safety where strangers can take shelter.

AFFLICTING: Give a gift to a happily married couple who are confirmed homebodies, but who could really use a chance to get out and do something different.

IN ARIES: Give them a gift that helps them get some exercise . . .

IN TAURUS: Give them a gift that clears up a financial burden . . .

IN GEMINI: Give them a gift that stimulates them intellectually . . .

IN CANCER: Give them a gift that makes their home more comfortable . . .

IN LEO: Give them a gift that allows them individual expression . . .

IN VIRGO: Give them a gift that helps them get organized . . .

IN LIBRA: Give them a gift that beautifies their surroundings . . .

IN SCORPIO: Give them a gift that sparks their passions . . .

IN SAGITTARIUS: Give them a gift that sends them out traveling . . .

IN CAPRICORN: Give them a gift that teaches them new skills . . .

IN AQUARIUS: Give them a gift that gets them doing something entirely new . . .

IN PISCES: Give them a gift that helps them to find spiritual comfort . . .

IN THE FIRST HOUSE: . . . in a way that makes them feel better about themselves physically.

IN THE SECOND HOUSE: . . . in a way that respects their values.

IN THE THIRD HOUSE: . . . in a way that stimulates conversation.

IN THE FOURTH HOUSE: . . . in a way that connects them to the past.

IN THE FIFTH HOUSE: . . . in a way that inspires creativity.

IN THE SIXTH HOUSE: . . . in a way that frees them up from some routine chore.

IN THE SEVENTH HOUSE: . . . in a way that they can enjoy only as a couple.

IN THE EIGHTH HOUSE: . . . in a way that lasts until their deaths and beyond.

IN THE NINTH HOUSE: . . . in a way that expands their horizons.

IN THE TENTH HOUSE: . . . in a way that helps them with their careers.

IN THE ELEVENTH HOUSE: . . . in a way that helps them bond with friends.

IN THE TWELFTH HOUSE: . . . in a way that makes them consider the flow of their life.

Moon Transiting Natal Mars

ENHANCING: Give a gift to a hard-driving double-career couple, especially two who work together on the same business, and who are trying to balance home and work.

AFFLICTING: Give a gift to a hard-driving double-career couple, especially two who work together on the same business but who are having great difficulty balancing home and work.

IN ARIES: Give them a gift that helps them get some exercise . . .

IN TAURUS: Give them a gift that clears up a financial burden . . .

IN GEMINI: Give them a gift that stimulates them intellectually . . .

IN CANCER: Give them a gift that makes their home more comfortable . . .

IN LEO: Give them a gift that allows them individual expression . . .

IN VIRGO: Give them a gift that helps them get organized . . .

IN LIBRA: Give them a gift that beautifies their surroundings . . .

IN SCORPIO: Give them a gift that sparks their passions . . .

IN SAGITTARIUS: Give them a gift that sends them out traveling . . .

IN CAPRICORN: Give them a gift that teaches them new skills . . .

IN AQUARIUS: Give them a gift that gets them doing something entirely new . . .

IN PISCES: Give them a gift that gives them spiritual comfort . . .

IN THE FIRST HOUSE: . . . in a way that makes them feel better about themselves physically.

IN THE SECOND HOUSE: . . . in a way that respects their values.

IN THE THIRD HOUSE: . . . in a way that stimulates conversation.

IN THE FOURTH HOUSE: . . . in a way that connects them to the past.

IN THE FIFTH HOUSE: . . . in a way that inspires creativity.

IN THE SIXTH HOUSE: . . . in a way that frees them up from some routine chore.

IN THE SEVENTH HOUSE: . . . in a way that they can enjoy only as a couple.

IN THE EIGHTH HOUSE: . . . in a way that lasts until their deaths and beyond.

IN THE NINTH HOUSE: . . . in a way that expands their horizons.

IN THE TENTH HOUSE: . . . in a way that helps them with their careers.

IN THE ELEVENTH HOUSE: . . . in a way that helps them bond with friends.

IN THE TWELFTH HOUSE: . . . in a way that makes them consider the flow of their life.

Moon Transiting Natal Jupiter

ENHANCING: Give a gift to a happy family who have plenty of resources that they share generously with others and whose home is open to many folk in need.

AFFLICTING: Give a gift to a family in crisis who have limited resources and whose home situation is in danger due to outside circumstances.

IN ARIES: Give them a gift that defends them against danger . . .

IN TAURUS: Give them a gift that clears up a financial burden . . .

IN GEMINI: Give them a gift that helps with local travel . . .

IN CANCER: Give them a gift that makes their home more secure . . .

IN LEO: Give them a gift that helps them feel proud as a family . . .

IN VIRGO: Give them a gift that helps them get organized . . .

IN LIBRA: Give them a gift that fights against injustice . . .

IN SCORPIO: Give them a gift that helps them deal with rage and frustration . . .

IN SAGITTARIUS: Give them a gift that helps with long-range transportation . . .

IN CAPRICORN: Give them a gift that teaches them new skills . . .

IN AQUARIUS: Give them a gift that gets them doing something entirely new . . .

IN PISCES: Give them a gift that gives them spiritual comfort . . .

IN THE FIRST HOUSE: . . . in a way that makes them feel better about how they look to the community.

IN THE SECOND HOUSE: . . . in a way that respects their values.

IN THE THIRD HOUSE: . . . in a way that stimulates ideas and conversation.

IN THE FOURTH HOUSE: . . . in a way that directly helps their home situation.

IN THE FIFTH HOUSE: . . . in a way that gives them some much-needed fun.

IN THE SIXTH HOUSE: . . . in a way that helps them with their health.

IN THE SEVENTH HOUSE: . . . in a way that helps the relationships of the adults.

IN THE EIGHTH HOUSE: . . . in a way that lasts until their deaths and beyond.

IN THE NINTH HOUSE: . . . in a way that helps them to keep faith.

IN THE TENTH HOUSE: . . . in a way that helps them with bureaucracies and agencies.

IN THE ELEVENTH HOUSE: . . . in a way that helps them make friends and allies.

IN THE TWELFTH HOUSE: . . . in a way that helps them get healing and counseling.

Moon Transiting Natal Saturn

ENHANCING: Give a gift to a child whose parents are no longer caring for them, but who is well cared for by grandparents.

AFFLICTING: Give a gift to a child whose family has been broken apart and who is living in foster care or in an institution.

IN ARIES: Give them a gift that helps them deal with anger . . .

IN TAURUS: Give them a gift that clears a financial blockage . . .

IN GEMINI: Give them a gift of written words . . .

IN CANCER: Give them a gift that helps their home life be more supportive of their goals . . .

IN LEO: Give them a gift that helps them express themselves . . .

IN VIRGO: Give them a gift that teaches them practical skills for the future . . .

IN LIBRA: Give them a gift that clears some small unfairness . . .

IN SCORPIO: Give them a gift that helps their will to survive . . .

IN SAGITTARIUS: Give them a gift that furthers their education . . .

IN CAPRICORN: Give them a gift that helps their future career . . .

IN AQUARIUS: Give them a gift that helps them feel good about being different . . .

IN PISCES: Give them a gift that relieves their stress and turmoil . . .

IN THE FIRST HOUSE: . . . in a way that tells them you appreciate them for who they are.

IN THE SECOND HOUSE: . . . in a way that reminds them of what is really important.

IN THE THIRD HOUSE: . . . in a way that inspires them to write or talk.

IN THE FOURTH HOUSE: . . . in a way that helps them feel like part of a family or tribe.

IN THE FIFTH HOUSE: . . . in a way that helps them take joy in life.

IN THE SIXTH HOUSE: . . . in a way that helps them take better care of their health.

IN THE SEVENTH HOUSE: . . . in a way that helps them feel like things are more fair.

IN THE EIGHTH HOUSE: . . . in a way that challenges them emotionally.

IN THE NINTH HOUSE: . . . in a way that expands their mind.

IN THE TENTH HOUSE: . . . in a way that helps to plan their future.

IN THE ELEVENTH HOUSE: . . . in a way that reminds them that they have friends.

IN THE TWELFTH HOUSE: . . . in a way that gives them a space in which to do some healing.

Moon Transiting Natal Uranus

ENHANCING: Give aid to an activist whose cause is helping children to thrive.

AFFLICTING: Give aid to an activist whose cause is helping children in crisis.

IN ARIES: Your gift should help some immediate emergency . . .

IN TAURUS: Your gift should help them obtain a solid foundation for their work . . .

IN GEMINI: Your gift should help make a change in their ability to disseminate information . . .

IN CANCER: Your gift should help make a change in their ability to work from home . . .

IN LEO: Your gift should help make a change in promoting them . . .

IN VIRGO: Your gift should help make a change in how they organize the details of their work . . .

IN LIBRA: Your gift should help make a change in their ability to find useful partners . . .

IN SCORPIO: Your gift should help make a change in their ability to face emotional adversity . . .

IN SAGITTARIUS: Your gift should help make a change in their ability to dream big . . .

IN CAPRICORN: Your gift should make a change in their ability to be seen as an authority . . .

IN AQUARIUS: Your gift should go directly toward their wildest goal . . .

IN PISCES: Your gift should make a change in their resources for handling stress . . .

IN THE FIRST HOUSE: . . . with regard to their public image.

IN THE SECOND HOUSE: . . . regarding financial solvency.

IN THE THIRD HOUSE: . . . regarding education about their cause.

IN THE FOURTH HOUSE: . . . regarding the ways their cause affects families.

IN THE FIFTH HOUSE: . . . regarding creative ways to spread the word.

IN THE SIXTH HOUSE: . . . regarding the ways their cause can be practically implemented.

IN THE SEVENTH HOUSE: . . . regarding the ways their cause is a natural ally of other causes.

IN THE EIGHTH HOUSE: . . . regarding financial aid from other parties.

IN THE NINTH HOUSE: . . . regarding the ways they can be heard in higher education.

IN THE TENTH HOUSE: . . . regarding the ways their cause can be a real career for them.

IN THE ELEVENTH HOUSE: . . . regarding the ways they can gain more volunteers.

IN THE TWELFTH HOUSE: . . . regarding the ways they can reach those who have no access.

Moon Transiting Natal Neptune

ENHANCING: Give a gift to a woman who practices women's spirituality and is an avatar of female magic and positive energy.

AFFLICTING: Give a gift to a woman who is afflicted with a mental illness or addiction and who needs spirituality in her life.

IN ARIES: Give them a gift that encourages them to face something that they fear . . .

IN TAURUS: Give them a gift that aids their financial situation . . .

IN GEMINI: Give them a book that concerns their spiritual path . . .

IN CANCER: Buy or cook them a meal that reflects their spiritual values regarding food . . .

IN LEO: Take them to a performance that celebrates aspects of their spirituality . . .

IN VIRGO: Give them a gift that helps them integrate spirituality into their ordinary work life . . .

IN LIBRA: Give them a gift of something beautiful that also inspires them . . .

IN SCORPIO: Give them a gift that encourages the mystical side of their faith . . .

IN SAGITTARIUS: Give them a gift that aids their religious education . . .

IN CAPRICORN: Give them a gift that celebrates the oldest traditions of their faith . . .

IN AQUARIUS: Give them a gift that reflects new and progressive developments in their faith . . .

IN PISCES: Give them a gift that encourages them to be alone and meditate . . .

IN THE FIRST HOUSE: . . . and provides unbiased information about how their faith looks to others.

IN THE SECOND HOUSE: . . . and honors their new spiritual values.

IN THE THIRD HOUSE: . . . and furthers communication between their faith and others.

IN THE FOURTH HOUSE: . . . and helps them integrate their spirituality and their home life.

IN THE FIFTH HOUSE: . . . and helps them to think about the spirituality of Love.

IN THE SIXTH HOUSE: . . . and helps them remember that their life still has a practical side.

IN THE SEVENTH HOUSE: . . . and aids them in finding a spiritual mentor of some kind.

IN THE EIGHTH HOUSE: . . . and helps them to weather this change of life.

IN THE NINTH HOUSE: . . . and encourages them to travel somewhere important to their faith.

IN THE TENTH HOUSE: . . . and encourages them to integrate their spiritual values with their career.

IN THE ELEVENTH HOUSE: . . . and encourages them to discover other interest groups.

IN THE TWELFTH HOUSE: . . . and encourages them to commune with the Divine in their own way.

Moon Transiting Natal Pluto

ENHANCING: Give a gift to a family who has been struck by chaos through war, death, disease, or other terrifying circumstances, and has survived the ordeal stronger than before.

AFFLICTING: Give a gift to a family who has been struck by chaos through war, death, disease, or other terrifying circumstances, and has been blown apart by it.

IN ARIES: Give them a gift that helps them deal with anger . . .

IN TAURUS: Give them a gift that clears a financial blockage . . .

IN GEMINI: Give them a gift of written words . . .

IN CANCER: Give them a gift that helps their home life be more supportive of their goals . . .

IN LEO: Give them a gift that helps them express themselves . . .

IN VIRGO: Give them a gift that teaches them practical skills for the future . . .

IN LIBRA: Give them a gift that clears some small unfairness . . .

IN SCORPIO: Give them a gift that helps their will to survive . . .

IN SAGITTARIUS: Give them a gift that furthers their education . . .

IN CAPRICORN: Give them a gift that helps their future career . . .

IN AQUARIUS: Give them a gift that helps them feel good about being different . . .

IN PISCES: Give them a gift that relieves their stress and turmoil . . .

IN THE FIRST HOUSE: . . . in a way that tells them you appreciate them for who they are.

IN THE SECOND HOUSE: . . . in a way that reminds them of what is really important.

IN THE THIRD HOUSE: . . . in a way that inspires them to write or talk.

IN THE FOURTH HOUSE: . . . in a way that helps them feel like part of a family or tribe.

IN THE FIFTH HOUSE: . . . in a way that helps them take joy in life.

IN THE SIXTH HOUSE: . . . in a way that helps them take better care of their health.

IN THE SEVENTH HOUSE: . . . in a way that helps them feel like things are more fair.

IN THE EIGHTH HOUSE: . . . in a way that challenges them emotionally.

IN THE NINTH HOUSE: . . . in a way that expands their mind.

IN THE TENTH HOUSE: . . . in a way that helps to plan their future.

IN THE ELEVENTH HOUSE: . . . in a way that reminds them that they have friends.

IN THE TWELFTH HOUSE: . . . in a way that gives them a space in which to do some healing.

Transiting Mercury

Burn incense on the appropriate altar.

Mercury Transiting Natal Sun

ENHANCING: Help out someone who writes and publishes books or articles about identity, self-discovery, confidence building, or autobiography, and whose work is going well.

AFFLICTING: Help out someone who writes books or articles about identity, self-discovery, confidence building, or autobiography, and who is struggling to be heard and published.

IN ARIES: Help them be enthusiastic about their work, and express your belief in them . . .

IN TAURUS: Give them a solid financial gift . . .

IN GEMINI: Let them bounce ideas off you, and help them clarify their thoughts . . .

IN CANCER: Give them a good nutritious meal . . .

IN LEO: Arrange for them to read their work in public . . .

IN VIRGO: Help them get better organized . . .

IN LIBRA: Correct some small unfairness in their life . . .

IN SCORPIO: Help them with any unusual research . . .

IN SAGITTARIUS: Arrange for them to speak at a place of higher education . . .

IN CAPRICORN: Help them in some way with their day job . . .

IN AQUARIUS: Introduce them to someone unusual who can help them . . .

IN PISCES: Let them cry on your shoulder . . .

IN THE FIRST HOUSE: . . . and help them remember to take care of their body.

IN THE SECOND HOUSE: . . . and get them some physical object that makes their life better.

IN THE THIRD HOUSE: . . . and help them with any writing, dictation, or transcription.

IN THE FOURTH HOUSE: . . . and help them create a more comfortable home space.

IN THE FIFTH HOUSE: . . . and help them get their creative juices flowing.

IN THE SIXTH HOUSE: . . . and help them with the scut work in the rest of their life.

IN THE SEVENTH HOUSE: . . . and be a partner to them in some difficult undertaking.

IN THE EIGHTH HOUSE: . . . and help them with something emotionally difficult.

IN THE NINTH HOUSE: . . . and introduce them to someone who can widen their horizons.

IN THE TENTH HOUSE: . . . and introduce them to someone who can help their career.

IN THE ELEVENTH HOUSE: . . . and introduce them to people worth networking with.

IN THE TWELFTH HOUSE: . . . and assist them in taking off a mental health day.

Mercury Transiting Natal Moon

ENHANCING: Give a gift to a child who has intellectual talent and who is doing good things with it toward their future.

AFFLICTING: Give a gift to a child who has intellectual talent, but who is blocked from being able to achieve their potential by unfortunate circumstances.

IN ARIES: Give them a gift that helps them keep up their enthusiasm for their projects . . .

IN TAURUS: Give them a gift that clears a financial blockage . . .

IN GEMINI: Give them a gift of written words . . .

IN CANCER: Give them a gift that helps their home life be more supportive of their goals . . .

IN LEO: Give them a place to show off their work . . .

IN VIRGO: Give them a gift of labor . . .

IN LIBRA: Give them a gift of that brings their environment some harmony . . .

IN SCORPIO: Give them a gift that stretches their ideas about controversial things . . .

IN SAGITTARIUS: Give them a gift that furthers their education . . .

IN CAPRICORN: Give them a gift that helps their future career . . .

IN AQUARIUS: Give them a gift that helps them feel good about being different . . .

IN PISCES: Give them a gift that relieves their stress and turmoil . . .

IN THE FIRST HOUSE: . . . in a way that tells them you appreciate them for who they are.

IN THE SECOND HOUSE: . . . in a way that reminds them of what is really important.

IN THE THIRD HOUSE: . . . in a way that inspires them to write or talk.

IN THE FOURTH HOUSE: . . . in a way that helps them feel like part of a family or tribe.

IN THE FIFTH HOUSE: . . . in a way that inspires them to have fun.

IN THE SIXTH HOUSE: . . . in a way that helps them learn to break down and finish tasks.

IN THE SEVENTH HOUSE: . . . in a way that helps them feel like things are more fair.

IN THE EIGHTH HOUSE: . . . in a way that challenges them emotionally.

IN THE NINTH HOUSE: . . . in a way that expands their mind.

IN THE TENTH HOUSE: . . . in a way that helps to plan their future.

IN THE ELEVENTH HOUSE: . . . in a way that reminds them that they have friends.

IN THE TWELFTH HOUSE: . . . in a way that reminds them that it's all right to be alone.

Mercury Transiting Natal Mercury

ENHANCING: Gift a gift to someone who is always talking, writing, and communicating.

AFFLICTING: Give a gift to someone who could use a lot of help in learning to communicate better with others.

IN ARIES: Give someone who communicates too loudly and aggressively . . .

IN TAURUS: Give someone whose communication is too slow and plodding . . .

IN GEMINI: Give someone whose talks too fast and says too little . . .

IN CANCER: Give someone whose emotions get in the way of their words . . .

IN LEO: Give someone who speaks too self-importantly . . .

IN VIRGO: Give someone whose communication is too flat and unexpressive . . .

IN LIBRA: Give someone whose opinions are too dependent on the opinions of others . . .

IN SCORPIO: Give someone who keeps too silent for too long . . .

IN SAGITTARIUS: Give someone who rambles and preaches too much . . .

IN CAPRICORN: Give someone whose communication style is too dour and intimidating . . .

IN AQUARIUS: Give someone whose communication style is too odd and erratic . . .

IN PISCES: Give someone whose communication style is too vague and unclear . . .

IN THE FIRST HOUSE: . . . a book on assertiveness training.

IN THE SECOND HOUSE: . . . a book on getting your priorities straight.

IN THE THIRD HOUSE: . . . a book on learning to be a better writer.

IN THE FOURTH HOUSE: . . . a book on effective mediation between family members.

IN THE FIFTH HOUSE: . . . a book on inspiring creative self-expression.

IN THE SIXTH HOUSE: . . . a book on getting organized and working more effectively.

IN THE SEVENTH HOUSE: . . . a book on how to have better relationships.

IN THE EIGHTH HOUSE: . . . a book on dealing with people in crisis.

IN THE NINTH HOUSE: . . . a book on ethnocentrism and communication between different cultures.

IN THE TENTH HOUSE: . . . a book on leadership in the public eye.

IN THE ELEVENTH HOUSE: . . . a book on group dynamics.

IN THE TWELFTH HOUSE: . . . a book on finding your inner quiet source.

Mercury Transiting Natal Venus

ENHANCING: Help out someone who writes and publishes poetry, love stories, or fantasy, and whose work is going well.

AFFLICTING: Help out someone who writes poetry, love stories, or fantasy, and who is struggling to be heard and published.

IN ARIES: Help them be enthusiastic about their work, and express your belief in them . . .

IN TAURUS: Give them a solid financial gift . . .

IN GEMINI: Let them bounce ideas off you, and help them clarify their thoughts . . .

IN CANCER: Give them a good nutritious meal . . .

IN LEO: Arrange for them to read their work in public . . .

IN VIRGO: Help them get better organized . . .

IN LIBRA: Correct some small unfairness in their life . . .

IN SCORPIO: Help them with any unusual research . . .

IN SAGITTARIUS: Arrange for them to speak at a place of higher education . . .

IN CAPRICORN: Help them in some way with their day job . . .

IN AQUARIUS: Introduce them to someone unusual who can help them . . .

IN PISCES: Let them cry on your shoulder . . .

IN THE FIRST HOUSE: . . . and help them remember to take care of their body.

IN THE SECOND HOUSE: . . . and get them some physical object that makes their life better.

IN THE THIRD HOUSE: . . . and help them with any writing, dictation, or transcription.

IN THE FOURTH HOUSE: . . . and help them create a more comfortable home space.

IN THE FIFTH HOUSE: . . . and help them get their creative juices flowing.

IN THE SIXTH HOUSE: . . . and help them with the scut work in the rest of their life.

IN THE SEVENTH HOUSE: . . . and be a partner to them in some difficult undertaking.

IN THE EIGHTH HOUSE: . . . and help them with something emotionally difficult.

IN THE NINTH HOUSE: . . . and introduce them to someone who can widen their horizons.

IN THE TENTH HOUSE: . . . and introduce them to someone who can help their career.

IN THE ELEVENTH HOUSE: . . . and introduce them to people worth networking with.

IN THE TWELFTH HOUSE: . . . and assist them in taking off a mental health day.

Mercury Transiting Natal Mars

ENHANCING: Help out someone who writes and publishes books or articles on war, violence, sports, or how to do things, and whose work is going well.

AFFLICTING: Help out someone who writes books or articles on war, violence, sports, or how to do things, and who is struggling to be heard and published.

IN ARIES: Help them be enthusiastic about their work, and express your belief in them . . .

IN TAURUS: Give them a solid financial gift . . .

IN GEMINI: Let them bounce ideas off you, and help them clarify their thoughts . . .

IN CANCER: Give them a good nutritious meal . . .

IN LEO: Arrange for them to read their work in public . . .

IN VIRGO: Help them get better organized . . .

IN LIBRA: Correct some small unfairness in their life . . .

IN SCORPIO: Help them with any unusual research . . .

IN SAGITTARIUS: Arrange for them to speak at a place of higher education . . .

IN CAPRICORN: Help them in some way with their day job . . .

IN AQUARIUS: Introduce them to someone unusual who can help them . . .

IN PISCES: Let them cry on your shoulder . . .

IN THE FIRST HOUSE: . . . and help them remember to take care of their body.

IN THE SECOND HOUSE: . . . and get them some physical object that makes their life better.

IN THE THIRD HOUSE: . . . and help them with any writing, dictation, or transcription.

IN THE FOURTH HOUSE: . . . and help them create a more comfortable home space.

IN THE FIFTH HOUSE: . . . and help them get their creative juices flowing.

IN THE SIXTH HOUSE: . . . and help them with the scut work in the rest of their life.

IN THE SEVENTH HOUSE: . . . and be a partner to them in some difficult undertaking.

IN THE EIGHTH HOUSE: . . . and help them with something emotionally difficult.

IN THE NINTH HOUSE: . . . and introduce them to someone who can widen their horizons.

IN THE TENTH HOUSE: . . . and introduce them to someone who can help their career.

IN THE ELEVENTH HOUSE: . . . and introduce them to people worth networking with.

IN THE TWELFTH HOUSE: . . . and assist them in taking off a mental health day.

Mercury Transiting Natal Jupiter

ENHANCING: Help out someone who writes and publishes books or articles that enable people to live better or think more positively, and whose work is going well.

AFFLICTING: Help out someone who writes books or articles that enable people to live better or think more positively, and who is struggling to be heard and published.

IN ARIES: Help them be enthusiastic about their work, and express your belief in them . . .

IN TAURUS: Give them a solid financial gift . . .

IN GEMINI: Let them bounce ideas off you, and help them clarify their thoughts . . .

IN CANCER: Give them a good nutritious meal . . .

IN LEO: Arrange for them to read their work in public . . .

IN VIRGO: Help them get better organized . . .

IN LIBRA: Correct some small unfairness in their life . . .

IN SCORPIO: Help them with any unusual research . . .

IN SAGITTARIUS: Arrange for them to speak at a place of higher education . . .

IN CAPRICORN: Help them in some way with their day job . . .

IN AQUARIUS: Introduce them to someone unusual who can help them . . .

IN PISCES: Let them cry on your shoulder . . .

IN THE FIRST HOUSE: . . . and help them remember to take care of their body.

IN THE SECOND HOUSE: . . . and get them some physical object that makes their life better.

IN THE THIRD HOUSE: . . . and help them with any writing, dictation, or transcription.

IN THE FOURTH HOUSE: . . . and help them create a more comfortable home space.

IN THE FIFTH HOUSE: . . . and help them get their creative juices flowing.

IN THE SIXTH HOUSE: . . . and help them with the scut work in the rest of their life.

IN THE SEVENTH HOUSE: . . . and be a partner to them in some difficult undertaking.

IN THE EIGHTH HOUSE: . . . and help them with something emotionally difficult.

IN THE NINTH HOUSE: . . . and introduce them to someone who can widen their horizons.

IN THE TENTH HOUSE: . . . and introduce them to someone who can help their career.

IN THE ELEVENTH HOUSE: . . . and introduce them to people worth networking with.

IN THE TWELFTH HOUSE: . . . and assist them in taking off a mental health day.

Mercury Transiting Natal Saturn

ENHANCING: Help out someone who writes and publishes books or articles about some aspect of disability or pain or ongoing struggle, and whose work is going well.

AFFLICTING: Help out someone who writes books or articles about some aspect of disability or pain or ongoing struggle, and who is struggling to be heard and published.

IN ARIES: Help them be enthusiastic about their work, and express your belief in them . . .

IN TAURUS: Give them a solid financial gift . . .

IN GEMINI: Let them bounce ideas off you, and help them clarify their thoughts . . .

IN CANCER: Give them a good nutritious meal . . .

IN LEO: Arrange for them to read their work in public . . .

IN VIRGO: Help them get better organized . . .

IN LIBRA: Correct some small unfairness in their life . . .

IN SCORPIO: Help them with any unusual research . . .

IN SAGITTARIUS: Arrange for them to speak at a place of higher education . . .

IN CAPRICORN: Help them in some way with their day job . . .

IN AQUARIUS: Introduce them to someone unusual who can help them . . .

IN PISCES: Let them cry on your shoulder . . .

IN THE FIRST HOUSE: . . . and help them remember to take care of their body.

IN THE SECOND HOUSE: . . . and get them some physical object that makes their life better.

IN THE THIRD HOUSE: . . . and help them with any writing, dictation, or transcription.

IN THE FOURTH HOUSE: . . . and help them create a more comfortable home space.

IN THE FIFTH HOUSE: . . . and help them get their creative juices flowing.

IN THE SIXTH HOUSE: . . . and help them with the scut work in the rest of their life.

IN THE SEVENTH HOUSE: . . . and be a partner to them in some difficult undertaking.

IN THE EIGHTH HOUSE: . . . and help them with something emotionally difficult.

IN THE NINTH HOUSE: . . . and introduce them to someone who can widen their horizons.

IN THE TENTH HOUSE: . . . and introduce them to someone who can help their career.

IN THE ELEVENTH HOUSE: . . . and introduce them to people worth networking with.

IN THE TWELFTH HOUSE: . . . and assist them in taking off a mental health day.

Mercury Transiting Natal Uranus

ENHANCING: Help out someone who writes and publishes books or articles about ways to make the world a better place, and whose work is going well.

AFFLICTING: Help out someone who writes books or articles about ways to make the world a better place, and who is struggling to be heard and published.

IN ARIES: Help them be enthusiastic about their work, and express your belief in them . . .

IN TAURUS: Give them a solid financial gift . . .

IN GEMINI: Let them bounce ideas off you, and help them clarify their thoughts . . .

IN CANCER: Give them a good nutritious meal . . .

IN LEO: Arrange for them to read their work in public . . .

IN VIRGO: Help them get better organized . . .

IN LIBRA: Correct some small unfairness in their life . . .

IN SCORPIO: Help them with any unusual research . . .

IN SAGITTARIUS: Arrange for them to speak at a place of higher education . . .

IN CAPRICORN: Help them in some way with their day job . . .

IN AQUARIUS: Introduce them to someone unusual who can help them . . .

IN PISCES: Let them cry on your shoulder . . .

IN THE FIRST HOUSE: . . . and help them remember to take care of their body.

IN THE SECOND HOUSE: . . . and get them some physical object that makes their life better.

IN THE THIRD HOUSE: . . . and help them with any writing, dictation, or transcription.

IN THE FOURTH HOUSE: . . . and help them create a more comfortable home space.

IN THE FIFTH HOUSE: . . . and help them get their creative juices flowing.

IN THE SIXTH HOUSE: . . . and help them with the scut work in the rest of their life.

IN THE SEVENTH HOUSE: . . . and be a partner to them in some difficult undertaking.

IN THE EIGHTH HOUSE: . . . and help them with something emotionally difficult.

IN THE NINTH HOUSE: . . . and introduce them to someone who can widen their horizons.

IN THE TENTH HOUSE: . . . and introduce them to someone who can help their career.

IN THE ELEVENTH HOUSE: . . . and introduce them to people worth networking with.

IN THE TWELFTH HOUSE: . . . and assist them in taking off a mental health day.

Mercury Transiting Natal Neptune

ENHANCING: Help out someone who writes and publishes books or articles about healing, cosmic mysteries, or spirituality, and whose work is going well.

AFFLICTING: Help out someone who writes books or articles about healing, cosmic mysteries, or spirituality, and who is struggling to be heard and published.

IN ARIES: Help them be enthusiastic about their work, and express your belief in them . . .

IN TAURUS: Give them a solid financial gift . . .

IN GEMINI: Let them bounce ideas off you, and help them clarify their thoughts . . .

IN CANCER: Give them a good nutritious meal . . .

IN LEO: Arrange for them to read their work in public . . .

IN VIRGO: Help them get better organized . . .

IN LIBRA: Correct some small unfairness in their life . . .

IN SCORPIO: Help them with any unusual research . . .

IN SAGITTARIUS: Arrange for them to speak at a place of higher education . . .

IN CAPRICORN: Help them in some way with their day job . . .

IN AQUARIUS: Introduce them to someone unusual who can help them . . .

IN PISCES: Let them cry on your shoulder . . .

IN THE FIRST HOUSE: . . . and help them remember to take care of their body.

IN THE SECOND HOUSE: . . . and get them some physical object that makes their life better.

IN THE THIRD HOUSE: . . . and help them with any writing, dictation, or transcription.

IN THE FOURTH HOUSE: . . . and help them create a more comfortable home space.

IN THE FIFTH HOUSE: . . . and help them get their creative juices flowing.

IN THE SIXTH HOUSE: . . . and help them with the scut work in the rest of their life.

IN THE SEVENTH HOUSE: . . . and be a partner to them in some difficult undertaking.

IN THE EIGHTH HOUSE: . . . and help them with something emotionally difficult.

IN THE NINTH HOUSE: . . . and introduce them to someone who can widen their horizons.

IN THE TENTH HOUSE: . . . and introduce them to someone who can help their career.

IN THE ELEVENTH HOUSE: . . . and introduce them to people worth networking with.

IN THE TWELFTH HOUSE: . . . and assist them in taking off a mental health day.

Mercury Transiting Natal Pluto

ENHANCING: Help out someone who writes and publishes books or articles about controversial subjects that most people don't want to hear, and whose work is going well.

AFFLICTING: Help out someone who writes books or articles about controversial subjects that most people don't want to hear, and who is struggling to be heard and published.

IN ARIES: Help them be enthusiastic about their work, and express your belief in them . . .

IN TAURUS: Give them a solid financial gift . . .

IN GEMINI: Let them bounce ideas off you, and help them clarify their thoughts . . .

IN CANCER: Give them a good nutritious meal . . .

IN LEO: Arrange for them to read their work in public . . .

IN VIRGO: Help them get better organized . . .

IN LIBRA: Correct some small unfairness in their life . . .

IN SCORPIO: Help them with any unusual research . . .

IN SAGITTARIUS: Arrange for them to speak at a place of higher education . . .

IN CAPRICORN: Help them in some way with their day job . . .

IN AQUARIUS: Introduce them to someone unusual who can help them . . .

IN PISCES: Let them cry on your shoulder . . .

IN THE FIRST HOUSE: . . . and help them remember to take care of their body.

IN THE SECOND HOUSE: . . . and get them some physical object that makes their life better.

IN THE THIRD HOUSE: . . . and help them with any writing, dictation, or transcription.

IN THE FOURTH HOUSE: . . . and help them create a more comfortable home space.

IN THE FIFTH HOUSE: . . . and help them get their creative juices flowing.

IN THE SIXTH HOUSE: . . . and help them with the scut work in the rest of their life.

IN THE SEVENTH HOUSE: . . . and be a partner to them in some difficult undertaking.

IN THE EIGHTH HOUSE: . . . and help them with something emotionally difficult.

IN THE NINTH HOUSE: . . . and introduce them to someone who can widen their horizons.

IN THE TENTH HOUSE: . . . and introduce them to someone who can help their career.

IN THE ELEVENTH HOUSE: . . . and introduce them to people worth networking with.

IN THE TWELFTH HOUSE: . . . and assist them in taking off a mental health day.

Transiting Venus
Place a chalice of wine or fruit juice on the appropriate altar.

Venus Transiting Natal Sun

AFFLICTING: Give a gift to an artist who is struggling and just can't seem to make it work.

ENHANCING: Give a gift to an artist who has struggled, but is making progress now.

IN ARIES: Give them a gift of enthusiasm for their projects . . .

IN TAURUS: Give them a gift that helps them sell their art . . .

IN GEMINI: Give them a gift of written words . . .

IN CANCER: Give them a gift of domestic comfort . . .

IN LEO: Give them a gift of admiration . . .

IN VIRGO: Give them a gift of labor . . .

IN LIBRA: Give them a gift of beauty . . .

IN SCORPIO: Give them a gift of insight into human behavior . . .

IN SAGITTARIUS: Give them a gift of new knowledge . . .

IN CAPRICORN: Give them a gift that helps their career . . .

IN AQUARIUS: Give them a gift of something new and different . . .

IN PISCES: Give them a gift of compassion and listening . . .

IN THE FIRST HOUSE: . . . in a way that tells them you appreciate them for who they are.

IN THE SECOND HOUSE: . . . in a way that reminds them of what is really important.

IN THE THIRD HOUSE: . . . in a way that inspires them to write or talk.

IN THE FOURTH HOUSE: . . . in a way that helps them feel like part of a family or tribe.

IN THE FIFTH HOUSE: . . . in a way that inspires them to create.

IN THE SIXTH HOUSE: . . . in a way that helps them learn to break down and finish tasks.

IN THE SEVENTH HOUSE: . . . in a way that helps them feel like things are more fair.

IN THE EIGHTH HOUSE: . . . in a way that challenges them emotionally.

IN THE NINTH HOUSE: . . . in a way that expands their mind.

IN THE TENTH HOUSE: . . . in a way that helps to build their reputation.

IN THE ELEVENTH HOUSE: . . . in a way that reminds them that they have friends.

IN THE TWELFTH HOUSE: . . . in a way that reminds them that true art comes from the depths.

Venus Transiting Natal Moon

ENHANCING: Give a gift to a child with a great deal of artistic or musical talent.

AFFLICTING: Give a gift to a child with a great deal of artistic or musical talent who is blocked from achieving their potential due to unfortunate circumstances.

IN ARIES: Give them a gift that helps them keep up their enthusiasm for their projects . . .

IN TAURUS: Give them a gift that clears a financial blockage . . .

IN GEMINI: Give them a gift of written words . . .

IN CANCER: Give them a gift that helps their home life be more supportive of their goals . . .

IN LEO: Give them a place to show off their work . . .

IN VIRGO: Give them a gift of labor . . .

IN LIBRA: Give them a gift of the kind of art to which they aspire . . .

IN SCORPIO: Give them a gift that stretches their ideas about their art . . .

IN SAGITTARIUS: Give them a gift that furthers their education . . .

IN CAPRICORN: Give them a gift that helps their future career . . .

IN AQUARIUS: Give them a gift that helps them feel good about being different . . .

IN PISCES: Give them a gift that relieves their stress and turmoil . . .

IN THE FIRST HOUSE: . . . in a way that tells them you appreciate them for who they are.

IN THE SECOND HOUSE: . . . in a way that reminds them of what is really important.

IN THE THIRD HOUSE: . . . in a way that inspires them to write or talk.

IN THE FOURTH HOUSE: . . . in a way that helps them feel like part of a family or tribe.

IN THE FIFTH HOUSE: . . . in a way that inspires them to create.

IN THE SIXTH HOUSE: . . . in a way that helps them learn to break down and finish tasks.

IN THE SEVENTH HOUSE: . . . in a way that helps them feel like things are more fair.

IN THE EIGHTH HOUSE: . . . in a way that challenges them emotionally.

IN THE NINTH HOUSE: . . . in a way that expands their mind.

IN THE TENTH HOUSE: . . . in a way that helps to plan their future.

IN THE ELEVENTH HOUSE: . . . in a way that reminds them that they have friends.

IN THE TWELFTH HOUSE: . . . in a way that reminds them that true art comes from the depths.

Venus Transiting Natal Mercury

ENHANCING: Give aid to a singer-songwriter who is doing well with their life and their creative pursuits.

AFFLICTING: Give aid to a singer-songwriter who is struggling with their life and their creative pursuits.

IN ARIES: Help them be enthusiastic about their work, and express your belief in them . . .

IN TAURUS: Give them a solid financial gift . . .

IN GEMINI: Let them bounce ideas off you, and help them clarify their thoughts . . .

IN CANCER: Give them a good nutritious meal . . .

IN LEO: Arrange for them to perform their work in public . . .

IN VIRGO: Help them get better organized . . .

IN LIBRA: Correct some small unfairness in their life . . .

IN SCORPIO: Help them with any unusual research . . .

IN SAGITTARIUS: Arrange for them to speak at a place of higher education . . .

IN CAPRICORN: Help them in some way with their day job . . .

IN AQUARIUS: Introduce them to someone unusual who can help them . . .

IN PISCES: Let them cry on your shoulder . . .

IN THE FIRST HOUSE: . . . and help them remember to take care of their body.

IN THE SECOND HOUSE: . . . and get them some physical object that makes their life better.

IN THE THIRD HOUSE: . . . and help them with any writing, dictation, or transcription.

IN THE FOURTH HOUSE: . . . and help them create a more comfortable home space.

IN THE FIFTH HOUSE: . . . and help them get their creative juices flowing.

IN THE SIXTH HOUSE: . . . and help them with the scut work in the rest of their life.

IN THE SEVENTH HOUSE: . . . and be a partner to them in some difficult undertaking.

IN THE EIGHTH HOUSE: . . . and help them with something emotionally difficult.

IN THE NINTH HOUSE: . . . and introduce them to someone who can widen their horizons.

IN THE TENTH HOUSE: . . . and introduce them to someone who can help their career.

IN THE ELEVENTH HOUSE: . . . and introduce them to people worth networking with.

IN THE TWELFTH HOUSE: . . . and assist them in taking a mental health day.

Venus Transiting Natal Venus

ENHANCING: Give a gift to a woman or a feminine person who embodies all the best qualities of Venus—charming, loving, artistic, aesthetic—and who has been healthily romantic with more than one person.

AFFLICTING: Give a gift to a woman or a feminine person to whom all the aforementioned qualities are important, and who is struggling to learn to embody them.

IN ARIES: Take them somewhere exciting . . .

IN TAURUS: Buy them a professional massage . . .

IN GEMINI: Buy them aesthetically beautiful books on a hobby that they like . . .

IN CANCER: Make or buy them food that makes them feel pampered . . .

IN LEO: Take them out to be shown off in public . . .

IN VIRGO: Buy them something to help them take care of their health . . .

IN LIBRA: Buy them a makeover, manicure, or some other beautification service . . .

IN SCORPIO: Buy them a sex toy that they can use with a partner . . .

IN SAGITTARIUS: Take them somewhere exotic and foreign . . .

IN CAPRICORN: Take them somewhere that allows them to pretend to be of a higher social class . . .

IN AQUARIUS: Encourage them to try an offbeat and different look . . .

IN PISCES: Take them to a spa, sauna, or luxurious pool . . .

IN THE FIRST HOUSE: . . . and take them shopping for new clothes.

IN THE SECOND HOUSE: . . . in a way that validates their feminine Venusian values.

IN THE THIRD HOUSE: . . . and pay their phone bill.

IN THE FOURTH HOUSE: . . . and get them something to beautify their home.

IN THE FIFTH HOUSE: . . . and take them to a creative performance.

IN THE SIXTH HOUSE: . . . and do some messy and dirty chore for them.

IN THE SEVENTH HOUSE: . . . and give them two tickets to an event for them and their partner.

IN THE EIGHTH HOUSE: . . . and take them to a performance that is intense and emotionally cathartic.

IN THE NINTH HOUSE: . . . and take them on a road trip of their choice.

IN THE TENTH HOUSE: . . . and give them a gift that brings beauty and comfort into their workplace.

IN THE ELEVENTH HOUSE: . . . and give them a night out with their friends.

IN THE TWELFTH HOUSE: . . . and give them a compassionate ear to listen to their troubles.

Venus Transiting Natal Mars

ENHANCING: Give a gift to a man or a masculine person who is very comfortable with their feminine side and who is able to embody positive Venus qualities as well as Mars ones.

AFFLICTING: Give a gift to a man or masculine person who desperately needs to become comfortable with their feminine side.

IN ARIES: Take them somewhere exciting . . .

IN TAURUS: Buy them a professional massage . . .

IN GEMINI: Buy them aesthetically beautiful books on a hobby that they like . . .

IN CANCER: Make or buy them food that makes them feel pampered . . .

IN LEO: Take them out to be shown off in public . . .

IN VIRGO: Buy them something to help them take care of their health . . .

IN LIBRA: Buy them a makeover, manicure, or some other beautification service . . .

IN SCORPIO: Buy them a sex toy that they can use with a partner . . .

IN SAGITTARIUS: Take them somewhere exotic and foreign . . .

IN CAPRICORN: Take them somewhere that allows them to pretend to be of a higher social class . . .

IN AQUARIUS: Encourage them to try an offbeat and different look . . .

IN PISCES: Take them to a spa, sauna, or luxurious pool . . .

IN THE FIRST HOUSE: . . . and take them shopping for new clothes.

IN THE SECOND HOUSE: . . . in a way that validates their feminine Venusian values.

IN THE THIRD HOUSE: . . . and pay their phone bill.

IN THE FOURTH HOUSE: . . . and get them something to beautify their home.

IN THE FIFTH HOUSE: . . . and take them to a creative performance.

IN THE SIXTH HOUSE: . . . and do some messy and dirty chore for them.

IN THE SEVENTH HOUSE: . . . and give them two tickets to an event for them and their partner.

IN THE EIGHTH HOUSE: . . . and take them to a performance that is intense and emotionally cathartic.

IN THE NINTH HOUSE: . . . and take them on a road trip of their choice.

IN THE TENTH HOUSE: . . . and give them a gift that brings beauty and comfort into their workplace.

IN THE ELEVENTH HOUSE: . . . and give them a night out with their friends.

IN THE TWELFTH HOUSE: . . . and give them a compassionate ear to listen to their troubles.

Venus Transiting Natal Jupiter

ENHANCING: Give a gift to a couple who have managed to go from poor to well-off, working as a team, and who still love each other deeply. The gift should take them somewhere.

AFFLICTING: Give a gift to a couple who have had many ups and downs, and perhaps a good deal of bad luck, but who still love each other deeply. The gift should take them somewhere.

IN ARIES: Give them tickets to something adventurous . . .

IN TAURUS: Give them tickets to something they would not normally be able to afford . . .

IN GEMINI: Give them tickets to something mentally stimulating . . .

IN CANCER: Give them tickets to something that reminds them of their childhoods . . .

IN LEO: Give them tickets to something that reminds them of their early courtship . . .

IN VIRGO: Give them tickets to something practical . . .

IN LIBRA: Give them tickets to something specifically for couples . . .

IN SCORPIO: Give them tickets to something about which they feel passionately . . .

IN SAGITTARIUS: Give them tickets that takes them on a trip . . .

IN CAPRICORN: Give them tickets to something where they can pretend they are richer . . .

IN AQUARIUS: Give them tickets to something very unusual . . .

IN PISCES: Give them tickets to something that helps them dream . . .

IN THE FIRST HOUSE: . . . that is out of character for their usual public appearances.

IN THE SECOND HOUSE: . . . that reflects their most important values.

IN THE THIRD HOUSE: . . . that gets them talking and discussing.

IN THE FOURTH HOUSE: . . . that isn't far from their home.

IN THE FIFTH HOUSE: . . . that makes them feel more romantic.

IN THE SIXTH HOUSE: . . . that helps them learn a new skill.

IN THE SEVENTH HOUSE: . . . that requires them to work as a team.

IN THE EIGHTH HOUSE: . . . that stimulates buried issues.

IN THE NINTH HOUSE: . . . that expands their horizons.

IN THE TENTH HOUSE: . . . that helps them expand their social circle.

IN THE ELEVENTH HOUSE: . . . that lets them spend time with friends.

IN THE TWELFTH HOUSE: . . . that stirs up old memories.

Venus Transiting Natal Saturn

ENHANCING: Give a gift to an ex-lover with whom you are on friendly terms.

AFFLICTING: Give a gift to an ex-lover with whom you are on less than friendly terms.

(If you are so lucky as to have no ex-lovers, use instead any former friends you loved

dearly but who are no longer friends.)

IN ARIES: Give an ex who gave you good practice in dealing with your anger . . .

IN TAURUS: Give an ex who gave you financial support, on whatever terms . . .

IN GEMINI: Give an ex with whom many lies were exchanged . . .

IN CANCER: Give an ex who triggered your parent issues . . .

IN LEO: Give an ex who you think you are superior to . . .

IN VIRGO: Give an ex who was very critical of you . . .

IN LIBRA: Give an ex who constantly argued with you . . .

IN SCORPIO: Give an ex with a lot of buried rage and suspicion . . .

IN SAGITTARIUS: Give an ex who had trouble committing . . .

IN CAPRICORN: Give an ex who was too emotionally closed . . .

IN AQUARIUS: Give an ex who was emotionally distant and cold . . .

IN PISCES: Give an ex who was clingy and dependent . . .

IN THE FIRST HOUSE: . . . a gift certificate to a gym or clothing store.

IN THE SECOND HOUSE: . . . a gift certificate to a department store.

IN THE THIRD HOUSE: . . . a gift certificate to a small bookstore.

IN THE FOURTH HOUSE: . . . a gift certificate to a home furnishings store.

IN THE FIFTH HOUSE: . . . a gift certificate to an arts and crafts store.

IN THE SIXTH HOUSE: . . . a gift certificate to a hardware store.

IN THE SEVENTH HOUSE: . . . a gift certificate to a place they might like to go with a
partner.

IN THE EIGHTH HOUSE: . . . a gift certificate to an unusual gift store.

IN THE NINTH HOUSE: . . . a gift certificate to a large bookstore.

IN THE TENTH HOUSE: . . . a gift certificate to a store that specializes in their
career.

IN THE ELEVENTH HOUSE: . . . a gift certificate to a club.

IN THE TWELFTH HOUSE: . . . a gift certificate to the movies.

Venus Transiting Natal Uranus

AFFLICTING: Give aid to an activist for a movement of people in nontraditional relationships who are suffering persecution.

ENHANCING: Give aid to an activist who works to improve life for people in nontraditional relationships.

IN ARIES: Your gift should help some immediate emergency . . .

IN TAURUS: Your gift should help them obtain a solid foundation for their work . . .

IN GEMINI: Your gift should help make a change in their ability to disseminate information . . .

IN CANCER: Your gift should help make a change in their ability to work from home . . .

IN LEO: Your gift should help make a change in promoting them . . .

IN VIRGO: Your gift should help make a change in how they organize the details of their work . . .

IN LIBRA: Your gift should help make a change in their ability to find useful partners . . .

IN SCORPIO: Your gift should help make a change in their ability to face emotional adversity . . .

IN SAGITTARIUS: Your gift should help make a change in their ability to dream big . . .

IN CAPRICORN: Your gift should make a change in their ability to be seen as an authority . . .

IN AQUARIUS: Your gift should go directly toward their wildest goal . . .

IN PISCES: Your gift should make a change in their resources for handling stress . . .

IN THE FIRST HOUSE: . . . with respect to their public image.

IN THE SECOND HOUSE: . . . regarding financial solvency.

IN THE THIRD HOUSE: . . . regarding education about their cause.

IN THE FOURTH HOUSE: . . . regarding the ways their cause affects families.

IN THE FIFTH HOUSE: . . . regarding the ways their cause affects children.

IN THE SIXTH HOUSE: . . . regarding the ways their cause can be practically implemented.

IN THE SEVENTH HOUSE: . . . regarding the ways their cause is a natural ally of other causes.

IN THE EIGHTH HOUSE: . . . regarding financial aid from other parties.

IN THE NINTH HOUSE: . . . regarding the ways they can be heard in higher education.

IN THE TENTH HOUSE: . . . regarding the ways their cause can be a real career for them.

IN THE ELEVENTH HOUSE: . . . regarding the ways they can gain more volunteers.

IN THE TWELFTH HOUSE: . . . regarding the ways they can reach those who have no access.

Venus Transiting Natal Neptune

ENHANCING: Give a poem to someone who you admire for their ability to achieve unconditional love for others.

AFFLICTING: Give a poem to someone who idealizes love—and their lovers—but who has difficulty separating the ideal from the reality.

IN ARIES: Give them a poem about courage . . .

IN TAURUS: Give them a poem about stability and endurance . . .

IN GEMINI: Give them a poem about the pull of dual urges . . .

IN CANCER: Give them a poem about maternal love . . .

IN LEO: Give them a poem that is an example of glorious self-expression . . .

IN VIRGO: Give them a poem about humble service . . .

IN LIBRA: Give them a poem about beauty . . .

IN SCORPIO: Give them a poem about emotional struggle . . .

IN SAGITTARIUS: Give them a poem about striving for one's horizon . . .

IN CAPRICORN: Give them a poem about overcoming obstacles . . .

IN AQUARIUS: Give them a strange and experimental poem . . .

IN PISCES: Give them a poem about self-sacrifice . . .

IN THE FIRST HOUSE: . . . that reminds them to be themselves.

IN THE SECOND HOUSE: . . . that shows strong values.

IN THE THIRD HOUSE: . . . that communicates its point succinctly.

IN THE FOURTH HOUSE: . . . that is nostalgic and old-fashioned.

IN THE FIFTH HOUSE: . . . that has humor to it.

IN THE SIXTH HOUSE: . . . that speaks like the words of a mentor.

IN THE SEVENTH HOUSE: . . . that is a love poem to a partner.

IN THE EIGHTH HOUSE: . . . that digs deep into the dark places of the psyche.

IN THE NINTH HOUSE: . . . that was written in a faraway culture.

IN THE TENTH HOUSE: . . . that was written by someone famous.

IN THE ELEVENTH HOUSE: . . . that extols the value of friendship.

IN THE TWELFTH HOUSE: . . . that is dreamy and full of evocative images.

Venus Transiting Natal Pluto

ENHANCING: Give a gift to someone who is involved with unusual and intense sexual practices as an activist, speaker, or performer.

AFFLICTING: Give a gift to someone who is involved with unusual and intense sexual practices, and who is struggling to figure out how this fits into their life and identity.

IN ARIES: Give someone who is out-front and public as a sex activist . . .

IN TAURUS: Give someone who talks about the spirituality of sensual massage . . .

IN GEMINI: Give someone who interviews and writes about people with strange sex lives . . .

IN CANCER: Give someone who talks about their childhood sexual experiences . . .

IN LEO: Give someone who is a sexual performance artist . . .

IN VIRGO: Give someone who teaches safer sex for those with unconventional sex lives . . .

IN LIBRA: Give someone who counsels couples with unusual sex lives . . .

IN SCORPIO: Give someone who works with sexual power exchange . . .

IN SAGITTARIUS: Give someone who talks about polyamory . . .

IN CAPRICORN: Give someone who speaks about sex and disability . . .

IN AQUARIUS: Give someone who speaks or writes about the sexual possibilities of the future . . .

IN PISCES: Give someone who teaches Tantric sex . . .

IN THE FIRST HOUSE: . . . erotic clothing of their choice.

IN THE SECOND HOUSE: . . . a bottle of massage oil.

IN THE THIRD HOUSE: . . . a book of sexual techniques.

IN THE FOURTH HOUSE: . . . a sensual blindfold.

IN THE FIFTH HOUSE: . . . an erotic video.

IN THE SIXTH HOUSE: . . . erotic restraints.

IN THE SEVENTH HOUSE: . . . a book of erotic love stories.

IN THE EIGHTH HOUSE: . . . new sex toys.

IN THE NINTH HOUSE: . . . transport to a conference on their subject.

IN THE TENTH HOUSE: . . . a class with someone they admire.

IN THE ELEVENTH HOUSE: . . . a meeting with an organization they are interested in.

IN THE TWELFTH HOUSE: . . . and book about sex and spirituality.

Transiting Mars

Light a candle on the appropriate altar.

Mars Transiting Natal Sun

ENHANCING: Give a gift to someone who is seriously into martial arts as a way to express the honorable warrior within.

AFFLICTING: Give a gift to someone who is struggling with finding a way to express the honorable warrior within.

IN ARIES: For either person, the gift should directly support some kind of martial art . . .

IN TAURUS: Take them to get a deep body-work massage . . .

IN GEMINI: Take them on a bicycle trip at high speed or on a motorcycle ride . . .

IN CANCER: Take them to a neighborhood watch group . . .

IN LEO: Take them dancing in a public place . . .

IN VIRGO: Take them to a drum circle . . .

IN LIBRA: Take them to see (or take part in) a debate . . .

IN SCORPIO: Take them on an endurance course . . .

IN SAGITTARIUS: Take them hiking up a mountain . . .

IN CAPRICORN: Take them to a job fair . . .

IN AQUARIUS: Take them to a protest or political rally . . .

IN PISCES: Take them to a loud concert with wild trance dancing . . .

IN THE FIRST HOUSE: . . . and encourage them to express their individuality.

IN THE SECOND HOUSE: . . . and get them to talk about what they'd do if they won the lottery.

IN THE THIRD HOUSE: . . . and get them to yell, loudly.

IN THE FOURTH HOUSE: . . . and get them to vent about whether their family supports their individuality.

IN THE FIFTH HOUSE: . . . and get them to talk about whether people appreciate them.

IN THE SIXTH HOUSE: . . . and get them to vent about being a cog for their day job.

IN THE SEVENTH HOUSE: . . . and get them to talk about whether their relationships repress them.

IN THE EIGHTH HOUSE: . . . and get them to talk about the compromises they make for their sex life.

IN THE NINTH HOUSE: . . . and get them to talk about some faraway place that they've always dreamed of visiting.

IN THE TENTH HOUSE: . . . and get them to talk about the career that would be most "them."

IN THE ELEVENTH HOUSE: . . . and get them to talk about how the groups they belong to support or repress their individuality.

IN THE TWELFTH HOUSE: . . . and get them to talk about their repressed anger.

Mars Transiting Natal Moon

ENHANCING: Give a gift to a child who has strong athletic talent and is making good progress toward polishing it.

AFFLICTING: Give a gift to a child who has strong athletic talent, but who is being prevented from taking it to its fullest potential by difficult circumstances.

IN ARIES: Give them a gift that helps them keep up their enthusiasm for their projects . . .

IN TAURUS: Give them a gift that clears a financial blockage . . .

IN GEMINI: Give them a gift of written words . . .

IN CANCER: Give them a gift that helps their home life be more supportive of their goals . . .

IN LEO: Give them a place to show off their skill . . .

IN VIRGO: Give them a gift of labor . . .

IN LIBRA: Give them a gift that clears away a small injustice . . .

IN SCORPIO: Give them a gift that gives them an outlet for strong emotions . . .

IN SAGITTARIUS: Give them a gift that furthers their education . . .

IN CAPRICORN: Give them a gift that helps them get good coaching . . .

IN AQUARIUS: Give them a gift that helps them feel good about being different . . .

IN PISCES: Give them a gift that relieves their worry and turmoil . . .

IN THE FIRST HOUSE: . . . in a way that tells them you appreciate them for who they are.

IN THE SECOND HOUSE: . . . in a way that reminds them of what is really important.

IN THE THIRD HOUSE: . . . in a way that helps them communicate the importance of their gift.

IN THE FOURTH HOUSE: . . . in a way that helps them feel like part of a family or tribe.

IN THE FIFTH HOUSE: . . . in a way that inspires them to have fun with it.

IN THE SIXTH HOUSE: . . . in a way that helps them learn to break down and finish tasks.

IN THE SEVENTH HOUSE: . . . in a way that helps them feel like things are more fair.

IN THE EIGHTH HOUSE: . . . in a way that challenges them emotionally.

IN THE NINTH HOUSE: . . . in a way that expands their mind.

IN THE TENTH HOUSE: . . . in a way that helps to plan their future.

IN THE ELEVENTH HOUSE: . . . in a way that reminds them that they have friends.

IN THE TWELFTH HOUSE: . . . in a way that helps them deal with their inner issues.

Mars Transiting Natal Mercury

ENHANCING: Give a gift to an attorney whose assertiveness and articulateness you admire.

AFFLICTING: Give a gift to an attorney (or would-be attorney) who is struggling with being assertive and articulate.

IN ARIES: Give them a book on assertiveness . . .

IN TAURUS: Give them a book on consolidating financial options . . .

IN GEMINI: Give them a book that is witty and amusing . . .

IN CANCER: Give them a book on social justice for children . . .

IN LEO: Give them a book on some kind of performance or self-expression . . .

IN VIRGO: Give them a book on practical organizational skills . . .

IN LIBRA: Give them a law book that they've always wanted . . .

IN SCORPIO: Give them a book on sexual ethics and the law . . .

IN SAGITTARIUS: Give them a book on religion and the law . . .

IN CAPRICORN: Give them a book on career success . . .

IN AQUARIUS: Give them a book on social justice for humanity . . .

IN PISCES: Give them a book on criminal psychology . . .

IN THE FIRST HOUSE: . . . and give them writings on how to appear more confident.

IN THE SECOND HOUSE: . . . and give them writings on social values.

IN THE THIRD HOUSE: . . . and give them writings on being a better communicator.

IN THE FOURTH HOUSE: . . . and give them writings on law of the past.

IN THE FIFTH HOUSE: . . . and give them writings on some creative project.

IN THE SIXTH HOUSE: . . . and give them writings on medicine and the law.

IN THE SEVENTH HOUSE: . . . and give them writings on divorce.

IN THE EIGHTH HOUSE: . . . and give them writings on death penalty issues.

IN THE NINTH HOUSE: . . . and give them writings on teaching law.

IN THE TENTH HOUSE: . . . and give them writings on starting one's own practice.

IN THE ELEVENTH HOUSE: . . . and give them writings on possible professional allies.

IN THE TWELFTH HOUSE: . . . and give them writings on dealing with mental stress.

Mars Transiting Natal Venus

ENHANCING: Give a gift to a woman or feminine person who is very comfortable with their masculine side and who is able to embody positive Mars qualities as well as Venus ones.

AFFLICTING: Give a gift to a woman or feminine person who desperately needs to become comfortable with their masculine side.

IN ARIES: Take them to watch or play a sports game . . .

IN TAURUS: Do something with them that is familiar and comfortable, but masculine . . .

IN GEMINI: Involve them in an intellectual game of a sort that entertains them . . .

IN CANCER: Make or buy them food that makes them feel secure . . .

IN LEO: Take them to a place where they can show off their talents . . .

IN VIRGO: Give them a gift that helps them take care of their health . . .

IN LIBRA: Give them a gift that allows them to fight an injustice . . .

IN SCORPIO: Give them a gift that aids their sex life . . .

IN SAGITTARIUS: Take them hiking or camping . . .

IN CAPRICORN: Take them to a place where they can pretend to be more important than they are . . .

IN AQUARIUS: Encourage them to try a wildly different hobby . . .

IN PISCES: Take them on a fishing trip . . .

IN THE FIRST HOUSE: . . . and take them shopping for some kind of purposeful clothing.

IN THE SECOND HOUSE: . . . and get them a masculine thing that they have wanted for a long time.

IN THE THIRD HOUSE: . . . and give them gas money for their car.

IN THE FOURTH HOUSE: . . . and take them on some activity connected with their childhood.

IN THE FIFTH HOUSE: . . . and take them to a place where they can have fun.

IN THE SIXTH HOUSE: . . . and help them with some craft or cleanup project.

IN THE SEVENTH HOUSE: . . . and give them two tickets to a place they can take their partner.

IN THE EIGHTH HOUSE: . . . and take them to a show or performance about warfare.

IN THE NINTH HOUSE: . . . and take them to an exotic and challenging place.

IN THE TENTH HOUSE: . . . and do something to aid in their career.

IN THE ELEVENTH HOUSE: . . . and give them a night out with their friends.

IN THE TWELFTH HOUSE: . . . and take them to a place where they can relax and release stress.

Mars Transiting Natal Mars

ENHANCING: Give a gift to a man or masculine person who best embodies all the qualities of Mars—honorable, assertive, healthily sexual, energetic, decisive.

AFFLICTING: Give a gift to a man or masculine person to whom the aforementioned qualities are important and who is struggling to learn to embody them.

IN ARIES: Take them to watch or play a sports game . . .

IN TAURUS: Do something with them that is familiar and comfortable . . .

IN GEMINI: Involve them in an intellectual game of a sort that entertains them . . .

IN CANCER: Make or buy them food that makes them feel secure . . .

IN LEO: Take them to a place where they can show off their talents . . .

IN VIRGO: Give them a gift that helps them take care of their health . . .

IN LIBRA: Give them a gift that allows them to fight an injustice . . .

IN SCORPIO: Give them a gift that aids their sex life . . .

IN SAGITTARIUS: Take them hiking or camping . . .

IN CAPRICORN: Take them to a place where they can pretend to be more important than they are . . .

IN AQUARIUS: Encourage them to try a wildly different hobby . . .

IN PISCES: Take them on a fishing trip . . .

IN THE FIRST HOUSE: . . . and take them shopping for some kind of purposeful clothing.

IN THE SECOND HOUSE: . . . and get them a thing that they have wanted for a long time.

IN THE THIRD HOUSE: . . . and give them gas money for their car.

IN THE FOURTH HOUSE: . . . and take them on some activity connected with their childhood.

IN THE FIFTH HOUSE: . . . and take them to a place where they can have fun.

IN THE SIXTH HOUSE: . . . and help them with some craft or cleanup project.

IN THE SEVENTH HOUSE: . . . and give them two tickets to a place they can take their partner.

IN THE EIGHTH HOUSE: . . . and take them to a show or performance about warfare.

IN THE NINTH HOUSE: . . . and take them to an exotic and challenging place.

IN THE TENTH HOUSE: . . . and do something to aid in their career.

IN THE ELEVENTH HOUSE: . . . and give them a night out with their friends.

IN THE TWELFTH HOUSE: . . . and take them to a place where they can relax and release stress.

Mars Transiting Natal Jupiter

ENHANCING: Give a gift to someone in a leadership role whose strong and assertive personality has helped them to be a good commander for their people.

AFFLICTING: Give a gift to someone in a leadership role whose strong and assertive personality has sometimes created problems in being a good commander for their people.

IN ARIES: Give them a gift that helps them get some exercise . . .

IN TAURUS: Give them a gift that clears up a financial burden . . .

IN GEMINI: Give them a gift that stimulates them intellectually . . .

IN CANCER: Give them a gift that makes their home more comfortable . . .

IN LEO: Give them a gift that allows them individual expression . . .

IN VIRGO: Give them a gift that helps them get organized . . .

IN LIBRA: Give them a gift that beautifies their surroundings . . .

IN SCORPIO: Give them a gift that sparks their passions . . .

IN SAGITTARIUS: Give them a gift that sends them out traveling . . .

IN CAPRICORN: Give them a gift that teaches them new skills . . .

IN AQUARIUS: Give them a gift that gets them doing something entirely new . . .

IN PISCES: Give them a gift that gives them spiritual comfort . . .

IN THE FIRST HOUSE: . . . in a way that makes them feel better about themselves physically.

IN THE SECOND HOUSE: . . . in a way that respects their values.

IN THE THIRD HOUSE: . . . in a way that stimulates conversation.

IN THE FOURTH HOUSE: . . . in a way that connects them to the past.

IN THE FIFTH HOUSE: . . . in a way that inspires creativity.

IN THE SIXTH HOUSE: . . . in a way that frees them up from some routine chore.

IN THE SEVENTH HOUSE: . . . in a way that encourages them to do something with a partner.

IN THE EIGHTH HOUSE: . . . in a way that lasts until their death and beyond.

IN THE NINTH HOUSE: . . . in a way that expands their horizons.

IN THE TENTH HOUSE: . . . in a way that helps them with their careers.

IN THE ELEVENTH HOUSE: . . . in a way that helps them bond with friends.

IN THE TWELFTH HOUSE: . . . in a way that makes them consider the flow of their life.

Mars Transiting Natal Saturn

ENHANCING: Give a gift to someone who has a long-standing difficulty expressing anger or assertiveness, but who has made great strides in overcoming the problem.

AFFLICTING: Give a gift to someone who has a long-standing difficulty expressing anger or assertiveness and who is finding it hard to make any progress.

IN ARIES: Get them a class in assertiveness training . . .

IN TAURUS: Get them a class in meditation . . .

IN GEMINI: Get them a class in debate . . .

IN CANCER: Get them a class on learning to nurture yourself . . .

IN LEO: Get them a class on public speaking . . .

IN VIRGO: Get them a class on yoga, nutrition, or health . . .

IN LIBRA: Get them a class on dance or creative movement . . .

IN SCORPIO: Get them a class in martial arts . . .

IN SAGITTARIUS: Get them a class in spiritual development . . .

IN CAPRICORN: Get them a class in a new career skill . . .

IN AQUARIUS: Get them a class in developing psychic powers . . .

IN PISCES: Get them a class on personal introspection . . .

IN THE FIRST HOUSE: . . . with a teacher who is outgoing and showy.

IN THE SECOND HOUSE: . . . with a teacher who expresses strong values.

IN THE THIRD HOUSE: . . . with a teacher who is a good communicator.

IN THE FOURTH HOUSE: . . . with a teacher who is warmly parental.

IN THE FIFTH HOUSE: . . . with a teacher who expresses themselves creatively.

IN THE SIXTH HOUSE: . . . with a teacher who is good at being practical.

IN THE SEVENTH HOUSE: . . . with a teacher who is fair.

IN THE EIGHTH HOUSE: . . . with a teacher who knows many unusual things.

IN THE NINTH HOUSE: . . . with a teacher who has academic credentials.

IN THE TENTH HOUSE: . . . with a teacher who is a public figure.

IN THE ELEVENTH HOUSE: . . . with a teacher who encourages group activity.

IN THE TWELFTH HOUSE: . . . with a teacher who has a mental health background.

Mars Transiting Natal Uranus

AFFLICTING: Give aid to an activist who helps the victims of violence.

ENHANCING: Give aid to an activist who works to prevent violence.

IN ARIES: Your gift should help some immediate emergency . . .

IN TAURUS: Your gift should help them obtain a solid foundation for their work . . .

IN GEMINI: Your gift should help make a change in their ability to disseminate information . . .

IN CANCER: Your gift should help make a change in their ability to work from home . . .

IN LEO: Your gift should help make a change in promoting them . . .

IN VIRGO: Your gift should help make a change in how they organize the details of their work . . .

IN LIBRA: Your gift should help make a change in their ability to achieve justice . . .

IN SCORPIO: Your gift should help make a change in their ability to face emotional adversity . . .

IN SAGITTARIUS: Your gift should help make a change in their ability to dream big . . .

IN CAPRICORN: Your gift should make a change in their ability to be seen as an authority . . .

IN AQUARIUS: Your gift should go directly toward their wildest goal . . .

IN PISCES: Your gift should make a change in their resources for healing survivors . . .

IN THE FIRST HOUSE: . . . with respect to their public image.

IN THE SECOND HOUSE: . . . regarding financial solvency.

IN THE THIRD HOUSE: . . . regarding education about their cause.

IN THE FOURTH HOUSE: . . . regarding the ways their cause affects families.

IN THE FIFTH HOUSE: . . . regarding the ways their cause affects children.

IN THE SIXTH HOUSE: . . . regarding the ways their cause can be practically implemented.

IN THE SEVENTH HOUSE: . . . regarding the ways their cause is a natural ally of other causes.

IN THE EIGHTH HOUSE: . . . regarding financial aid from other parties.

IN THE NINTH HOUSE: . . . regarding the ways they can be heard in higher education.

IN THE TENTH HOUSE: . . . regarding the ways their cause can be a real career for them.

IN THE ELEVENTH HOUSE: . . . regarding the ways they can gain more volunteers.

IN THE TWELFTH HOUSE: . . . regarding the ways they can reach those who have no access.

Mars Transiting Natal Neptune

ENHANCING: Give a gift to a man who practices men's spirituality and who is an avatar of male magic and positive energy.

AFFLICTING: Give a gift to a man who is afflicted with mental illness or addiction and who could use some spirituality in his life.

IN ARIES: Give them a gift that encourages them to face something they fear

IN TAURUS: Give them a gift that aids their financial situation . . .

IN GEMINI: Give them a book that concerns their spiritual path . . .

IN CANCER: Buy or cook them a meal that reflects their spiritual values regarding food . . .

IN LEO: Take them to a performance that celebrates aspects of their spirituality . . .

IN VIRGO: Give them a gift that helps them integrate spirituality into their ordinary work life . . .

IN LIBRA: Give them a gift of something beautiful that also inspires them . . .

IN SCORPIO: Give them a gift that encourages the mystical side of their faith . . .

IN SAGITTARIUS: Give them a gift that aids their religious education . . .

IN CAPRICORN: Give them a gift that celebrates the oldest traditions of their faith . . .

IN AQUARIUS: Give them a gift that reflects new and progressive developments in their faith . . .

IN PISCES: Give them a gift that encourages them to be alone and meditate . . .

IN THE FIRST HOUSE: . . . and provides unbiased information about how their faith looks to others.

IN THE SECOND HOUSE: . . . and honors their new spiritual values.

IN THE THIRD HOUSE: . . . and furthers communication between their faith and others.

IN THE FOURTH HOUSE: . . . and helps them integrate their spirituality and their home life.

IN THE FIFTH HOUSE: . . . and helps them to think about the spirituality of Love.

IN THE SIXTH HOUSE: . . . and helps them remember that their life still has a practical side.

IN THE SEVENTH HOUSE: . . . and aids them in finding a spiritual mentor of some kind.

IN THE EIGHTH HOUSE: . . . and helps them to weather this change of life.

IN THE NINTH HOUSE: . . . and encourages them to travel somewhere important to their faith.

IN THE TENTH HOUSE: . . . and encourages them to integrate their spiritual values with their career.

IN THE ELEVENTH HOUSE: . . . and encourages them to discover other interest groups.

IN THE TWELFTH HOUSE: . . . and encourages them to commune with the Divine in their own way.

Mars Transiting Natal Pluto

ENHANCING: Give a gift to someone whose past is a wreckage of anger and destructive lack of self-control, but who has managed to pull themselves out and live a different life through sheer willpower.

AFFLICTING: Give a gift to someone who is struggling to emerge from a life of anger and destructive lack of self-control.

IN ARIES: Give them a gift that helps them get some exercise . . .

IN TAURUS: Give them a gift that clears up a financial burden . . .

IN GEMINI: Give them a gift that stimulates them intellectually . . .

IN CANCER: Give them a gift that makes their home more comfortable . . .

IN LEO: Give them a gift that allows them individual expression . . .

IN VIRGO: Give them a gift that helps them build discipline . . .

IN LIBRA: Give them a gift that beautifies their surroundings . . .

IN SCORPIO: Give them a gift that helps with anger management . . .

IN SAGITTARIUS: Give them a gift that sends them out traveling . . .

IN CAPRICORN: Give them a gift that teaches them new skills . . .

IN AQUARIUS: Give them a gift that gets them doing something entirely new . . .

IN PISCES: Give them a gift that gives them spiritual comfort . . .

IN THE FIRST HOUSE: . . . in a way that makes them feel better about themselves physically.

IN THE SECOND HOUSE: . . . in a way that respects their values.

IN THE THIRD HOUSE: . . . in a way that stimulates conversation.

IN THE FOURTH HOUSE: . . . in a way that connects them to the past.

IN THE FIFTH HOUSE: . . . in a way that gives them a light-hearted moment.

IN THE SIXTH HOUSE: . . . in a way that frees them up from some routine chore.

IN THE SEVENTH HOUSE: . . . in a way that encourages them to deal fairly with others.

IN THE EIGHTH HOUSE: . . . in a way that lasts until their death and beyond.

IN THE NINTH HOUSE: . . . in a way that expands their horizons.

IN THE TENTH HOUSE: . . . in a way that helps them with their careers.

IN THE ELEVENTH HOUSE: . . . in a way that helps them bond with friends.

IN THE TWELFTH HOUSE: . . . in a way that helps them deal with their inner demons.

Transiting Jupiter

Place coins upon the appropriate altar.

Jupiter Transiting Natal Sun

ENHANCING: Give aid to a group or nonprofit organization that gives grant money to successful people seeking to follow their dreams.

AFFLICTING: Give aid to a group or nonprofit organization that gives grant money to struggling, high-risk individuals attempting to follow their dreams.

IN ARIES: The grant should fund athletes . . .

IN TAURUS: The grant should fund small business entrepreneurs . . .

IN GEMINI: The grant should fund writers . . .

IN CANCER: The grant should fund housewives returning to work . . .

IN LEO: The grant should fund performers . . .

IN VIRGO: The grant should fund craftspeople . . .

IN LIBRA: The grant should fund artists . . .

IN SCORPIO: The grant should fund a controversial and passionate dream . . .

IN SAGITTARIUS: The grant should fund people who want to travel as part of their dream . . .

IN CAPRICORN: The grant should fund small business owners who want to expand . . .

IN AQUARIUS: The grant should fund people with unusual and innovative ideas . . .

IN PISCES: The grant should fund people in the healing professions . . .

IN THE FIRST HOUSE: . . . and help them with physical needs.

IN THE SECOND HOUSE: . . . and help them financially.

IN THE THIRD HOUSE: . . . and help them with the media.

IN THE FOURTH HOUSE: . . . and help them keep a roof over their heads.

IN THE FIFTH HOUSE: . . . and help with a creative endeavor.

IN THE SIXTH HOUSE: . . . and help with practical daily organization.

IN THE SEVENTH HOUSE: . . . and help them find mentors.

IN THE EIGHTH HOUSE: . . . and help them acquire more sources of funding.

IN THE NINTH HOUSE: . . . and help them with training and education.

IN THE TENTH HOUSE: . . . and help them with bureaucracies.

IN THE ELEVENTH HOUSE: . . . and help them network with allies.

IN THE TWELFTH HOUSE: . . . and aid them in getting more private creative time.

Jupiter Transiting Natal Moon

ENHANCING: Give a gift to a child who is lucky and blessed, with a good home and family life and few problems in their existence.

AFFLICTING: Give a gift to a child who has suffered a great deal of bad luck and misfortune in their life.

IN ARIES: Give them a gift that helps them deal with anger . . .

IN TAURUS: Give them a gift that clears a financial blockage . . .

IN GEMINI: Give them a gift of written words . . .

IN CANCER: Give them a gift that helps their home life be more supportive of their goals . . .

IN LEO: Give them a gift that helps them express themselves . . .

IN VIRGO: Give them a gift that teaches them practical skills for the future . . .

IN LIBRA: Give them a gift that clears some small unfairness . . .

IN SCORPIO: Give them a gift that helps their will to survive . . .

IN SAGITTARIUS: Give them a gift that furthers their education . . .

IN CAPRICORN: Give them a gift that helps their future career . . .

IN AQUARIUS: Give them a gift that helps them feel good about being different . . .

IN PISCES: Give them a gift that relieves their stress and turmoil . . .

IN THE FIRST HOUSE: . . . in a way that tells them you appreciate them for who they are.

IN THE SECOND HOUSE: . . . in a way that reminds them of what is really important.

IN THE THIRD HOUSE: . . . in a way that inspires them to write or talk.

IN THE FOURTH HOUSE: . . . in a way that helps them feel like part of a family or tribe.

IN THE FIFTH HOUSE: . . . in a way that helps them take joy in life.

IN THE SIXTH HOUSE: . . . in a way that helps them learn to break down and finish tasks.

IN THE SEVENTH HOUSE: . . . in a way that helps them feel like things are more fair.

IN THE EIGHTH HOUSE: . . . in a way that challenges them emotionally.

IN THE NINTH HOUSE: . . . in a way that expands their mind.

IN THE TENTH HOUSE: . . . in a way that helps to plan their future.

IN THE ELEVENTH HOUSE: . . . in a way that reminds them that they have friends.

IN THE TWELFTH HOUSE: . . . in a way that gives them a space in which to do some healing.

Jupiter Transiting Natal Mercury

ENHANCING: Give a gift to someone who has the gift of fast-talking and who has used it to inspire people and to help them be the best they can be.

AFFLICTING: Give a gift to someone who has the gift of fast-talking, but who has had to learn the hard way that it should not be misused.

IN ARIES: Give them a book of action stories . . .

IN TAURUS: Give them a book on making money . . .

IN GEMINI: Give them a book of short stories . . .

IN CANCER: Give them a book of sentimental fiction . . .

IN LEO: Give them a book of jokes . . .

IN VIRGO: Give them a book on learning a practical skill . . .

IN LIBRA: Give them a book on forming partnerships . . .

IN SCORPIO: Give them a sarcastically written book . . .

IN SAGITTARIUS: Give them a book of adventures . . .

IN CAPRICORN: Give them a book on politics . . .

IN AQUARIUS: Give them a book on something controversial . . .

IN PISCES: Give them a book on spirituality . . .

IN THE FIRST HOUSE: . . . that reminds them how they look to others.

IN THE SECOND HOUSE: . . . that improves their poor values and validates their good ones.

IN THE THIRD HOUSE: . . . that gives them tips on better communication.

IN THE FOURTH HOUSE: . . . that teaches them something about their heritage.

IN THE FIFTH HOUSE: . . . that gives them a fun read.

IN THE SIXTH HOUSE: . . . that encourages them to be of service to others.

IN THE SEVENTH HOUSE: . . . that helps them make up their mind on an important decision.

IN THE EIGHTH HOUSE: . . . that helps them wrestle with their inner demons.

IN THE NINTH HOUSE: . . . that expands their mind.

IN THE TENTH HOUSE: . . . that helps them with their career.

IN THE ELEVENTH HOUSE: . . . that shows them a picture of a better future.

IN THE TWELFTH HOUSE: . . . that helps them find compassion for others.

Jupiter Transiting Natal Venus

ENHANCING: Give a gift to a couple who have been happily married for many decades and still deeply love each other. The gift should take them somewhere.

AFFLICTING: Give a gift to someone who has had many lovers, but none that seemed to last.

IN ARIES: Give them tickets to something adventurous . . .

IN TAURUS: Give them tickets to something they would not normally be able to afford . . .

IN GEMINI: Give them tickets to something mentally stimulating . . .

IN CANCER: Give them tickets to something that reminds them of their childhoods . . .

IN LEO: Give them tickets to something that reminds them of their early courtship . . .

IN VIRGO: Give them tickets to something practical . . .

IN LIBRA: Give them tickets to something specifically for couples . . .

IN SCORPIO: Give them tickets to something about which they feel passionately . . .

IN SAGITTARIUS: Give them tickets that take them on a trip . . .

IN CAPRICORN: Give them tickets to something where they can pretend they are richer . . .

IN AQUARIUS: Give them tickets to something very unusual . . .

IN PISCES: Give them tickets to something that helps them dream . . .

IN THE FIRST HOUSE: . . . that is out of character for their usual public appearances.

IN THE SECOND HOUSE: . . . that reflects their most important values.

IN THE THIRD HOUSE: . . . that gets them talking and discussing.

IN THE FOURTH HOUSE: . . . that isn't far from their home.

IN THE FIFTH HOUSE: . . . that makes them feel more romantic.

IN THE SIXTH HOUSE: . . . that helps them learn a new skill.

IN THE SEVENTH HOUSE: . . . that requires them to work as a team.

IN THE EIGHTH HOUSE: . . . that stimulates buried issues.

IN THE NINTH HOUSE: . . . that expands their horizons.

IN THE TENTH HOUSE: . . . that helps them expand their social circle.

IN THE ELEVENTH HOUSE: . . . that lets them spend time with friends.

IN THE TWELFTH HOUSE: . . . that stirs up old memories.

Jupiter Transiting Natal Mars

ENHANCING: Give a gift to someone whose actions exemplify the principle of using devout, personally fulfilling religious beliefs as a moral touchstone.

AFFLICTING: Give a gift to someone who attempts to use devout, personally fulfilling religious beliefs as a moral touchstone, but who often fails in these attempts and does not respect the beliefs of others.

IN ARIES: Give them a gift that helps them get some exercise . . .

IN TAURUS: Give them a gift that clears up a financial burden . . .

IN GEMINI: Give them a gift that stimulates them intellectually . . .

IN CANCER: Give them a gift that makes their home more comfortable . . .

IN LEO: Give them a gift that allows them individual expression . . .

IN VIRGO: Give them a gift that helps them get organized . . .

IN LIBRA: Give them a gift that beautifies their surroundings . . .

IN SCORPIO: Give them a gift that sparks their passions . . .

IN SAGITTARIUS: Give them a gift that sends them out traveling . . .

IN CAPRICORN: Give them a gift that teaches them new skills . . .

IN AQUARIUS: Give them a gift that gets them doing something entirely new . . .

IN PISCES: Give them a gift that gives them spiritual comfort . . .

IN THE FIRST HOUSE: . . . in a way that makes them feel better about themselves physically.

IN THE SECOND HOUSE: . . . in a way that respects their values.

IN THE THIRD HOUSE: . . . in a way that stimulates conversation.

IN THE FOURTH HOUSE: . . . in a way that connects them to the past.

IN THE FIFTH HOUSE: . . . in a way that inspires creativity.

IN THE SIXTH HOUSE: . . . in a way that frees them up from some routine chore.

IN THE SEVENTH HOUSE: . . . in a way that encourages them to do something with a partner.

IN THE EIGHTH HOUSE: . . . in a way that lasts until their death and beyond.

IN THE NINTH HOUSE: . . . in a way that expands their horizons.

IN THE TENTH HOUSE: . . . in a way that helps them with their careers.

IN THE ELEVENTH HOUSE: . . . in a way that helps them bond with friends.

IN THE TWELFTH HOUSE: . . . in a way that makes them consider the flow of their life.

Jupiter Transiting Natal Jupiter

ENHANCING: Give a gift to someone who is incredibly lucky and whose luck has pulled them through life.

AFFLICTING: Give a gift to someone who is incredibly unlucky and who has had to work hard for everything they have gained.

IN ARIES: Help out with a problem that makes them angry . . .

IN TAURUS: Help out with a problem that strains their patience . . .

IN GEMINI: Help out with a problem that they are of two minds about . . .

IN CANCER: Get them a good home-cooked meal . . .

IN LEO: Encourage their self-expression . . .

IN VIRGO: Help them learn a new system of organization . . .

IN LIBRA: Help with some small unfairness in their life . . .

IN SCORPIO: Help out with a problem that pushes their deep emotional triggers . . .

IN SAGITTARIUS: Encourage them to be more generous with people . . .

IN CAPRICORN: Encourage them to think about how they use their authority . . .

IN AQUARIUS: Encourage them to go out and join more groups . . .

IN PISCES: Encourage them to be more compassionate to people . . .

IN THE FIRST HOUSE: . . . and help them do right with their physical body.

IN THE SECOND HOUSE: . . . and help them understand that you get what you give.

IN THE THIRD HOUSE: . . . and help out with a communication problem.

IN THE FOURTH HOUSE: . . . and help them in a way that benefits their home and family life.

IN THE FIFTH HOUSE: . . . and help them with creative projects.

IN THE SIXTH HOUSE: . . . and offer to help with boring tasks.

IN THE SEVENTH HOUSE: . . . and give aid that allows them to go out with a partner.

IN THE EIGHTH HOUSE: . . . and give aid that helps them end some painful habit.

IN THE NINTH HOUSE: . . . and help them with transportation somewhere.

IN THE TENTH HOUSE: . . . and give aid that helps them in their career.

IN THE ELEVENTH HOUSE: . . . and encourage them to spend more time with outside interest groups.

IN THE TWELFTH HOUSE: . . . and find them someone who can advise them about their path.

Jupiter Transiting Natal Saturn

ENHANCING: Give a gift to someone who frequently mentors others on their path, through simple generosity, but who could always use someone to talk to.

AFFLICTING: Give a gift to someone who is clearly in need of a mentor on their path.

IN ARIES: Connect them with someone who is an idealist . . .

IN TAURUS: Connect them with someone who is earthy and practical . . .

IN GEMINI: Connect them with someone who is articulate . . .

IN CANCER: Connect them with someone who is a parent (or child) figure . . .

IN LEO: Connect them with someone who is a showy public figure . . .

IN VIRGO: Connect them with someone who can give constructive criticism . . .

IN LIBRA: Connect them with someone who gives good advice about love . . .

IN SCORPIO: Connect them with someone who is comfortable with darkness . . .

IN SAGITTARIUS: Connect them with someone who is optimistic about the future . . .

IN CAPRICORN: Connect them with someone who will aid them in their career . . .

IN AQUARIUS: Connect them with someone who has radical ideas . . .

IN PISCES: Connect them with someone who talks about spirituality . . .

IN THE FIRST HOUSE: . . . and who is a model of being oneself.

IN THE SECOND HOUSE: . . . and who has strong values.

IN THE THIRD HOUSE: . . . and who communicates well.

IN THE FOURTH HOUSE: . . . and who has a strong sense of family and tribe.

IN THE FIFTH HOUSE: . . . and who is a natural performer.

IN THE SIXTH HOUSE: . . . and who has a strong work ethic.

IN THE SEVENTH HOUSE: . . . and who has a strong primary relationship.

IN THE EIGHTH HOUSE: . . . and who understands catharsis.

IN THE NINTH HOUSE: . . . and who travels a lot.

IN THE TENTH HOUSE: . . . and who is socially successful.

IN THE ELEVENTH HOUSE: . . . and who networks a great deal.

IN THE TWELFTH HOUSE: . . . and who is very introspective.

Jupiter Transiting Natal Uranus

AFFLICTING: Give aid to an activist who is trying to change the world in a way that seems impossible, a dedicated Don Quixote.

ENHANCING: Give aid to an activist who is trying to change the world and is making progress in their field.

IN ARIES: Your gift should help some immediate emergency . . .

IN TAURUS: Your gift should help them obtain a solid foundation for their work . . .

IN GEMINI: Your gift should help make a change in their ability to disseminate information . . .

IN CANCER: Your gift should help make a change in their ability to work from home . . .

IN LEO: Your gift should help make a change in promoting them . . .

IN VIRGO: Your gift should help make a change in how they organize the details of their work . . .

IN LIBRA: Your gift should help make a change in their ability to find useful partners . . .

IN SCORPIO: Your gift should help make a change in their ability to face emotional adversity . . .

IN SAGITTARIUS: Your gift should help make a change in their ability to dream big . . .

IN CAPRICORN: Your gift should make a change in their ability to be seen as an authority . . .

IN AQUARIUS: Your gift should go directly toward their wildest goal . . .

IN PISCES: Your gift should make a change in their resources for handling stress . . .

IN THE FIRST HOUSE: . . . with respect to their public image.

IN THE SECOND HOUSE: . . . regarding financial solvency.

IN THE THIRD HOUSE: . . . regarding education about their cause.

IN THE FOURTH HOUSE: . . . regarding the ways their cause affects families.

IN THE FIFTH HOUSE: . . . regarding the ways their cause affects children.

IN THE SIXTH HOUSE: . . . regarding the ways their cause can be practically implemented.

IN THE SEVENTH HOUSE: . . . regarding the ways their cause is a natural ally of other causes.

IN THE EIGHTH HOUSE: . . . regarding financial aid from other parties.

IN THE NINTH HOUSE: . . . regarding the ways they can be heard in higher education.

IN THE TENTH HOUSE: . . . regarding the ways their cause can be a real career for them.

IN THE ELEVENTH HOUSE: . . . regarding the ways they can gain more volunteers.

IN THE TWELFTH HOUSE: . . . regarding the ways they can reach those who have no access.

Jupiter Transiting Natal Neptune

ENHANCING: Give aid to a clergyperson for a large and well-established religion.

AFFLICTING: Give aid to a clergyperson for a small and misunderstood religion.

IN ARIES: Help out with a problem that makes them angry . . .

IN TAURUS: Help out with a problem that strains their patience . . .

IN GEMINI: Help out with a problem that they are of two minds about . . .

IN CANCER: Get them a good home-cooked meal . . .

IN LEO: Encourage their self-expression . . .

IN VIRGO: Help them learn a new system of organization . . .

IN LIBRA: Help with some small unfairness in their life . . .

IN SCORPIO: Help out with a problem that pushes their deep emotional triggers . . .

IN SAGITTARIUS: Encourage them to talk about their religious faith . . .

IN CAPRICORN: Encourage them to think about how they use their authority . . .

IN AQUARIUS: Encourage them to go out more among the people they minister to . . .

IN PISCES: Give aid that allows them more time to pray . . .

IN THE FIRST HOUSE: . . . and help them do right with their physical body.

IN THE SECOND HOUSE: . . . and encourage them to talk about their conflicting issues with money.

IN THE THIRD HOUSE: . . . and help out with a communication problem.

IN THE FOURTH HOUSE: . . . and help them in a way that benefits their home and family life.

IN THE FIFTH HOUSE: . . . and help them with creative projects.

IN THE SIXTH HOUSE: . . . and offer to help with boring tasks.

IN THE SEVENTH HOUSE: . . . and give aid that allows them to go out with a partner.

IN THE EIGHTH HOUSE: . . . and give aid that helps them end some painful habit.

IN THE NINTH HOUSE: . . . and help them with transportation somewhere.

IN THE TENTH HOUSE: . . . and give aid that helps them in their career.

IN THE ELEVENTH HOUSE: . . . and encourage them to spend more time with outside interest groups.

IN THE TWELFTH HOUSE: . . . and encourage them to meditate quietly, alone.

Jupiter Transiting Natal Pluto

ENHANCING: Give a gift to someone who embodies the concept of faith that can move mountains.

AFFLICTING: Give a gift to someone who has had a crisis of faith and needs something to believe in.

IN ARIES: Take them up a mountain . . .

IN TAURUS: Take them somewhere luxurious . . .

IN GEMINI: Take them to hear an inspirational speaker . . .

IN CANCER: Take them to a place that reminds them of the good parts of their childhood . . .

IN LEO: Take them to an inspirational performance . . .

IN VIRGO: Take them to do some public service work together . . .

IN LIBRA: Take them somewhere beautiful . . .

IN SCORPIO: Take them to a particularly intense performance . . .

IN SAGITTARIUS: Take them on an adventurous road trip . . .

IN CAPRICORN: Take them somewhere that has practical uses for their life . . .

IN AQUARIUS: Take them to a place where they could never imagine themselves being . . .

IN PISCES: Take them to a sacred place . . .

IN THE FIRST HOUSE: . . . and encourage them to express their individuality.

IN THE SECOND HOUSE: . . . and get them to talk about their priorities.

IN THE THIRD HOUSE: . . . and get them to talk about whatever they like, so long as they talk.

IN THE FOURTH HOUSE: . . . and get them to vent about whether their family supports their individuality.

IN THE FIFTH HOUSE: . . . and get them to talk about whether people appreciate them.

IN THE SIXTH HOUSE: . . . and get them to vent about being a cog for their day job.

IN THE SEVENTH HOUSE: . . . and get them to talk about whether their relationships repress them.

IN THE EIGHTH HOUSE: . . . and get them to talk about the compromises they make for their sex life.

IN THE NINTH HOUSE: . . . and get them to talk about some faraway place that they've always dreamed of visiting.

IN THE TENTH HOUSE: . . . and get them to talk about the career that would be most "them."

IN THE ELEVENTH HOUSE: . . . and get them to talk about how the groups they belong to support or repress their individuality.

IN THE TWELFTH HOUSE: . . . and get them to talk about their hopes for the future.

Transiting Saturn

Place coins upon the appropriate altar.

Saturn Transiting Natal Sun

ENHANCING: Give aid to your grandparents or to someone who has successfully acted like a grandparent to you in the past.

AFFLICTING: Give aid to someone else's grandparent who is having a difficult time.

IN ARIES: Give them a gift that encourages them to exercise . . .

IN TAURUS: Give them a gift that makes them more comfortable . . .

IN GEMINI: Give them a gift that stimulates them intellectually . . .

IN CANCER: Give them a gift that helps them spend more quality time with the grandkids . . .

IN LEO: Give them a gift that makes them feel young again . . .

IN VIRGO: Give them a gift that helps them get organized . . .

IN LIBRA: Give them a gift to remedy some injustice in their life . . .

IN SCORPIO: Give them a gift of something they feel passionately intense about . . .

IN SAGITTARIUS: Give them a gift that broadens their horizons . . .

IN CAPRICORN: Give them a gift that makes them feel respected as a wise elder . . .

IN AQUARIUS: Give them a gift that must be used with a group of friends . . .

IN PISCES: Give them a gift that shows how much compassion you have for them . . .

IN THE FIRST HOUSE: . . . and tell them that they are courageous not to have given up.

IN THE SECOND HOUSE: . . . and help them build something useful.

IN THE THIRD HOUSE: . . . and have a good conversation with them.

IN THE FOURTH HOUSE: . . . and help out around the house.

IN THE FIFTH HOUSE: . . . and take them to some entertainment.

IN THE SIXTH HOUSE: . . . and help them clean grubby things.

IN THE SEVENTH HOUSE: . . . and give them two tickets that they can use as they wish.

IN THE EIGHTH HOUSE: . . . and let them use some resource of yours.

IN THE NINTH HOUSE: . . . and drive them somewhere.

IN THE TENTH HOUSE: . . . and give them a job reference or referral.

IN THE ELEVENTH HOUSE: . . . and spend time just being a friend.

IN THE TWELFTH HOUSE: . . . and tell them that they are not too old to follow their dreams.

Saturn Transiting Natal Moon

ENHANCING: Give a gift to a disabled child.

AFFLICTING: Give a gift to a child with a terminal illness.

IN ARIES: Give them a gift that gives them more energy . . .

IN TAURUS: Give them a gift that clears a financial blockage . . .

IN GEMINI: Give them a gift of written words . . .

IN CANCER: Give them a gift that helps their parents care for them . . .

IN LEO: Give them a gift that gets them out into the world . . .

IN VIRGO: Give them a gift that helps their health . . .

IN LIBRA: Give them a gift of the kind of art to which they aspire . . .

IN SCORPIO: Give them a gift that stretches their ideas about their art . . .

IN SAGITTARIUS: Give them a small adventure . . .

IN CAPRICORN: Give them a gift that helps with difficult and painful tasks . . .

IN AQUARIUS: Give them a gift that helps them feel good about being different . . .

IN PISCES: Give them a gift that relieves their stress and turmoil . . .

IN THE FIRST HOUSE: . . . in a way that tells them you appreciate them for who they are.

IN THE SECOND HOUSE: . . . in a way that reminds them of what is really important.

IN THE THIRD HOUSE: . . . in a way that inspires them to write or talk.

IN THE FOURTH HOUSE: . . . in a way that makes their home environment easier.

IN THE FIFTH HOUSE: . . . in a way that allows them to do something fun.

IN THE SIXTH HOUSE: . . . in a way that helps with their medical care.

IN THE SEVENTH HOUSE: . . . in a way that helps them find someone to talk to.

IN THE EIGHTH HOUSE: . . . in a way that helps them face their limits.

IN THE NINTH HOUSE: . . . in a way that allows them to get around better.

IN THE TENTH HOUSE: . . . in a way that gets them help from bureaucracies.

IN THE ELEVENTH HOUSE: . . . in a way that reminds them that they have friends.

IN THE TWELFTH HOUSE: . . . in a way that makes their lives more comfortable.

Saturn Transiting Natal Mercury

ENHANCING: Give a gift of words to someone who has a learning disability and who has done great work to compensate for it.

AFFLICTING: Give a gift of words to someone who is struggling with a learning disability.

IN ARIES: Let the words be about courage . . .

IN TAURUS: Let the words be about strength . . .

IN GEMINI: Let the words be about eloquence . . .

IN CANCER: Let the words be about honoring the emotions . . .

IN LEO: Let the words be about letting oneself shine . . .

IN VIRGO: Let the words be about self-improvement . . .

IN LIBRA: Let the words be about justice . . .

IN SCORPIO: Let the words be about anger . . .

IN SAGITTARIUS: Let the words be about truth . . .

IN CAPRICORN: Let the words be about understanding one's limitations . . .

IN AQUARIUS: Let the words be about valuing individuality . . .

IN PISCES: Let the words be about compassion . . .

IN THE FIRST HOUSE: . . . and the ability to be oneself.

IN THE SECOND HOUSE: . . . and the ability to be grateful for what one has.

IN THE THIRD HOUSE: . . . and the ability to stretch one's mind.

IN THE FOURTH HOUSE: . . . and the ability to overcome childhood trauma.

IN THE FIFTH HOUSE: . . . and the ability to take a risk.

IN THE SIXTH HOUSE: . . . and the ability to work hard.

IN THE SEVENTH HOUSE: . . . and the ability to work with others.

IN THE EIGHTH HOUSE: . . . and the ability to meet your destiny.

IN THE NINTH HOUSE: . . . and the ability to find your path.

IN THE TENTH HOUSE: . . . and the ability to command respect.

IN THE ELEVENTH HOUSE: . . . and the ability to defend your people.

IN THE TWELFTH HOUSE: . . . and the ability to know yourself.

Saturn Transiting Natal Venus

AFFLICTING: Help out someone who has just been through, or is going through, a nasty divorce.

ENHANCING: Help out someone who has recently been divorced and has managed to handle it skillfully without too many problems.

IN ARIES: Take them to a place where they can breathe fresh air . . .

IN TAURUS: Help them with some practical project . . .

IN GEMINI: Give them some easy conversation time . . .

IN CANCER: Help around the house or with family matters . . .

IN LEO: Take them to a place where they can be in charge . . .

IN VIRGO: Help them clean up a mess . . .

IN LIBRA: Help them go on a date with someone else . . .

IN SCORPIO: Take them to a public place with a lot of sexual energy . . .

IN SAGITTARIUS: Take them on a road trip . . .

IN CAPRICORN: Take them to a place where they can learn skills for their new life . . .

IN AQUARIUS: Take them somewhere that offers a mind-stretching experience for them . . .

IN PISCES: Be a sympathetic ear and let them vent . . .

IN THE FIRST HOUSE: . . . and give them an objective view of how they are seen by others.

IN THE SECOND HOUSE: . . . and remind them of their priorities.

IN THE THIRD HOUSE: . . . and remind them to communicate and use their words.

IN THE FOURTH HOUSE: . . . and remind them that you consider them family.

IN THE FIFTH HOUSE: . . . and remind them that they are talented.

IN THE SIXTH HOUSE: . . . and give them organizational advice on a hard task.

IN THE SEVENTH HOUSE: . . . and give them an opposing view on their opinions.

IN THE EIGHTH HOUSE: . . . and remind them to be ready for the unexpected.

IN THE NINTH HOUSE: . . . and remind them of their dreams and goals.

IN THE TENTH HOUSE: . . . and remind them of their reputation.

IN THE ELEVENTH HOUSE: . . . and remind them that you are a friend.

IN THE TWELFTH HOUSE: . . . and remind them that the subconscious cannot be neglected.

Saturn Transiting Natal Mars

ENHANCING: Do something to help someone who has anger management problems under control and who you use as a role model on the subject.

AFFLICTING: Do something to help someone who has anger management problems that they are managing with difficulty.

IN ARIES: Take them to a place where they can breathe fresh air . . .

IN TAURUS: Help them with some practical project . . .

IN GEMINI: Let them vent about anything they want . . .

IN CANCER: Help them around the house or with family matters . . . .

IN LEO: Take them to a place where they can be in charge of things . . .

IN VIRGO: Help them clean up a mess . . .

IN LIBRA: Take them to a place that you know is beautiful to them . . .

IN SCORPIO: Let them vent to you about their most horrible fantasy . . . .

IN SAGITTARIUS: Take them on a road trip . . .

IN CAPRICORN: Take them to a place where they can be the authority about something . . .

IN AQUARIUS: Take them somewhere that offers a mind-stretching experience for them . . .

IN PISCES: Let them vent to you about their pain at feeling set apart . . .

IN THE FIRST HOUSE: . . . and give them an objective view of how they are seen by others.

IN THE SECOND HOUSE: . . . and remind them of their priorities.

IN THE THIRD HOUSE: . . . and remind them to communicate and use their words.

IN THE FOURTH HOUSE: . . . and remind them that you consider them family.

IN THE FIFTH HOUSE: . . . and remind them that they are talented.

IN THE SIXTH HOUSE: . . . and give them organizational advice on a hard task.

IN THE SEVENTH HOUSE: . . . and give them an opposing view of their opinions.

IN THE EIGHTH HOUSE: . . . and remind them to be ready for the unexpected.

IN THE NINTH HOUSE: . . . and remind them of their dreams and goals.

IN THE TENTH HOUSE: . . . and remind them of their reputation.

IN THE ELEVENTH HOUSE: . . . and remind them that you are a friend.

IN THE TWELFTH HOUSE: . . . and remind them that the subconscious cannot be neglected.

Saturn Transiting Natal Jupiter

ENHANCING: Give aid to someone who has had reasonably good luck throughout their life, but who has recently had a run of bad luck, which is forcing them to become a more disciplined person.

AFFLICTING: Give aid to someone who has had reasonably good luck throughout their life, but who has recently had a run of bad luck, and it is dragging them down.

IN ARIES: Help someone who is a veteran or who self-identifies as a warrior . . .

IN TAURUS: Help someone who used to have money . . .

IN GEMINI: Help someone who is finding it difficult to communicate . . .

IN CANCER: Help someone who has become homeless . . .

IN LEO: Help someone who used to feel important and powerful . . .

IN VIRGO: Help someone who is unemployed . . .

IN LIBRA: Help someone going through a divorce . . .

IN SCORPIO: Help someone who is going through a mental breakdown . . .

IN SAGITTARIUS: Help someone who has come a long way and has no friends here . . .

IN CAPRICORN: Help someone who has lost their social standing . . .

IN AQUARIUS: Help someone who has had a change of ideals . . .

IN PISCES: Help someone who has been imprisoned . . .

IN THE FIRST HOUSE: . . . and your gift should help them do right with their physical body.

IN THE SECOND HOUSE: . . . and your gift should help them prioritize things.

IN THE THIRD HOUSE: . . . and your gift should be books or computer help.

IN THE FOURTH HOUSE: . . . and your gift should benefit their home and family life.

IN THE FIFTH HOUSE: . . . and your gift should help them with creative projects.

IN THE SIXTH HOUSE: . . . and your should offer to help with boring tasks.

IN THE SEVENTH HOUSE: . . . and your gift should allow them to go out with a partner.

IN THE EIGHTH HOUSE: . . . and your gift should help them end some painful habit.

IN THE NINTH HOUSE: . . . and your gift should help them with transportation somewhere.

IN THE TENTH HOUSE: . . . and your gift should help them in their career.

IN THE ELEVENTH HOUSE: . . . and your gift should help them find friends.

IN THE TWELFTH HOUSE: . . . and your gift should help them heal internally.

Saturn Transiting Natal Saturn

ENHANCING: Give a gift to an elderly person who is living alone and needs some aid.

AFFLICTING: Give a gift to an elderly person who is in an institution.

IN ARIES: Give them a gift that gives them more energy . . .

IN TAURUS: Give them a gift that clears a financial blockage . . .

IN GEMINI: Give them a gift of written words . . .

IN CANCER: Help them do things around the house . . .

IN LEO: Give them a gift that gets them out into the world . . .

IN VIRGO: Give them a gift that helps their health . . .

IN LIBRA: Give them a gift that beautifies their surroundings . . .

IN SCORPIO: Give them a gift that helps them in times of anger and resentment . . .

IN SAGITTARIUS: Give them a small adventure . . .

IN CAPRICORN: Give them a gift that helps with difficult and painful tasks . . .

IN AQUARIUS: Give them a gift that introduces them to something new . . .

IN PISCES: Give them a compassionate ear to hear them talk . . .

IN THE FIRST HOUSE: . . . in a way that tells them you appreciate them for who they are.

IN THE SECOND HOUSE: . . . in a way that reminds them of what is really important.

IN THE THIRD HOUSE: . . . in a way that inspires them to write or talk.

IN THE FOURTH HOUSE: . . . in a way that makes their home environment easier.

IN THE FIFTH HOUSE: . . . in a way that allows them to do something fun.

IN THE SIXTH HOUSE: . . . in a way that helps with their medical care.

IN THE SEVENTH HOUSE: . . . in a way that helps them find someone to talk to.

IN THE EIGHTH HOUSE: . . . in a way that helps them face their limits.

IN THE NINTH HOUSE: . . . in a way that allows them to get around better.

IN THE TENTH HOUSE: . . . in a way that gets them help from bureaucracies.

IN THE ELEVENTH HOUSE: . . . in a way that reminds them that they have friends.

IN THE TWELFTH HOUSE: . . . in a way that helps with their fears or the reality of institutionalization.

Saturn Transiting Natal Uranus

ENHANCING: Give aid to an activist who focuses on creating benefits for disabled people.

AFFLICTING: Give aid to an activist who focuses on the treatment of disabled people.

IN ARIES: Your gift should help some immediate emergency . . .

IN TAURUS: Your gift should help them obtain a solid foundation for their work . . .

IN GEMINI: Your gift should help make a change in their ability to disseminate information . . .

IN CANCER: Your gift should help make a change in their ability to work from home . . .

IN LEO: Your gift should help make a change in promoting them . . .

IN VIRGO: Your gift should help make a change in how they organize the details of their work . . .

IN LIBRA: Your gift should help make a change in their ability to find useful partners . . .

IN SCORPIO: Your gift should help make a change in their ability to face emotional adversity . . .

IN SAGITTARIUS: Your gift should help make a change in their ability to dream big . . .

IN CAPRICORN: Your gift should make a change in their ability to be seen as an authority . . .

IN AQUARIUS: Your gift should go directly toward their wildest goal . . .

IN PISCES: Your gift should make a change in their resources for handling stress . . .

IN THE FIRST HOUSE: . . . with respect to their public image.

IN THE SECOND HOUSE: . . . regarding financial solvency.

IN THE THIRD HOUSE: . . . regarding education about their cause.

IN THE FOURTH HOUSE: . . . regarding the ways their cause affects families.

IN THE FIFTH HOUSE: . . . regarding the ways their cause affects children.

IN THE SIXTH HOUSE: . . . regarding the ways their cause can be practically implemented.

IN THE SEVENTH HOUSE: . . . regarding the ways their cause is a natural ally of other causes.

IN THE EIGHTH HOUSE: . . . regarding financial aid from other parties.

IN THE NINTH HOUSE: . . . regarding the ways they can be heard in higher education.

IN THE TENTH HOUSE: . . . regarding the ways their cause can be a real career for them.

IN THE ELEVENTH HOUSE: . . . regarding the ways they can gain more volunteers.

IN THE TWELFTH HOUSE: . . . regarding the ways they can reach those who have no access.

Saturn Transiting Natal Neptune

ENHANCING: Give aid to someone who has successfully beaten mental illness or addiction.

AFFLICTING: Give aid to someone who is struggling with mental illness or addiction.

IN ARIES: Take them to a place where they can release pent-up rage and aggression . . .

IN TAURUS: Do something comfortable and unthreatening with them . . .

IN GEMINI: Give them a book on mental health . . .

IN CANCER: Keep them company during a period when they must stay home . . .

IN LEO: Take them to a club or coffeehouse where sobriety is the rule . . .

IN VIRGO: Help pay for some of their medical treatment . . .

IN LIBRA: Help them get through some small injustice . . .

IN SCORPIO: Take them to a performance that does not shy away from cathartic emotions . . .

IN SAGITTARIUS: Take them on a road trip to someplace interesting . . .

IN CAPRICORN: Help them navigate authorities and bureaucracies . . .

IN AQUARIUS: Bring them to help volunteer for humans in worse straits than them . . .

IN PISCES: Give them a compassionate ear to complain to . . .

IN THE FIRST HOUSE: . . . and take them shopping for something to wear.

IN THE SECOND HOUSE: . . . and do something that clearly supports the values of self-improvement.

IN THE THIRD HOUSE: . . . and give them a book on how to communicate better.

IN THE FOURTH HOUSE: . . . and do something to help them break out of old patterns.

IN THE FIFTH HOUSE: . . . and take them somewhere low-risk to have fun.

IN THE SIXTH HOUSE: . . . and help pay for part of any medications they may be taking.

IN THE SEVENTH HOUSE: . . . and help them find a mentor.

IN THE EIGHTH HOUSE: . . . and help them get access to outside resources.

IN THE NINTH HOUSE: . . . and drive them to their appointments.

IN THE TENTH HOUSE: . . . and help them focus on important tasks.

IN THE ELEVENTH HOUSE: . . . and take them to a support group.

IN THE TWELFTH HOUSE: . . . and give them support to get through their psych appointments.

Saturn Transiting Natal Pluto

ENHANCING: Give a gift to someone who has recovered from a severe illness or injury, but has permanent damage from its effects.

AFFLICTING: Give a gift to someone who is suffering from a terminal illness.

IN ARIES: Lend them some strength to get through an ordeal that frightens them . . .

IN TAURUS: Give them a gift of a steady hand in a frustrating task . . .

IN GEMINI: Give them a gift of several days of conversation on their favorite topics . . .

IN CANCER: Make or buy them food that warms their soul . . .

IN LEO: Do something to make them feel beautiful and admired . . .

IN VIRGO: Do some scut-work task that they have been dreading . . .

IN LIBRA: Give them a gift that beautifies their environment . . .

IN SCORPIO: Give them a gift of writings about death . . .

IN SAGITTARIUS: Give them a trip to someplace new . . .

IN CAPRICORN: Give them a gift that provides practical aid for their physical condition . . .

IN AQUARIUS: Give them a gift of a new experience they never thought they would get . . .

IN PISCES: Give them a gift of a compassionate ear to listen to them . . .

IN THE FIRST HOUSE: . . . and do something for their physical well-being.

IN THE SECOND HOUSE: . . . and buy them something that they have always wanted.

IN THE THIRD HOUSE: . . . and pay their phone bill.

IN THE FOURTH HOUSE: . . . and help them get their house in order.

IN THE FIFTH HOUSE: . . . and take them to have some fun.

IN THE SIXTH HOUSE: . . . and help organize a task that has fallen behind.

IN THE SEVENTH HOUSE: . . . and arrange to let them spend time with someone they like.

IN THE EIGHTH HOUSE: . . . and encourage them to talk about their fears.

IN THE NINTH HOUSE: . . . and provide for some degree of transportation.

IN THE TENTH HOUSE: . . . and support them in dealing with authority figures.

IN THE ELEVENTH HOUSE: . . . and let them know that they have a friend.

IN THE TWELFTH HOUSE: . . . and give them support and aid in dealing with doctors and hospitals.

Transiting Uranus

Burn incense on the appropriate altar.

Uranus Transiting Natal Sun

AFFLICTING: Give a gift of time or resources to a progressive group or nonprofit organization that specializes in fighting for the rights of those with minority identities.

ENHANCING: Give a gift of time or resources to a progressive group or nonprofit organization that provides benefits to those with minority identities.

IN ARIES: The group should have an active, in-your-face policy . . .

IN TAURUS: The group should be focused on strong positive values . . .

IN GEMINI: The group should be primarily information based . . .

IN CANCER: The group should work with needy minority parents or children . . .

IN LEO: The group should have a street-theater approach to activism . . .

IN VIRGO: The group should be well organized and have hard workers . . .

IN LIBRA: The group should focus on social justice . . .

IN SCORPIO: The group should be a sexual minority . . .

IN SAGITTARIUS: The group should have a spiritual or religious slant . . .

IN CAPRICORN: The group should provide aid in getting ahead in the world . . .

IN AQUARIUS: The group should be serving the needs of the weirdest of the weird . . .

IN PISCES: The group should focus on healing the abused . . .

IN THE FIRST HOUSE: . . . and your gift should clear up an immediate and urgent problem.

IN THE SECOND HOUSE: . . . and your gift should reward the group for their positive values.

IN THE THIRD HOUSE: . . . and your gift should be directed toward the dissemination of information.

IN THE FOURTH HOUSE: . . . and your gift should give their employees some comfort.

IN THE FIFTH HOUSE: . . . and your gift should be high profile and flashy.

IN THE SIXTH HOUSE: . . . and your gift should be many hours of scut-work labor.

IN THE SEVENTH HOUSE: . . . and your gift should aid in their legal battles.

IN THE EIGHTH HOUSE: . . . and your gift should be self-sustaining for a long time.

IN THE NINTH HOUSE: . . . and your gift should help them network with many other groups.

IN THE TENTH HOUSE: . . . and your gift should help give their employees practical benefits.

IN THE ELEVENTH HOUSE: . . . and your gift should go toward their future as an organization.

IN THE TWELFTH HOUSE: . . . and your gift should be anonymous.

Uranus Transiting Natal Moon

AFFLICTING: Give a gift of time or resources to a group or nonprofit organization that specializes in fighting for the rights of children and families in troubled situations.

ENHANCING: Give a gift of time or resources to a group or nonprofit organization that specializes in providing benefits for children and families in troubled situations.

IN ARIES: The group should focus on heroic emergency efforts such as providing assistance after natural disasters . . .

IN TAURUS: The group should be solid and have a long-term reputation . . .

IN GEMINI: The group should focus on the dissemination of information . . .

IN CANCER: The group should focus on the needs of food and shelter . . .

IN LEO: The group should focus on the needs of teenagers . . .

IN VIRGO: The group should aid them in connecting to programs, resources, and paperwork . . .

IN LIBRA: The group should have a strong social justice focus . . .

IN SCORPIO: The group should have a strong mental health slant . . .

IN SAGITTARIUS: The group should work with immigrants or refugees from other countries . . .

IN CAPRICORN: The group should work with existing governmental agencies . . .

IN AQUARIUS: The group should specialize in GLBT youth/parents or nontraditional families . . .

IN PISCES: The group should focus on issues of healing abuse . . .

IN THE FIRST HOUSE: . . . and your gift should help them get more attention.

IN THE SECOND HOUSE: . . . and your gift should ease a financial burden.

IN THE THIRD HOUSE: . . . and your gift should go directly toward books, pamphlets, or information.

IN THE FOURTH HOUSE: . . . and your gift should go toward finding them shelter.

IN THE FIFTH HOUSE: . . . and your gift should go toward working with very young children.

IN THE SIXTH HOUSE: . . . and your gift should go toward finding them food or health care.

IN THE SEVENTH HOUSE: . . . and your gift should address an immediate injustice.

IN THE EIGHTH HOUSE: . . . and your gift should address their issues of deep emotional trauma.

IN THE NINTH HOUSE: . . . and your gift should help them acquire transportation.

IN THE TENTH HOUSE: . . . and your gift should help them find financial backers.

IN THE ELEVENTH HOUSE: . . . and your gift should go toward their long-term goals.

IN THE TWELFTH HOUSE: . . . and your gift should address healing abuse.

Uranus Transiting Natal Mercury

AFFLICTING: Give a gift of time or resources to a progressive group or nonprofit organization that specializes in educating the public about dangerously ignorant lies and misunderstandings.

ENHANCING: Give a gift of time or resources to a progressive group or nonprofit organization that specializes in the dissemination of useful information.

IN ARIES: The group should be fighting passionately for a cause . . .

IN TAURUS: The group should give out useful and practical information . . .

IN GEMINI: The group should involve a telephone hotline or info line . . .

IN CANCER: The group should aid children or families in some way . . .

IN LEO: The group should be highly visible and charismatic . . .

IN VIRGO: The group should be a low-profile, low-money, hard-working edifice . . .

IN LIBRA: The group should specialize in legal issues . . .

IN SCORPIO: The group should specialize in uncovering and exposing hidden facts . . .

IN SAGITTARIUS: The group should be building an extensive library . . .

IN CAPRICORN: The group should work with local businesses . . .

IN AQUARIUS: The group should have an unusual and futuristic philosophy . . .

IN PISCES: The group should be aiding those who cannot speak for themselves . . .

IN THE FIRST HOUSE: . . . and your gift should go straight to the group's public interface.

IN THE SECOND HOUSE: . . . and your gift should reflect the values you have in common.

IN THE THIRD HOUSE: . . . and your gift should go directly into information dissemination.

IN THE FOURTH HOUSE: . . . and your gift should go toward getting the information to more homes.

IN THE FIFTH HOUSE: . . . and your gift should make their medium more appealing.

IN THE SIXTH HOUSE: . . . and your gift should go toward bookkeeping or accounting.

IN THE SEVENTH HOUSE: . . . and your gift should help the group make alliances with other groups.

IN THE EIGHTH HOUSE: . . . and your gift should be used for serious research.

IN THE NINTH HOUSE: . . . and your gift should be used to help the group expand geographically.

IN THE TENTH HOUSE: . . . and your gift should sponsor the group's public speakers.

IN THE ELEVENTH HOUSE: . . . and your gift should go toward educating other groups about them.

IN THE TWELFTH HOUSE: . . . and your gift should get the info to those unable to see, hear, or read.

Uranus Transiting Natal Venus

AFFLICTING: Give a gift of time or resources to a group or nonprofit organization that specializes in fighting for the rights of people with nontraditional relationships.

ENHANCING: Give a gift of time or resources to a group or nonprofit organization that specializes in providing benefits for people with nontraditional relationships.

IN ARIES: The group should use aggressive, in-your-face tactics . . .

IN TAURUS: The group should be quiet and comparatively conservative . . .

IN GEMINI: The group should disseminate a lot of writing on the subject . . .

IN CANCER: The group should focus on alternative families with children . . .

IN LEO: The group should be a high-profile organization . . .

IN VIRGO: The group should work with sexual health issues . . .

IN LIBRA: The group should work with issues of equal treatment . . .

IN SCORPIO: The group should work with a sexual minority that makes you uncomfortable . . .

IN SAGITTARIUS: The group should work with issues of sexual freedom . . .

IN CAPRICORN: The group should work with issues of career equality . . .

IN AQUARIUS: The group's demographic and methods should be highly controversial . . .

IN PISCES: The group should focus on healing emotional wounds in victims . . .

IN THE FIRST HOUSE: . . . and your gift should help with public awareness.

IN THE SECOND HOUSE: . . . and your gift should help them manage their money.

IN THE THIRD HOUSE: . . . and your gift should help disseminate information.

IN THE FOURTH HOUSE: . . . and your gift should help repair damaged family bonds.

IN THE FIFTH HOUSE: . . . and your gift should educate children.

IN THE SIXTH HOUSE: . . . and your gift should be diligent scut work.

IN THE SEVENTH HOUSE: . . . and your gift should help educate about alternative marriages.

IN THE EIGHTH HOUSE: . . . and your gift should help prevent violence and death.

IN THE NINTH HOUSE: . . . and your gift should help academic research on the subject.

IN THE TENTH HOUSE: . . . and your gift should help educate employers.

IN THE ELEVENTH HOUSE: . . . and your gift should help educate other organizations.

IN THE TWELFTH HOUSE: . . . and your gift should aid the healing of those damaged by hate crimes.

Uranus Transiting Natal Mars

AFFLICTING: Give a gift of time or resources to a group or nonprofit organization that fights against the perpetrators of violence.

ENHANCING: Give a gift of time or resources to a group or nonprofit organization that gives aid to the victims of violence.

IN ARIES: The group should use aggressive, in-your-face tactics . . .

IN TAURUS: The group should have a solid history of success . . .

IN GEMINI: The group should use education to prevent violence . . .

IN CANCER: The group should target violence among children . . .

IN LEO: The group should employ many public speakers . . .

IN VIRGO: The group should focus on harassment of silent minorities . . .

IN LIBRA: The group should focus on battering within couples . . .

IN SCORPIO: The group should specialize in sexual violence . . .

IN SAGITTARIUS: The group should challenge stereotypes that incite violence . . .

IN CAPRICORN: The group should work with government agencies . . .

IN AQUARIUS: The group should specialize in outreach over the Internet . . .

IN PISCES: The group should teach self-defense to the chronically passive eternal victim type . . .

IN THE FIRST HOUSE: . . . and your gift should help them with community visibility.

IN THE SECOND HOUSE: . . . and your gift should help them raise funding.

IN THE THIRD HOUSE: . . . and your gift should go toward brochures or printed materials.

IN THE FOURTH HOUSE: . . . and your gift should add comfort to the volunteers' work environment.

IN THE FIFTH HOUSE: . . . and your gift should go toward educating adolescents.

IN THE SIXTH HOUSE: . . . and your gift should help relieve them of small niggling tasks.

IN THE SEVENTH HOUSE: . . . and your gift should help with legal funding.

IN THE EIGHTH HOUSE: . . . and your gift should aid them in acquiring grant money.

IN THE NINTH HOUSE: . . . and your gift should help them fund transportation.

IN THE TENTH HOUSE: . . . and your gift should help get them more community respect.

IN THE ELEVENTH HOUSE: . . . and your gift should benefit long-term dreams that have been shelved.

IN THE TWELFTH HOUSE: . . . and your gift should help get people counseling to heal.

Uranus Transiting Natal Jupiter

AFFLICTING: Give a gift of time or resources to a group or nonprofit organization that is trying to change the world in a way that emphasizes preventing disaster.

ENHANCING: Give a gift of time or resources to a group or nonprofit organization that is trying to change the world in a way that emphasizes bringing long-term, positive benefits.

IN ARIES: The group should deal with issues of war and large-scale violence . . .

IN TAURUS: The group should deal with issues of world poverty . . .

IN GEMINI: The group should focus on disseminating controversial writings . . .

IN CANCER: The group should deal with the preservation of the environment . . .

IN LEO: The group should focus on the right to self-expression . . .

IN VIRGO: The group should deal with issues of public health care . . .

IN LIBRA: The group should focus on justice for the oppressed . . .

IN SCORPIO: The group should focus on local violence . . .

IN SAGITTARIUS: The group should deal with issues of higher education of minorities . . .

IN CAPRICORN: The group should deal with corporate ethics and fair business . . .

IN AQUARIUS: The group should directly address changing people's ideas and worldviews . . .

IN PISCES: The group should deal with justice for prisoners . . .

IN THE FIRST HOUSE: . . . and your gift should aid publicity of their issue.

IN THE SECOND HOUSE: . . . and your gift should help their financial situation.

IN THE THIRD HOUSE: . . . and your gift should help with disseminating educational material.

IN THE FOURTH HOUSE: . . . and your gift should help them reach families and private homes.

IN THE FIFTH HOUSE: . . . and your gift should fund speakers in children's schools.

IN THE SIXTH HOUSE: . . . and your gift should be one of labor on small niggling tasks.

IN THE SEVENTH HOUSE: . . . and your gift should directly aid their legal matters.

IN THE EIGHTH HOUSE: . . . and your gift should help them get grant money from outside.

IN THE NINTH HOUSE: . . . and your gift should fund speakers at colleges and universities.

IN THE TENTH HOUSE: . . . and your gift should help them lobby government agencies.

IN THE ELEVENTH HOUSE: . . . and your gift should help them network with other organizations.

IN THE TWELFTH HOUSE: . . . and your gift should help them reach an unreachable population.

Uranus Transiting Natal Saturn

AFFLICTING: Give a gift of time or resources to a group or nonprofit organization that aids those suffering from a disability or health problem.

ENHANCING: Give a gift of time or resources to a group or nonprofit organization that specializes in preventing disabilities or health problems.

IN ARIES: The group should work with war veterans . . .

IN TAURUS: The group should work with the deaf . . .

IN GEMINI: The group should work with diseases of motor control and nerve degeneration . . .

IN CANCER: The group should work with children or pregnant women . . .

IN LEO: The group should work with the blind . . .

IN VIRGO: The group should work with epidemic diseases . . .

IN LIBRA: The group should put a high value on fair access to medical treatment . . .

IN SCORPIO: The group should focus on sexually transmitted diseases . . .

IN SAGITTARIUS: The group should focus on walking disabilities . . .

IN CAPRICORN: The group should work with the afflictions of elderly people . . .

IN AQUARIUS: The group should work with rare genetic disorders . . .

IN PISCES: The group should focus on mental disabilities . . .

IN THE FIRST HOUSE: . . . and your gift should help with public awareness.

IN THE SECOND HOUSE: . . . and your gift should help them manage their money.

IN THE THIRD HOUSE: . . . and your gift should help disseminate information.

IN THE FOURTH HOUSE: . . . and your gift should help people get better access to housing.

IN THE FIFTH HOUSE: . . . and your gift should support new and creative ideas for aid.

IN THE SIXTH HOUSE: . . . and your gift should be diligent scut work.

IN THE SEVENTH HOUSE: . . . and your gift should help create alliances between groups.

IN THE EIGHTH HOUSE: . . . and your gift should help prevent deaths.

IN THE NINTH HOUSE: . . . and your gift should help research on the subject.

IN THE TENTH HOUSE: . . . and your gift should help them obtain corporate sponsors.

IN THE ELEVENTH HOUSE: . . . and your gift should help educate other organizations.

IN THE TWELFTH HOUSE: . . . and your gift should promote emotional support for sufferers.

Uranus Transiting Natal Uranus

AFFLICTING: Give a gift of time or resources to a group or nonprofit organization that researches new technology to aid the afflicted.

ENHANCING: Give a gift of time or resources to a group or nonprofit organization that researches new technology for the love of discovery.

IN ARIES: The focus of the research should be alternative energy . . .

IN TAURUS: The focus of the research should be organic and alternative agriculture . . .

IN GEMINI: The focus of the research should be studying the brain . . .

IN CANCER: The focus of the research should be prenatal development . . .

IN LEO: The focus of the research should be issues of adolescence . . .

IN VIRGO: The focus of the research should be on curing diseases . . .

IN LIBRA: The focus of the research should be on human sexual problems . . .

IN SCORPIO: The focus of the research should be on death . . .

IN SAGITTARIUS: The focus of the research should be extraplanetary travel . . .

IN CAPRICORN: The focus of the research should be on helping disabled people . . .

IN AQUARIUS: The focus of the research should be artificial intelligence . . .

IN PISCES: The focus of the research should be mental illness . . .

IN THE FIRST HOUSE: . . . and your gift should help with public awareness.

IN THE SECOND HOUSE: . . . and your gift should help them manage their money.

IN THE THIRD HOUSE: . . . and your gift should help disseminate information.

IN THE FOURTH HOUSE: . . . and your gift should aid future generations.

IN THE FIFTH HOUSE: . . . and your gift should support new and creative ideas.

IN THE SIXTH HOUSE: . . . and your gift should be diligent scut work.

IN THE SEVENTH HOUSE: . . . and your gift should help create alliances between groups.

IN THE EIGHTH HOUSE: . . . and your gift should help them get the financial aid of others.

IN THE NINTH HOUSE: . . . and your gift should help research at colleges.

IN THE TENTH HOUSE: . . . and your gift should help them obtain corporate sponsors.

IN THE ELEVENTH HOUSE: . . . and your gift should help support future goals.

IN THE TWELFTH HOUSE: . . . and your gift should help with quality control of hidden problems.

Uranus Transiting Natal Neptune

AFFLICTING: Give a gift of time or resources to a group or nonprofit organization in the human services field that concentrates on helping people in crisis.

ENHANCING: Give a gift of time or resources to a group or nonprofit organization in the human services field that gives spiritual and psychological aid to their target clients.

IN ARIES: The group should help confront spiritual assumptions about war and violence . . .

IN TAURUS: The group should help confront spiritual assumptions . . .

IN GEMINI: The group should help confront spiritual assumptions about past research . . .

IN CANCER: The group should help confront spiritual assumptions about family values . . .

IN LEO: The group should help confront spiritual assumptions about individual needs . . .

IN VIRGO: The group should help confront spiritual assumptions about service . . .

IN LIBRA: The group should help confront spiritual assumptions about marriage . . .

IN SCORPIO: The group should help confront spiritual assumptions about sex . . .

IN SAGITTARIUS: The group should help confront spiritual assumptions about religious blindness . . .

IN CAPRICORN: The group should help confront spiritual assumptions about class and access . . .

IN AQUARIUS: The group should help confront spiritual assumptions about race and culture . . .

IN PISCES: The group should help confront spiritual assumptions about victimization . . .

IN THE FIRST HOUSE: . . . but in turn it should give aid that honors individual situations and needs.

IN THE SECOND HOUSE: . . . but in turn it should give examples of positive values.

IN THE THIRD HOUSE: . . . but in turn it should give written documentation for its beliefs.

IN THE FOURTH HOUSE: . . . but in turn it should take people's upbringings into consideration.

IN THE FIFTH HOUSE: . . . but in turn it should use humor to get through to people.

IN THE SIXTH HOUSE: . . . but in turn it should give practical help with everyday problems.

IN THE SEVENTH HOUSE: . . . but in turn it should give examples of ways to improve relationships.

IN THE EIGHTH HOUSE: . . . but in turn it should show a clear path to self-transformation.

IN THE NINTH HOUSE: . . . but in turn it should find ways to reach members of traditional religions.

IN THE TENTH HOUSE: . . . but in turn it should find ways to reach members of different classes.

IN THE ELEVENTH HOUSE: . . . but in turn it should be flexible enough to work with other groups that have different values.

IN THE TWELFTH HOUSE: . . . but in turn it should take people's individual spiritual paths into account.

Uranus Transiting Natal Pluto

ENHANCING: Give a gift of time or resources to a group or nonprofit organization that specializes in research into controversial areas.

AFFLICTING: Give a gift of time or resources to a group or nonprofit organization that specializes in support for people involved in controversial issues.

IN ARIES: The group should focus on victims of violence or war . . .

IN TAURUS: The group should focus on illness from agricultural or industrial chemicals . . .

IN GEMINI: The group should focus on honesty in the media . . .

IN CANCER: The group should focus on child sexual abuse . . .

IN LEO: The group should focus on some aspect of looksism . . .

IN VIRGO: The group should focus on socially stigmatized health problems . . .

IN LIBRA: The group should focus on some controversial social injustice . . .

IN SCORPIO: The group should focus on unusual sexual practices . . .

IN SAGITTARIUS: The group should focus on religious honesty and hypocrisy . . .

IN CAPRICORN: The group should focus on government honesty and fairness . . .

IN AQUARIUS: The group should focus on inhumane treatment of minorities . . .

IN PISCES: The group should focus on issues of the mentally ill or addicted . . .

IN THE FIRST HOUSE: . . . and your gift should help with public awareness.

IN THE SECOND HOUSE: . . . and your gift should help them manage their money.

IN THE THIRD HOUSE: . . . and your gift should help disseminate information.

IN THE FOURTH HOUSE: . . . and your gift should aid future generations.

IN THE FIFTH HOUSE: . . . and your gift should support new and creative ideas.

IN THE SIXTH HOUSE: . . . and your gift should be diligent scut work.

IN THE SEVENTH HOUSE: . . . and your gift should help create alliances between groups.

IN THE EIGHTH HOUSE: . . . and your gift should help them get the financial aid of others.

IN THE NINTH HOUSE: . . . and your gift should help research at colleges.

IN THE TENTH HOUSE: . . . and your gift should help them obtain corporate sponsors.

IN THE ELEVENTH HOUSE: . . . and your gift should help support future goals.

IN THE TWELFTH HOUSE: . . . and your gift should help with quality control of hidden problems.

Transiting Neptune

Place a chalice of wine upon the appropriate altar.

Neptune Transiting Natal Sun

ENHANCING: Give aid to a large, public, and thriving religious or spiritual organization that promotes the idea of dissolving one's ego in the spiritual realm.

AFFLICTING: Give aid to a small and struggling religious or spiritual organization that promotes the idea of dissolving one's ego in the spiritual realm.

IN ARIES: Your gift should aid their foremost project . . .

IN TAURUS: Your gift should help with maintenance of a building . . .

IN GEMINI: Your gift should go toward building their library . . .

IN CANCER: Your gift should go toward child care . . .

IN LEO: Your gift should be flamboyant and visible . . .

IN VIRGO: Your gift should help them get organized . . .

IN LIBRA: Your gift should help them defend themselves legally . . .

IN SCORPIO: Your gift should help with community members who are in crisis . . .

IN SAGITTARIUS: Your gift should help with the higher education of community members . . .

IN CAPRICORN: Your gift should help them gain status in the outer community . . .

IN AQUARIUS: Your gift should create an innovation . . .

IN PISCES: Your gift should aid healing and counseling . . .

IN THE FIRST HOUSE: . . . and aid how they are seen by the community.

IN THE SECOND HOUSE: . . . and reflect their values.

IN THE THIRD HOUSE: . . . and help them communicate their message more effectively.

IN THE FOURTH HOUSE: . . . and directly aid the core group of the organization.

IN THE FIFTH HOUSE: . . . and help with a creative project.

IN THE SIXTH HOUSE: . . . and help with the physical health of their community members.

IN THE SEVENTH HOUSE: . . . and aid them in providing counseling for couples.

IN THE EIGHTH HOUSE: . . . and help them transform their ideas around something important.

IN THE NINTH HOUSE: . . . and help with travel expenses.

IN THE TENTH HOUSE: . . . and help them deal with government regulations.

IN THE ELEVENTH HOUSE: . . . and help them network with allies.

IN THE TWELFTH HOUSE: . . . and help them to better serve the unconscious needs of their community.

Neptune Transiting Natal Moon

ENHANCING: Give aid to a religious or spiritual organization that puts a high value on women and their experience and perspective.

AFFLICTING: Give aid to a religious or spiritual organization that is working hard to put a higher value on women and their experience and perspective than they have in the past.

IN ARIES: Your gift should aid their foremost project . . .

IN TAURUS: Your gift should help with maintenance of a building . . .

IN GEMINI: Your gift should go toward building their library . . .

IN CANCER: Your gift should go toward child care . . .

IN LEO: Your gift should be flamboyant and visible . . .

IN VIRGO: Your gift should help them get organized . . .

IN LIBRA: Your gift should help them defend themselves legally . . .

IN SCORPIO: Your gift should help with community members who are in crisis . . .

IN SAGITTARIUS: Your gift should help with the higher education of community members . . .

IN CAPRICORN: Your gift should help them gain status in the outer community . . .

IN AQUARIUS: Your gift should create an innovation . . .

IN PISCES: Your gift should aid healing and counseling . . .

IN THE FIRST HOUSE: . . . and aid how they are seen by the community.

IN THE SECOND HOUSE: . . . and reflect their values.

IN THE THIRD HOUSE: . . . and help them communicate their message more effectively.

IN THE FOURTH HOUSE: . . . and directly aid the core group of the organization.

IN THE FIFTH HOUSE: . . . and help with a creative project.

IN THE SIXTH HOUSE: . . . and help with the physical health of their community members.

IN THE SEVENTH HOUSE: . . . and aid them in providing counseling for couples.

IN THE EIGHTH HOUSE: . . . and help them transform their ideas around something important.

IN THE NINTH HOUSE: . . . and help with travel expenses.

IN THE TENTH HOUSE: . . . and help them deal with government regulations.

IN THE ELEVENTH HOUSE: . . . and help them network with allies.

IN THE TWELFTH HOUSE: . . . and help them to better serve the unconscious needs of their community.

Neptune Transiting Natal Mercury

ENHANCING: Give aid to a poet, songwriter, or someone who embodies the ideal of the bard, and whose writing is spiritual in nature.

AFFLICTING: Give aid to a poet or songwriter who is struggling or to someone who is attempting to achieve the status of a bard, and whose struggles are spiritual in nature.

IN ARIES: Help them get out and exercise . . .

IN TAURUS: Give or buy them a stress-relieving massage . . .

IN GEMINI: Help them get books that they've wanted for a long time . . .

IN CANCER: Buy or cook them an aesthetically beautiful meal . . .

IN LEO: Take them to a place where they can read aloud or perform for an audience . . .

IN VIRGO: Get them something practical that helps organize their life . . .

IN LIBRA: Give them a gift of words that deal with justice or beauty . . .

IN SCORPIO: Give them a gift of words that deal with pain and power . . .

IN SAGITTARIUS: Give them a gift that frees up their time . . .

IN CAPRICORN: Give them a gift that helps stave off a looming bureaucracy . . .

IN AQUARIUS: Encourage them to do something uncharacteristic . . .

IN PISCES: Take them to a spiritual function that you think they'll enjoy . . .

IN THE FIRST HOUSE: . . . and help them polish their demeanor to be more effective in their work.

IN THE SECOND HOUSE: . . . and give them a gift that shows they are worth a lot.

IN THE THIRD HOUSE: . . . and arrange to have them speak to interested audiences.

IN THE FOURTH HOUSE: . . . and help them around the house.

IN THE FIFTH HOUSE: . . . and take them to a concert, art gallery, or someplace creative and beautiful.

IN THE SIXTH HOUSE: . . . and do some scut work for them that they have been dreading.

IN THE SEVENTH HOUSE: . . . and give aid that allows them to spend time with a partner.

IN THE EIGHTH HOUSE: . . . and give them poetry that deals with transformation.

IN THE NINTH HOUSE: . . . and give them a gift that helps with their education.

IN THE TENTH HOUSE: . . . and do something to aid their career.

IN THE ELEVENTH HOUSE: . . . and encourage them to spend time with a peer group.

IN THE TWELFTH HOUSE: . . . and encourage them to spend time alone, meditating.

Neptune Transiting Natal Venus

ENHANCING: Give aid to someone who writes, speaks, or teaches about the sacredness of sexuality, or who embodies the archetype of the sacred prostitute, and who is comfortable with their path.

AFFLICTING: Give aid to someone who writes, speaks, or teaches about the sacredness of sexuality, or who embodies the archetype of the sacred prostitute, and who is struggling with their path.

IN ARIES: Help them get out and exercise . . .

IN TAURUS: Give or buy them a stress-relieving massage . . .

IN GEMINI: Help them get books that they've wanted for a long time . . .

IN CANCER: Buy or cook them an aesthetically beautiful meal . . .

IN LEO: Take them out dancing or to a place where they can show off . . .

IN VIRGO: Get them something practical that helps organize their life . . .

IN LIBRA: Give them something that brings beauty into their life . . .

IN SCORPIO: Give them a gift that they can use for ritual sex . . .

IN SAGITTARIUS: Give them a gift that frees up their time . . .

IN CAPRICORN: Give them a gift that helps stave off a looming bureaucracy . . .

IN AQUARIUS: Encourage them to do something uncharacteristic . . .

IN PISCES: Take them to a spiritual function that you think they'll enjoy . . .

IN THE FIRST HOUSE: . . . and take them shopping for new clothes.

IN THE SECOND HOUSE: . . . and give them a gift that shows they are worth a lot.

IN THE THIRD HOUSE: . . . and arrange to have them speak to interested audiences.

IN THE FOURTH HOUSE: . . . and help them around the house.

IN THE FIFTH HOUSE: . . . and take them to a concert, art gallery, or someplace creative and beautiful.

IN THE SIXTH HOUSE: . . . and offer to serve them in some way, instead of them serving you.

IN THE SEVENTH HOUSE: . . . and give aid that allows them to spend time with a partner.

IN THE EIGHTH HOUSE: . . . and give them poetry that expresses the sacredness of sexuality.

IN THE NINTH HOUSE: . . . and give them a gift that helps with their education.

IN THE TENTH HOUSE: . . . and do something to aid their positive public image.

IN THE ELEVENTH HOUSE: . . . and encourage them to spend time with a peer group.

IN THE TWELFTH HOUSE: . . . and encourage them to spend time alone, meditating.

Neptune Transiting Natal Mars

ENHANCING: Give aid to someone who successfully embodies the archetype of the spiritual warrior, regardless of what battlefield they have chosen.

AFFLICTING: Give aid to someone who is attempting to live the path of the spiritual warrior, but who is struggling with it.

IN ARIES: Give them a weapon, real or symbolic . . .

IN TAURUS: Give or buy them a stress-relieving massage . . .

IN GEMINI: Help them get books that they've wanted for a long time . . .

IN CANCER: Buy or cook them an aesthetically beautiful meal . . .

IN LEO: Give them a gift that makes them feel admired and appreciated . . .

IN VIRGO: Get them something practical that helps organize their life . . .

IN LIBRA: Give them something that brings beauty into their life . . .

IN SCORPIO: Give them a gift that helps them release anger or sexual frustration . . .

IN SAGITTARIUS: Give them a gift that frees up their time . . .

IN CAPRICORN: Give them a gift that helps stave off a looming bureaucracy . . .

IN AQUARIUS: Encourage them to do something uncharacteristic . . .

IN PISCES: Take them to a spiritual function that you think they'll enjoy . . .

IN THE FIRST HOUSE: . . . and take them to a place where they can be themselves.

IN THE SECOND HOUSE: . . . and the gift should acknowledge their sense of honor.

IN THE THIRD HOUSE: . . . and arrange to have them speak to interested audiences.

IN THE FOURTH HOUSE: . . . and help them around the house.

IN THE FIFTH HOUSE: . . . and take them to a concert, art gallery, or someplace creative and beautiful.

IN THE SIXTH HOUSE: . . . and offer to serve them in some way.

IN THE SEVENTH HOUSE: . . . and give aid that allows them to spend time with a partner.

IN THE EIGHTH HOUSE: . . . and give them a gift of words about spiritual struggle.

IN THE NINTH HOUSE: . . . and give them a gift that helps with their education.

IN THE TENTH HOUSE: . . . and do something to aid their career.

IN THE ELEVENTH HOUSE: . . . and encourage them to spend time with a peer group.

IN THE TWELFTH HOUSE: . . . and encourage them to spend time alone, meditating.

Neptune Transiting Natal Jupiter

ENHANCING: Give aid to a religious or spiritual organization with a strong focus on charitable and philanthropic activities.

AFFLICTING: Give aid to a religious or spiritual organization that is struggling to increase its level of charitable and philanthropic activities.

IN ARIES: Your gift should aid their foremost project . . .

IN TAURUS: Your gift should help with maintenance of a building . . .

IN GEMINI: Your gift should go toward building their library . . .

IN CANCER: Your gift should go toward child care . . .

IN LEO: Your gift should be flamboyant and visible . . .

IN VIRGO: Your gift should help them get organized . . .

IN LIBRA: Your gift should help them defend themselves legally . . .

IN SCORPIO: Your gift should help with community members who are in crisis . . .

IN SAGITTARIUS: Your gift should help with the higher education of community members . . .

IN CAPRICORN: Your gift should help them gain status in the outer community . . .

IN AQUARIUS: Your gift should create an innovation . . .

IN PISCES: Your gift should aid healing and counseling . . .

IN THE FIRST HOUSE: . . . and aid how they are seen by the community.

IN THE SECOND HOUSE: . . . and reflect their values.

IN THE THIRD HOUSE: . . . and help them communicate their message more effectively.

IN THE FOURTH HOUSE: . . . and directly aid the core group of the organization.

IN THE FIFTH HOUSE: . . . and help with a creative project.

IN THE SIXTH HOUSE: . . . and help with the physical health of their community members.

IN THE SEVENTH HOUSE: . . . and aid them in providing counseling for couples.

IN THE EIGHTH HOUSE: . . . and help them transform their ideas around something important.

IN THE NINTH HOUSE: . . . and help with travel expenses.

IN THE TENTH HOUSE: . . . and help them deal with government regulations.

IN THE ELEVENTH HOUSE: . . . and help them network with allies.

IN THE TWELFTH HOUSE: . . . and help them to better serve the unconscious needs of their community.

Neptune Transiting Natal Saturn

ENHANCING: Give aid to a large and successful religious or spiritual organization with a strong focus on aiding the elderly, the poor, and the underprivileged.

AFFLICTING: Give aid to a small and struggling religious or spiritual organization with a strong focus on aiding the elderly, the poor, and the underprivileged.

IN ARIES: Your gift should aid their foremost project . . .

IN TAURUS: Your gift should help with maintenance of a building . . .

IN GEMINI: Your gift should go toward building their library . . .

IN CANCER: Your gift should go toward child care . . .

IN LEO: Your gift should be flamboyant and visible . . .

IN VIRGO: Your gift should help with aid to the poor . . .

IN LIBRA: Your gift should help them defend themselves legally . . .

IN SCORPIO: Your gift should help with community members who are in crisis . . .

IN SAGITTARIUS: Your gift should help with aid to immigrants . . .

IN CAPRICORN: Your gift should help them with aid to the elderly . . .

IN AQUARIUS: Your gift should help with humanitarian projects . . .

IN PISCES: Your gift should aid healing and counseling . . .

IN THE FIRST HOUSE: . . . and aid how they are seen by the community.

IN THE SECOND HOUSE: . . . and reflect their values.

IN THE THIRD HOUSE: . . . and help them communicate their message more effectively.

IN THE FOURTH HOUSE: . . . and directly aid the core group of the organization.

IN THE FIFTH HOUSE: . . . and help with a creative project.

IN THE SIXTH HOUSE: . . . and help with the physical health of their community members.

IN THE SEVENTH HOUSE: . . . and aid them in providing counseling for couples.

IN THE EIGHTH HOUSE: . . . and help them transform their ideas around something important.

IN THE NINTH HOUSE: . . . and help with travel expenses.

IN THE TENTH HOUSE: . . . and help them deal with government regulations.

IN THE ELEVENTH HOUSE: . . . and help them network with allies.

IN THE TWELFTH HOUSE: . . . and help them to better serve those in prison or institutions.

Neptune Transiting Natal Uranus

AFFLICTING: Give aid to an activist who challenges religious and spiritual assumptions.

ENHANCING: Give aid to an activist who works with religious and spiritual organizations.

IN ARIES: Your gift should help some immediate emergency . . .

IN TAURUS: Your gift should help them obtain a solid foundation for their work . . .

IN GEMINI: Your gift should help make a change in their ability to disseminate information . . .

IN CANCER: Your gift should help make a change in their ability to work from home . . .

IN LEO: Your gift should help make a change in promoting them . . .

IN VIRGO: Your gift should help make a change in how they organize the details of their work . . .

IN LIBRA: Your gift should help make a change in their ability to find useful partners . . .

IN SCORPIO: Your gift should help make a change in their ability to face emotional adversity . . .

IN SAGITTARIUS: Your gift should help make a change in their ability to dream big . . .

IN CAPRICORN: Your gift should make a change in their ability to be seen as an authority . . .

IN AQUARIUS: Your gift should go directly toward their wildest goal . . .

IN PISCES: Your gift should make a change in their resources for handling stress . . .

IN THE FIRST HOUSE: . . . with respect to their public image.

IN THE SECOND HOUSE: . . . regarding financial solvency.

IN THE THIRD HOUSE: . . . regarding education about their cause.

IN THE FOURTH HOUSE: . . . regarding the ways their cause affects families.

IN THE FIFTH HOUSE: . . . regarding the ways their cause affects children.

IN THE SIXTH HOUSE: . . . regarding the ways their cause can be practically implemented.

IN THE SEVENTH HOUSE: . . . regarding the ways their cause is a natural ally of other causes.

IN THE EIGHTH HOUSE: . . . regarding financial aid from other parties.

IN THE NINTH HOUSE: . . . regarding the ways they can be heard in higher education.

IN THE TENTH HOUSE: . . . regarding the ways their cause can be a real career for them.

IN THE ELEVENTH HOUSE: . . . regarding the ways they can gain more volunteers.

IN THE TWELFTH HOUSE: . . . regarding the ways they can reach those who have no access.

Neptune Transiting Natal Neptune

ENHANCING: Gift a gift to a religious or spiritual group that you find to be the embodiment of positive spirituality or as close to it as you can come.

AFFLICTING: Give a gift to a religious or spiritual group that you find to be hopeful in its message, but scattered and vague in its organization.

IN ARIES: Your gift should aid their foremost project . . .

IN TAURUS: Your gift should help with maintenance of a building . . .

IN GEMINI: Your gift should go toward building their library . . .

IN CANCER: Your gift should go toward child care . . .

IN LEO: Your gift should be flamboyant and visible . . .

IN VIRGO: Your gift should help them get organized . . .

IN LIBRA: Your gift should help them defend themselves legally . . .

IN SCORPIO: Your gift should help with community members who are in crisis . . .

IN SAGITTARIUS: Your gift should help with the higher education of community members . . .

IN CAPRICORN: Your gift should help them gain status in the outer community . . .

IN AQUARIUS: Your gift should create an innovation . . .

IN PISCES: Your gift should aid healing and counseling . . .

IN THE FIRST HOUSE: . . . and aid how they are seen by the community.

IN THE SECOND HOUSE: . . . and reflect their values.

IN THE THIRD HOUSE: . . . and help them communicate their message more effectively.

IN THE FOURTH HOUSE: . . . and directly aid the core group of the organization.

IN THE FIFTH HOUSE: . . . and help with a creative project.

IN THE SIXTH HOUSE: . . . and help with the physical health of their community members.

IN THE SEVENTH HOUSE: . . . and aid them in providing counseling for couples.

IN THE EIGHTH HOUSE: . . . and help them transform their ideas around something important.

IN THE NINTH HOUSE: . . . and help with travel expenses.

IN THE TENTH HOUSE: . . . and help them deal with government regulations.

IN THE ELEVENTH HOUSE: . . . and help them network with allies.

IN THE TWELFTH HOUSE: . . . and help them to better serve the unconscious needs of their community.

Neptune Transiting Natal Pluto

ENHANCING: Give aid to a large and well-organized religious or spiritual organization that puts emphasis on sexual issues, death, or intense personal transformation.

AFFLICTING: Give aid to a small and struggling religious or spiritual organization that puts emphasis on sexual issues, death, or intense personal transformation.

IN ARIES: Your gift should aid their foremost project . . .

IN TAURUS: Your gift should help with maintenance of a building . . .

IN GEMINI: Your gift should go toward building their library . . .

IN CANCER: Your gift should go toward child care . . .

IN LEO: Your gift should be flamboyant and visible . . .

IN VIRGO: Your gift should help them get organized . . .

IN LIBRA: Your gift should help them defend themselves legally . . .

IN SCORPIO: Your gift should help with community members who are in crisis . . .

IN SAGITTARIUS: Your gift should help with the higher education of community members . . .

IN CAPRICORN: Your gift should help them gain status in the outer community . . .

IN AQUARIUS: Your gift should create an innovation . . .

IN PISCES: Your gift should aid healing and counseling . . .

IN THE FIRST HOUSE: . . . and aid how they are seen by the community.

IN THE SECOND HOUSE: . . . and reflect their values.

IN THE THIRD HOUSE: . . . and help them communicate their message more effectively.

IN THE FOURTH HOUSE: . . . and directly aid the core group of the organization.

IN THE FIFTH HOUSE: . . . and help with a creative project.

IN THE SIXTH HOUSE: . . . and help with the physical health of their community members.

IN THE SEVENTH HOUSE: . . . and aid them in providing counseling for couples.

IN THE EIGHTH HOUSE: . . . and help them transform their ideas around something important.

IN THE NINTH HOUSE: . . . and help with travel expenses.

IN THE TENTH HOUSE: . . . and help them deal with government regulations.

IN THE ELEVENTH HOUSE: . . . and help them network with allies.

IN THE TWELFTH HOUSE: . . . and help them to better serve the unconscious needs of their community.

Transiting Pluto
Light a candle on the appropriate altar.

Pluto Transiting Natal Sun

ENHANCING: Give aid to an organization that disseminates information about some class of people whose lives and identities change drastically.

AFFLICTING: Give aid to an organization that gives support to some class of people whose lives and identities change drastically.

IN ARIES: The organization should aid soldiers who can no longer do their jobs . . .

IN TAURUS: The organization should aid those who become suddenly impoverished . . .

IN GEMINI: The organization should aid those who suffer brain damage . . .

IN CANCER: The organization should aid children who have any physical, mental, or social disadvantages . . .

IN LEO: The organization should aid those who go blind . . .

IN VIRGO: The organization should aid those who go deaf . . .

IN LIBRA: The organization should aid those who are released from many years in prison . . .

IN SCORPIO: The organization should aid those who come down with a possibly fatal illness . . .

IN SAGITTARIUS: The organization should aid refugees from countries in turmoil . . .

IN CAPRICORN: The organization should aid people who become severely physically disabled . . .

IN AQUARIUS: The organization should aid people who undergo sex reassignment . . .

IN PISCES: The organization should aid people who come down with chronic mental illness . . .

IN THE FIRST HOUSE: . . . and the gift should go toward publicity for the organization.

IN THE SECOND HOUSE: . . . and the gift should go toward a financial goal.

IN THE THIRD HOUSE: . . . and the gift should go toward spreading information to those in need.

IN THE FOURTH HOUSE: . . . and the gift should go toward finding appropriate shelter for clients.

IN THE FIFTH HOUSE: . . . and the gift should go toward funding speakers.

IN THE SIXTH HOUSE: . . . and the gift should go toward medical care for clients.

IN THE SEVENTH HOUSE: . . . and the gift should go toward supporting mentors for clients.

IN THE EIGHTH HOUSE: . . . and the gift should go toward suicide prevention for clients.

IN THE NINTH HOUSE: . . . and the gift should go toward education of future service providers.

IN THE TENTH HOUSE: . . . and the gift should go toward getting aid from larger organizations.

IN THE ELEVENTH HOUSE: . . . and the gift should go toward some far future goal.

IN THE TWELFTH HOUSE: . . . and the gift should go toward therapy or healing for clients.

Pluto Transiting Natal Moon

ENHANCING: Give aid to a large and thriving organization that specializes in healing emotional trauma.

AFFLICTING: Give aid to a small and struggling organization that specializes in healing emotional trauma.

IN ARIES: The organization should help those traumatized by war . . .

IN TAURUS: The organization should help those traumatized by growing up poor and disadvantaged . . .

IN GEMINI: The organization should focus on runaways . . .

IN CANCER: The organization should focus on child abuse . . .

IN LEO: The organization should focus on the trauma of teenagers . . .

IN VIRGO: The organization should focus on those afflicted with illnesses . . .

IN LIBRA: The organization should focus on spousal abuse . . .

IN SCORPIO: The organization should focus on rape survivors . . .

IN SAGITTARIUS: The organization should focus on religious abuse . . .

IN CAPRICORN: The organization should focus on elder abuse . . .

IN AQUARIUS: The organization should focus on those abused by governments . . .

IN PISCES: The organization should focus on abuse of prisoners . . .

IN THE FIRST HOUSE: . . . and the gift should go toward publicity for the organization.

IN THE SECOND HOUSE: . . . and the gift should go toward a financial goal.

IN THE THIRD HOUSE: . . . and the gift should go toward spreading information to those in need.

IN THE FOURTH HOUSE: . . . and the gift should go toward finding appropriate shelter for clients.

IN THE FIFTH HOUSE: . . . and the gift should go toward funding speakers.

IN THE SIXTH HOUSE: . . . and the gift should go toward medical care for clients.

IN THE SEVENTH HOUSE: . . . and the gift should go toward supporting mentors for clients.

IN THE EIGHTH HOUSE: . . . and the gift should go toward suicide prevention for clients.

IN THE NINTH HOUSE: . . . and the gift should go toward education of future service providers.

IN THE TENTH HOUSE: . . . and the gift should go toward getting aid from larger organizations.

IN THE ELEVENTH HOUSE: . . . and the gift should go toward some far future goal.

IN THE TWELFTH HOUSE: . . . and the gift should go toward therapy or healing for clients.

Pluto Transiting Natal Mercury

ENHANCING: Give aid to an organization that supports those who speak the unspeakable and that is doing well at its mission.

AFFLICTING: Give aid to an organization that supports those who speak the unspeakable and that is struggling in its mission.

IN ARIES: Give a gift of enthusiasm and energetic work . . .

IN TAURUS: Give a financial gift . . .

IN GEMINI: Give a gift of books . . .

IN CANCER: Give a gift of food . . .

IN LEO: Give a public and visible gift . . .

IN VIRGO: Give a gift of scut work . . .

IN LIBRA: Give a gift that solves some small injustice . . .

IN SCORPIO: Give a gift of speaking out a hard truth to others . . .

IN SAGITTARIUS: Give a gift of transportation . . .

IN CAPRICORN: Give a gift of bureaucratic aid . . .

IN AQUARIUS: Give a gift of computer equipment . . .

IN PISCES: Give a gift that de-stresses the workers . . .

IN THE FIRST HOUSE: . . . to an organization that talks about the dangers of social conformity.

IN THE SECOND HOUSE: . . . to an organization that talks about the scourge of poverty.

IN THE THIRD HOUSE: . . . to an organization that talks about the evils of censorship.

IN THE FOURTH HOUSE: . . . to an organization that talks about preventing childhood sexual abuse.

IN THE FIFTH HOUSE: . . . to an organization that talks about violence and cruelty among children.

IN THE SIXTH HOUSE: . . . to an organization that talks about the health risks of pollution.

IN THE SEVENTH HOUSE: . . . to an organization that talks about preventing spousal abuse.

IN THE EIGHTH HOUSE: . . . to an organization that talks about preventing rape.

IN THE NINTH HOUSE: . . . to an organization that talks about issues of immigration.

IN THE TENTH HOUSE: . . . to an organization that talks about corporate greed.

IN THE ELEVENTH HOUSE: . . . to an organization that talks about fair international trade.

IN THE TWELFTH HOUSE: . . . to an organization that talks about justice for the mentally ill.

Pluto Transiting Natal Venus

ENHANCING: Give a gift to an organization that supports unusual sexual practices that you are familiar with or approve of.

AFFLICTING: Give a gift to an organization that supports unusual sexual practices that make you uncomfortable, due to your personal preferences. Get your horizons stretched by the experience.

IN ARIES: The organization should be lobbying for political rights . . .

IN TAURUS: The organization should be quiet and discreet . . .

IN GEMINI: The organization should support the dissemination of erotica . . .

IN CANCER: The organization should support alternative families with children . . .

IN LEO: The organization should support the sexual rights of teens . . .

IN VIRGO: The organization should teach safer sex of all kinds . . .

IN LIBRA: The organization should support justice for alternative sexualities . . .

IN SCORPIO: The organization should support BDSM play . . .

IN SAGITTARIUS: The organization should support polyamory . . .

IN CAPRICORN: The organization should support those who prefer sexual hierarchies . . .

IN AQUARIUS: The organization should support GLBT practices . . .

IN PISCES: The organization should teach Tantric sex . . .

IN THE FIRST HOUSE: . . . and your gift should help their public image.

IN THE SECOND HOUSE: . . . and your gift should be in keeping with their values.

IN THE THIRD HOUSE: . . . and your gift should help them disseminate information.

IN THE FOURTH HOUSE: . . . and your gift should provide child care for their workers.

IN THE FIFTH HOUSE: . . . and you should give their workers something fun.

IN THE SIXTH HOUSE: . . . and your gift should go toward organizing.

IN THE SEVENTH HOUSE: . . . and you should bring some of their values into your own personal relationships.

IN THE EIGHTH HOUSE: . . . and you should, for at least a short time, immerse yourself in the most difficult of their practices.

IN THE NINTH HOUSE: . . . and your gift should help them get information to an academic audience.

IN THE TENTH HOUSE: . . . and your gift should help them with some government bureaucracy.

IN THE ELEVENTH HOUSE: . . . and your gift should help them create support groups.

IN THE TWELFTH HOUSE: . . . and you should help with finding resources for counseling.

Pluto Transiting Natal Mars

ENHANCING: Give aid to a large and successful organization that helps fallen warriors and disabled veterans.

AFFLICTING: Give aid to a small and struggling organization that helps fallen warriors and disabled veterans.

IN ARIES: The group should have an active, in-your-face policy . . .

IN TAURUS: The group should be focused on strong positive values . . .

IN GEMINI: The group should be primarily information-based . . .

IN CANCER: The group should work with the families of the clients as well . . .

IN LEO: The group should be public and easy to access . . .

IN VIRGO: The group should be well organized and have hard workers . . .

IN LIBRA: The group should focus on social justice . . .

IN SCORPIO: The group should work with POWs . . .

IN SAGITTARIUS: The group should have a spiritual or religious slant . . .

IN CAPRICORN: The group should be funded by the government or corporations . . .

IN AQUARIUS: The group should have a strongly progressive policy . . .

IN PISCES: The group should focus on a gentle, healing method of aid . . .

IN THE FIRST HOUSE: . . . and your gift should go toward clothing for their clients.

IN THE SECOND HOUSE: . . . and your gift should go toward financial help for their clients.

IN THE THIRD HOUSE: . . . and your gift should go toward computer access for their clients.

IN THE FOURTH HOUSE: . . . and your gift should go toward housing for their clients.

IN THE FIFTH HOUSE: . . . and your gift should go toward recreation for their clients.

IN THE SIXTH HOUSE: . . . and your gift should go toward health care for their clients.

IN THE SEVENTH HOUSE: . . . and your gift should go toward legal fees for their clients.

IN THE EIGHTH HOUSE: . . . and your gift should go toward funeral costs for their clients.

IN THE NINTH HOUSE: . . . and your gift should go toward education for their clients.

IN THE TENTH HOUSE: . . . and your gift should go toward getting government aid for their clients.

IN THE ELEVENTH HOUSE: . . . and your gift should go toward support groups for their clients.

IN THE TWELFTH HOUSE: . . . and your gift should go toward counseling for their clients.

Pluto Transiting Natal Jupiter

ENHANCING: Give aid to an organization that works peacefully for religious reform.

AFFLICTING: Give aid to an organization that fights loudly against religious oppression.

IN ARIES: The group should have an active, in-your-face policy . . .

IN TAURUS: The group should be focused on strong positive values . . .

IN GEMINI: The group should be primarily information-based . . .

IN CANCER: The group should work with families and children . . .

IN LEO: The group should have a street-theater approach to activism . . .

IN VIRGO: The group should be well organized and have hard workers . . .

IN LIBRA: The group should focus on social justice . . .

IN SCORPIO: The group should be a sexual minority . . .

IN SAGITTARIUS: The group should be working to affect academia . . .

IN CAPRICORN: The group should be willing to work with socially conservative people . . .

IN AQUARIUS: The group should be fairly radical . . .

IN PISCES: The group should focus on healing the abused . . .

IN THE FIRST HOUSE: . . . and your gift should go toward polishing the organization's image.

IN THE SECOND HOUSE: . . . and your gift should go toward financial help.

IN THE THIRD HOUSE: . . . and your gift should go toward computer access.

IN THE FOURTH HOUSE: . . . and your gift should go toward making their message accessible and nonthreatening for all family members.

IN THE FIFTH HOUSE: . . . and your gift should go toward public speakers.

IN THE SIXTH HOUSE: . . . and your gift should go toward organizing.

IN THE SEVENTH HOUSE: . . . and your gift should go toward legal fees.

IN THE EIGHTH HOUSE: . . . and your gift should go toward transforming some aspect of their work.

IN THE NINTH HOUSE: . . . and your gift should go toward academic speakers.

IN THE TENTH HOUSE: . . . and your gift should go toward government lobbying.

IN THE ELEVENTH HOUSE: . . . and your gift should go toward support groups.

IN THE TWELFTH HOUSE: . . . and your gift should go toward counseling.

Pluto Transiting Natal Saturn

ENHANCING: Give a gift to an organization that specializes in giving aid to people with terminal illnesses.

AFFLICTING: Give a gift to an organization that specializes in granting the last wishes of people with terminal illnesses.

IN ARIES: Your gift should help someone have an adventure . . .

IN TAURUS: Your gift should help pay for some object that a client wants . . .

IN GEMINI: Your gift should be computer-related . . .

IN CANCER: Your gift should help them in their home . . .

IN LEO: Your gift should help them see a performance . . .

IN VIRGO: Your gift should be one of service . . .

IN LIBRA: Your gift should beautify their world . . .

IN SCORPIO: Your gift should give them a place to rage . . .

IN SAGITTARIUS: Your gift should be a trip to someplace they've always wanted to go . . .

IN CAPRICORN: Your gift should be some practical thing that they need . . .

IN AQUARIUS: Your gift should be something unusual . . .

IN PISCES: Your gift should be something magical . . .

IN THE FIRST HOUSE: . . . and should make them feel better about the way they look.

IN THE SECOND HOUSE: . . . and should help financially in some way.

IN THE THIRD HOUSE: . . . and should go toward communication in some way.

IN THE FOURTH HOUSE: . . . and should pay a client's rent or mortgage.

IN THE FIFTH HOUSE: . . . and should pay for a client's recreation in some way.

IN THE SIXTH HOUSE: . . . and should help with their health care.

IN THE SEVENTH HOUSE: . . . and should help repair some small injustice for a client.

IN THE EIGHTH HOUSE: . . . and should go toward some client's future funeral costs.

IN THE NINTH HOUSE: . . . and should go toward transportation costs.

IN THE TENTH HOUSE: . . . and should go toward helping them get out in public.

IN THE ELEVENTH HOUSE: . . . and should go toward giving them time with friends.

IN THE TWELFTH HOUSE: . . . and should have a spiritual purpose.

Pluto Transiting Natal Uranus

AFFLICTING: Give aid to an activist for a cause that most people find controversial and frightening.

ENHANCING: Give aid to an activist for a cause that most people find powerful and moving.

IN ARIES: Your gift should help some immediate emergency . . .

IN TAURUS: Your gift should help them obtain a solid foundation for their work . . .

IN GEMINI: Your gift should help make a change in their ability to disseminate information . . .

IN CANCER: Your gift should help make a change in their ability to work from home . . .

IN LEO: Your gift should help make a change in promoting them . . .

IN VIRGO: Your gift should help make a change in how they organize the details of their work . . .

IN LIBRA: Your gift should help make a change in their ability to find useful partners . . .

IN SCORPIO: Your gift should help make a change in their ability to face emotional adversity . . .

IN SAGITTARIUS: Your gift should help make a change in their ability to dream big . . .

IN CAPRICORN: Your gift should make a change in their ability to be seen as an authority . . .

IN AQUARIUS: Your gift should go directly toward their wildest goal . . .

IN PISCES: Your gift should make a change in their resources for handling stress . . .

IN THE FIRST HOUSE: . . . with respect to their public image.

IN THE SECOND HOUSE: . . . regarding financial solvency.

IN THE THIRD HOUSE: . . . regarding education about their cause.

IN THE FOURTH HOUSE: . . . regarding the ways their cause affects families.

IN THE FIFTH HOUSE: . . . regarding the ways their cause affects children.

IN THE SIXTH HOUSE: . . . regarding the ways their cause can be practically implemented.

IN THE SEVENTH HOUSE: . . . regarding the ways their cause is a natural ally of other causes.

IN THE EIGHTH HOUSE: . . . regarding financial aid from other parties.

IN THE NINTH HOUSE: . . . regarding the ways they can be heard in higher education.

IN THE TENTH HOUSE: . . . regarding the ways their cause can be a real career for them.

IN THE ELEVENTH HOUSE: . . . regarding the ways they can gain more volunteers.

IN THE TWELFTH HOUSE: . . . regarding the ways they can reach those who have no access.

Pluto Transiting Natal Neptune

ENHANCING: Give aid to an organization that specializes in giving support to people in recovery from addiction and to their families.

AFFLICTING: Give aid to an organization that specializes in helping addicts in crisis.

IN ARIES: Your gift should fund immediate intervention . . .

IN TAURUS: Your gift should help make the association more stable . . .

IN GEMINI: Your gift should help fund hotlines . . .

IN CANCER: Your gift should help families and children . . .

IN LEO: Your gift should help fund speakers . . .

IN VIRGO: Your gift should help with organization and efficiency . . .

IN LIBRA: Your gift should help with legal issues . . .

IN SCORPIO: Your gift should help fund emergency intervention . . .

IN SAGITTARIUS: Your gift should help with widespread education . . .

IN CAPRICORN: Your gift should help fund the group's bigger ambitions . . .

IN AQUARIUS: Your gift should help with peer support groups . . .

IN PISCES: Your gift should help get people therapy . . .

IN THE FIRST HOUSE: . . . and help with the group's public image.

IN THE SECOND HOUSE: . . . and help with a financial blockage.

IN THE THIRD HOUSE: . . . and assist with the dissemination of information.

IN THE FOURTH HOUSE: . . . and help find people housing.

IN THE FIFTH HOUSE: . . . and assist with finding creative outlets instead of addictions.

IN THE SIXTH HOUSE: . . . and assist with getting people better job skills.

IN THE SEVENTH HOUSE: . . . and assist with getting addicts sponsors and mentors.

IN THE EIGHTH HOUSE: . . . and help with addicts who need to reshape their whole lives.

IN THE NINTH HOUSE: . . . and assist with transportation.

IN THE TENTH HOUSE: . . . and assist them in getting help from the government.

IN THE ELEVENTH HOUSE: . . . and help them network with other groups.

IN THE TWELFTH HOUSE: . . . and help with addicts who are currently in hospitals and clinics.

Pluto Transiting Natal Pluto

ENHANCING: Give aid to a large and successful organization that helps the victims of natural disasters.

AFFLICTING: Give aid to a small and struggling organization that helps the victims of natural disasters.

IN ARIES: The organization should work on the disaster spot, not from a distance . . .

IN TAURUS: The organization should help with financial compensation . . .

IN GEMINI: The organization should advertise for help for those in need . . .

IN CANCER: The organization should give food to those affected . . .

IN LEO: The organization should be public and proactive . . .

IN VIRGO: The organization should be local and quiet . . .

IN LIBRA: The organization should help families who are affected . . .

IN SCORPIO: The organization should help the bereaved . . .

IN SAGITTARIUS: The organization should help the displaced . . .

IN CAPRICORN: The organization should be government funded . . .

IN AQUARIUS: The organization should help to predict disasters . . .

IN PISCES: The organization should give counseling to the grieving . . .

IN THE FIRST HOUSE: . . . and your gift should help them advertise.

IN THE SECOND HOUSE: . . . and your gift should reflect their priorities.

IN THE THIRD HOUSE: . . . and your gift should help rebuild communication lines.

IN THE FOURTH HOUSE: . . . and your gift should help families find new homes.

IN THE FIFTH HOUSE: . . . and your gift should provide optimism for children.

IN THE SIXTH HOUSE: . . . and your gift should assist in cleanup.

IN THE SEVENTH HOUSE: . . . and your gift should help reunite families.

IN THE EIGHTH HOUSE: . . . and your gift should aid the families of those who have died.

IN THE NINTH HOUSE: . . . and your gift should help with travel for the displaced.

IN THE TENTH HOUSE: . . . and your gift should help the organization deal with governments.

IN THE ELEVENTH HOUSE: . . . and your gift should help a network of different organizations.

IN THE TWELFTH HOUSE: . . . and your gift should help with counseling and emotional healing.

17
Planetary Hours
Shortcuts to Scheduling

Planetary hours have been used by ceremonial magicians for centuries. The concept centers on the idea that certain hours of the day are associated with certain planets and can thus be used to provide a smaller version of the "thrust" given to a spell when it's done on an astrologically auspicious date. They are kind of a "shortcut," in that one does not need to do major calculations to find a (at least slightly) more propitious time. They work well for activities like bringing absent energies into one's life. They are also used for scheduling important appointments, rituals, special activities, and other significant events. As they only follow the planets and don't include signs or houses, if the emphasis is on a sign or a house, use the hour for the planet that rules them.

You'll notice when you peruse the following charts that the first hour of each day is the planet supposedly associated with that day—for example, Saturn for Saturday. If you speak a Romance language such as Italian, Spanish, or French, it's obvious what the ruling planet of that day is—Mercury's day is Miercoles in Spanish, Jove's day is Jueves, and so on. We take our day names from the Anglo-Saxons, a Germanic-speaking people who attempted, rather clumsily, to copy the Roman names for deities/planets by associating the days with their own very different gods—for instance, "Woden travels a lot, that must mean he's like Mercury!"—leaving us with Tyr's Day, Woden's Day, Thor's Day, and Freya's Day.

PLANETARY HOURS

HOURS OF THE DAY, FROM SUNRISE UNTIL SUNSET

HOUR	SUN	MON	TUES	WED	THURS	FRI	SAT
1	Sun	Moon	Mars	Mercury	Jupiter	Venus	Saturn
2	Venus	Saturn	Sun	Moon	Mars	Mercury	Jupiter
3	Mercury	Jupiter	Venus	Saturn	Sun	Moon	Mars
4	Moon	Mars	Mercury	Jupiter	Venus	Saturn	Sun
5	Saturn	Sun	Moon	Mars	Mercury	Jupiter	Venus
6	Jupiter	Venus	Saturn	Sun	Moon	Mars	Mercury
7	Mars	Mercury	Jupiter	Venus	Saturn	Sun	Moon
8	Sun	Moon	Mars	Mercury	Jupiter	Venus	Saturn
9	Venus	Saturn	Sun	Moon	Mars	Mercury	Jupiter
10	Mercury	Jupiter	Venus	Saturn	Sun	Moon	Mars
11	Moon	Mars	Mercury	Jupiter	Venus	Saturn	Sun
12	Saturn	Sun	Moon	Mars	Mercury	Jupiter	Venus

HOURS OF THE NIGHT, FROM SUNSET UNTIL SUNRISE

HOUR	SUN	MON	TUE	WED	THURS	FRI	SAT
1	Jupiter	Venus	Saturn	Sun	Moon	Mars	Mercury
2	Mars	Mercury	Jupiter	Venus	Saturn	Sun	Moon
3	Sun	Moon	Mars	Mercury	Jupiter	Venus	Saturn

HOUR	SUN	MON	TUE	WED	THURS	FRI	SAT
4	Venus	Saturn	Sun	Moon	Mars	Mercury	Jupiter
5	Mercury	Jupiter	Venus	Saturn	Sun	Moon	Mars
6	Moon	Mars	Mercury	Jupiter	Venus	Saturn	Sun
7	Saturn	Sun	Moon	Mars	Mercury	Jupiter	Venus
8	Jupiter	Venus	Saturn	Sun	Moon	Mars	Mercury
9	Mars	Mercury	Jupiter	Venus	Saturn	Sun	Moon
10	Sun	Moon	Mars	Mercury	Jupiter	Venus	Saturn
11	Venus	Saturn	Sun	Moon	Mars	Mercury	Jupiter
12	Mercury	Jupiter	Venus	Saturn	Sun	Moon	Mars

CALCULATING THE PLANETARY HOURS

The planetary hours are not figured as even sixty-minute slices of time beginning at midnight. The day begins at dawn, and the daytime, sunrise to sunset, is divided into twelve hours of equal length. The nighttime is also divided into twelve hours of equal length, from sunset to sunrise, but except very near an equinox these hours will be of a different length than the daylight hours. That is why these are called the unequal hours, as they vary from each other and with the season.

We can calculate the planetary hours using some basic math and the times of sunrise and sunset for the day and location in question. These can be obtained by looking them up in an almanac, by checking the U.S. Naval Observatory's astronomical data website (http://aa.usno.navy.mil), or by observing the Sun.

As an example, let's say I have an important meeting (or ritual) next Tuesday at 2 pm and want to find out what planetary hour that is.

First I find the number of minutes from sunrise to sunset (for a time during the day) or from sunset to sunrise (for a time during the night) at the desired location. In this example, I check my almanac and find that next Tuesday the sun rises at 7:16 am and sets at 4:36 pm, my latitude and longitude. That is a New England winter day with 9 hours and 20 minutes of daylight, or 560 minutes. I divide that by 12 and find that each daylight hour is 46 2/3 minutes long.

By marking down each hour, I get the following list for next Tuesday:

PLANETARY HOURS FOR TUESDAY		
HOUR OF DAYLIGHT	TIME	MINUTES PAST MIDNIGHT
1	7:16 am	436
2	8:03 am	483
3	8:49 am	529
4	9:36 am	576
5	10:23 am	623
6	11:09 am	669
7	11:56 am	716
8	12:43 pm	763
9	1:29 pm	809
10	2:16 pm	856
11	3:03 pm	903
12	3:49 pm	949

From the Planetary Hours chart, we can see that my meeting would start in the ninth hour of the day on Tuesday, ruled by the Sun, but by 2:16 we would be in Venus's hour. If it ran past three, we would be in the hour of Mercury. I have devised a worksheet to help you with these calculations.

WORKSHEET FOR PLANETARY HOURS

The equations below are best utilized by making a zerox copy of the blank pages so you can re-use the templates as many times as desired.

1. **What time will the Sun rise and set on the day in question?**

    Be sure to check that the time zone is correct for your location and that you've taken daylight savings time into account. If you cannot look up times for your exact location, check that the location used for your calculations isn't substantially farther north or south than your actual location.

Sunrise [   ] : [   ] am   Sunset [   ] : [   ] pm
      hour   minute   hour   minute

2. **How many minutes past midnight is that?**

    Times written like 3:15 pm or 6:30 am are difficult to multiply and add together, so we'll convert them to a form that is easier to work with.

    Hours of Sunrise equation:

    Hour of sunrise: [   ]
                         x 60
                         [   ]
    Minute of sunrise: + [   ]
    Sunrise is   [   ] minutes past midnight.

    Hours of Sunset equation:

    Hour of sunset: [   ]
                         + 12
                         [   ]
                         x 60
                         [   ]
    Minute of sunrise: + [   ]
    Sunset is   [   ] minutes past midnight.

3. **For daylight hours, how many minutes are between sunrise and sunset? For nighttime hours, how many minutes are between sunset and sunrise?** Divide this number by 12 to find the length of each planetary hour.

Calculate daylight hours as follows:

```
    [    ]  Sunset, minutes past midnight
 -  [    ]  Sunrise, minutes past midnight
    [    ]  Length of the day, in minutes
    ÷ 12
    [    ]  Length of each daytime planetary hour
```

Calculate nighttime hours as follows:

```
    1440   The number of minutes in a day
 +  [    ]  Sunrise, minutes past midnight
    [    ]
 -  [    ]  Sunset, minutes past midnight
    [    ]  Length of the night, in minutes
    ÷ 12
    [    ]  Length of each nighttime planetary hour
```

4. When does each hour begin?

The first daylight hour begins at sunrise. The first nighttime hour begins at sunset.

Add the planetary hour length to the first hour to get the beginning of the second hour.

Add the planetary hour length to second hour to get the beginning of the third hour.

And so on . . .

Hour 1 begins	[ ]	minutes past midnight
+	[ ]	planetary hour length
Hour 2 begins	[ ]	minutes past midnight
+	[ ]	planetary hour length
Hour 3 begins	[ ]	minutes past midnight
+	[ ]	planetary hour length
Hour 4 begins	[ ]	minutes past midnight
+	[ ]	planetary hour length
Hour 5 begins	[ ]	minutes past midnight
+	[ ]	planetary hour length
Hour 6 begins	[ ]	minutes past midnight
+	[ ]	planetary hour length
Hour 7 begins	[ ]	minutes past midnight
+	[ ]	planetary hour length
Hour 8 begins	[ ]	minutes past midnight
+	[ ]	planetary hour length
Hour 9 begins	[ ]	minutes past midnight
+	[ ]	planetary hour length
Hour 10 begins	[ ]	minutes past midnight
+	[ ]	planetary hour length
Hour 11 begins	[ ]	minutes past midnight
+	[ ]	planetary hour length
Hour 12 begins	[ ]	minutes past midnight

5. What times are those in hours and minutes?

Convert all these minutes past midnight into times and fill them in on the chart.

Example 1: What time is 574 minutes past midnight?

$$574 \div 60 = 9.5666$$

So, the hour is 9 a.m., but how many minutes past 9 a.m. is it?

$$9.5666 - 9 \times 60 = 33.996$$

We'll round up and call that 9:34 a.m.

Example 2: What time is 949 minutes past midnight?

$$949 \div 60 = 15.8166$$

So, it is 15 hours past midnight, which is 3 p.m. How many minutes past 3 p.m.?

$$15.8166 - 15 \times 60 = 48.999$$

We'll round up and call that 3:49 p.m.

Example 3: What time is 1623 minutes past midnight?

$$574 \div 60 = 27.05$$

So, is it 27 hours past midnight, which is 3 a.m. the next day. How many minutes past 3 a.m.?

$$27.05 - 27 \times 60 = 3$$

That is 3:05 a.m.

	PLANETARY HOURS CHART	
1		
2		
3		
4		
5		
6		
7		
8		
9		
10		
11		
12		

6. Look up the ruling planets for that day of the week on the Planetary Hours chart and use the information to fill in the box.

Recommended Reading

If you want to learn the basics of astrology—such as how to interpret a birth chart, how to compare two (or more) charts, how to manage a composite, how to do more complex transits, and more—I strongly recommend the following books by Steven and Jodie Forrest:

The Changing Sky: A Practical Guide to Predictive Astrology, by Steven Forrest. San Diego: ACS, 1999.

The Inner Sky: How to Make Wiser Choices for a More Fulfilling Life, by Steven Forrest. San Diego: ACS, 1989.

Skymates: Love, Sex and Evolutionary Astrology, by Steven Forrest and Jodie Forrest. Chapel Hill, N.C.: Seven Paws Press, 2002.

Skymates, Volume Two: The Composite Chart, by Steven Forrest and Jodie Forrest. Chapel Hill, N.C.: Seven Paws Press, 2005.

The following books are useful for further research into the subtler meanings and energies of the astrological planets, signs, houses, and aspects. They're my favorites, but hundreds of good books are out there, many of them concentrating on a single planet or sign. Astrology books are in vogue right now, and they are coming out by the hundreds, so you'll have plenty to look through.

An Astrological Guide to Self-Awareness, by Donna Cunningham. Sebastopol, Calif.: CRCS Publications, 1994.

The Astrology of Fate, by Liz Greene. Newburyport, Mass.: Weiser Books, 1984.

Astrology for Lovers, by Liz Greene. Newburyport, Mass.: Weiser Books, 1989.

The Astrology of Self-Discovery, by Tracy Marks. Sebastopol, Calif.: CRCS Publications, 1985.

Meet Your Planets: Fun with Astrology, by Roy Alexander. Woodbury, Minn.: Llewellyn Publications, 1997.

MythAstrology: Exploring Planets & Pantheons, by Raven Kaldera. Woodbury, Minn.: Llewellyn Publications, 2004.

Pagan Polyamory, by Raven Kaldera. Woodbury, Minn.: Llewellyn Publications, 2005.

Planets in Composite: Analyzing Human Relationships, by Robert Hand. Atglen, Pa.: Schiffer Publishing, 1975.

Index

BOOKS OF RELATED INTEREST

Drawing Down the Spirits
The Traditions and Techniques of Spirit Possession
by Kenaz Filan and Raven Kaldera

The Pagan Book of Days
A Guide to the Festivals, Traditions, and Sacred Days of the Year
by Nigel Pennick

A Druid's Herbal for the Sacred Earth Year
by Ellen Evert Hopman

Magic and the Power of the Goddess
Initiation, Worship, and Ritual in the Western Mystery Tradition
by Gareth Knight

The Pagan Mysteries of Halloween
Celebrating the Dark Half of the Year
by Jean Markale

The Return of the Dead
Ghosts, Ancestors, and the Transparent Veil of the Pagan Mind
by Claude Lecouteux

Witches, Werewolves, and Fairies
Shapeshifters and Astral Doubles in the Middle Ages
by Claude Lecouteux

Witchcraft Medicine
Healing Arts, Shamanic Practices, and Forbidden Plants
by Claudia Müller-Ebeling, Christian Rätsch, and Wolf-Dieter Storl

INNER TRADITIONS • BEAR & COMPANY
P.O. Box 388
Rochester, VT 05767
1-800-246-8648
www.InnerTraditions.com

Or contact your local bookseller